MILK THE BELOVED COUNTRY

ALSO BY SIHLE KHUMALO

Dark Continent My Black Arse (2007)
Heart of Africa (2009)
Almost Sleeping My Way to Timbuktu (2013)
Rainbow Nation My Zulu Arse (2018)

Sihle Khumalo

MILK THE BELOVED COUNTRY

UMUZI

Published in 2023 by *Umuzi*,
an imprint of Penguin Random House South Africa (Pty) Ltd
Company Reg. No. 1953/000441/07
The Estuaries No. 4, Oxbow Crescent, Century Avenue,
Century City, 7441, South Africa
PO Box 1144, Cape Town, 8000, South Africa
www.penguinrandomhouse.co.za

First edition, first printing 2023
1 3 5 7 9 8 6 4 2

ISBN 978-1-4152-1096-3 (Print)

ISBN 978-1-4152-1120-5 (ePub)

Cover design by MR Design
Cover photography:
M2 highway with taxi: iStock/THEGIFT777
Cow: iStock/Clara Bastian
Speed sign: iStock/Sandra Daengeli
Back cover: iStock/Clara Bastian
Text design by Chérie Collins
Set in 10.8 on 14 pt Sabon LT Std

Printed and bound by Novus Print, a Novus Holdings company

MIX
Paper from
responsible sources
FSC® C022948

This book is dedicated –

with 100% approval from my wife –

to two other women in my life:

Rebecca Duduzile 'RD' Sithole and

Phumzile Penelope 'PP' Mvelase.

CONTENTS

PART III
Ama-Reflections: Let us pause and ponder

INTRODUCTION

South Africa: the country that keeps giving – without fail – only to a select few. If South Africa was a cow, it would have a humungous udder which – against all thuggery and theft – never runs out of the goodies that keep the greedy coming back for more, and more. Maybe this explains why some politicians call our country a 'cowntry'. The suckers are milking the country almost dry, but it keeps giving. Until when?

While traversing my own country in 2016, one of the things that struck me was that there is rich history behind the names of certain cities, towns, streets and so on.

That 2016 adventure, covering all nine provinces, culminated in my book *Rainbow Nation My Zulu Arse* (Umuzi, 2018). There was still so much I wanted to say about my homeland, however – so here I am, back again, for another bite at this very rich yet very poor country called the Republic of South Africa – my country, our cowntry.

For starters, as a country we do not even have a name. What we have is a geographic location masquerading as a name.

Modern-day Namibia, while colonised, was South West Africa, which is also a geographic location; Kenya was part of so-called British East Africa; and modern-day Burkina Faso was 'Upper Volta' (basically, the upper part of the Volta River). We, meanwhile, occupy a piece of land on the southern tip of the African continent, and that coincidentally happens to be, ahem, the name of our country. Even

'Mzansi', the colloquial term for South Africa, refers to a geographic location: technically 'mazantsi', it's the Xhosa word for 'south'.

Therefore, if you ask me, obsessing about name changes of cities, towns and streets when we as a country have no meaningful name not only entirely misses the bigger picture but also suggests that we lack the context and foundation on which all the other names should be based. And that could explain why, as has been witnessed, whenever the government attempts to change the names of cities, towns or streets, it becomes a highly emotional issue, and at times legal battles ensue.

While doing research on the history of town names for this book, I was taken aback by how the Dutch and British governors, as part of the colonisation project, went on naming sprees. Some British governors even named towns after their fathers-in-law who never visited South Africa.

Not to be outdone, the British royal family also gave their names to towns and cities. Even more interesting, at least for me, is how pastors, soldiers and magistrates were enthusiastic participants in these naming sprees. Believe it or not, dear reader, there is even a town in this country that's named after a horse. A dead horse.

The issue of old and new names is not the only topical issue in Mzansi, of course. In fact, our country is complex and, as such, trying to deal with its challenges means, among other things, that you have to cover a whole lot of themes and subjects. So the various parts of this book might feel totally different from each other, because that is exactly how our country is, in its true sense. You cross the road from Sandton to Alexandra, or vice versa, and it looks and feels as if you are in a different country altogether. Within half an hour of leaving the informal settlements of Khayelitsha, you are in the picturesque multimillion-rand wine farms of Stellenbosch. You read about multibillion-rand deals, and in the same newspaper there is a story about how the substantial part of the population lives below the poverty line.

We are a complex country partly because our past is complex and convoluted. We are the only country in sub-Saharan Africa that had two waves of independence: in 1910 we became a self-governing state of the British Empire called the Union of South Africa, and in 1961 we became a fully sovereign state called the Republic of South Africa. In both these instances, the minority of the population continued in power, and this was so for more than eight decades. This, therefore, means there was a third wave of independence: freedom for all, in 1994.

We, as people of this land, are not a product of just one thing or another. We are a product of everything. And more. Even victors are victims, to an extent. You might have your riches but you have no peace of mind. You have to constantly and consistently watch your back. Just in case.

Victims, on the other hand, can claim victories of some sort – that first person in the family to get a university degree or buy a car or buy property in the suburbs, for example. These are often highlighted as a case of the triumph of the human spirit. But, in essence, it is, I strongly feel, victims of the system claiming some sort of victory.

Nothing, I think, illustrates how victims had to improvise and make the best of a dire situation like the gumboot dance. It all started in the late 1800s when miners had to find a way to communicate between themselves without the mine bosses knowing. Bear in mind that at the time mine bosses were so obsessed with employee control that even mere conversation between workers was a highly regulated affair. In time, and as part of fighting boredom in the hostels, gumboot dancing became a social phenomenon. Before you knew it, mine workers had exported gumboot dancing home and, voilà, today it is part and parcel of our diverse cultural heritage.

This is the story of South Africa. It is a country steeped in a colonial past, and shaped and moulded by the apartheid project. And it is a country in which, besides the rhetoric and cosmetic changes where young black people are being indoctrinated to be tenderpreneurs while the adult black population has internalised playing small in a white economic space through black economic empowerment (BEE) deals and ineffective affirmative-action policies, darkies by and large remain in the economic and social darkness.

Of course, all of us have had an electoral voice since 1994. Some of the duly elected leaders have spent so much time, effort and energy enriching themselves (and their friends, families, mistresses, boyfriends and partners) that some among us have started missing certain things that used to work properly during the apartheid years. You know that the government, which is predominantly black and is predominantly voted into power by black people, has failed when some black people start thinking – and even hoping – that white people will run the country again.

Whenever I see a politician, part of me knows that I am looking at an actor or an actress. Otherwise, how do you explain that some of them, if not all, publicly act as if they care about the poor, when they do not only not give a fuck about them, but also exploit them? Could it be that you cannot be a politician unless you are emotionally dead? The same could be said of capitalists – the vast majority of the global population: can it be that you cannot be a capitalist unless you are emotionally dead?

Or is it the other way around: you have to be emotionally dead first, before you can become a politician? You must be able to stand in front of people and promise them heaven, then, once in power, screw the little fuckers and give them hell.

As I grew older, I started questioning if politicians had the power – real power – that is needed to change our country, or any country. I started thinking that maybe, just maybe, there were some puppet-masters who ruled from the shadows.

I am not saying that all the 'power broker' groups I mention in this book manipulate politicians for their own selfish benefit. My point is that there are groups in this country who had (and some of whom still have) loads of power, be it economic, social, cultural or otherwise. The jury is still out on how these individuals use that power to influence, manipulate and dictate terms to the state. Are the politicians we see on the news every day just puppets who are controlled by these powerful groups or wealthy individuals?

The final part of this book is about reflection. I am not just reflecting on certain key episodes in our country's story, I am at the same time questioning things that, to an extent, have not received the contemplation and deliberation they deserved. This lack of comprehensive analysis of our country can be attributed, I think, to the fact that there is so much happening not only politically but also socially, technologically and economically, that we as a people hardly have time to pause and reflect on historic events. And as such we, as some among us often say, 'just carry on'.

But I am saying, 'Hang on! Not so fast! Before we carry on …' I am asking questions that in our busyness and in our quest to make a living we seem to have skimmed over. I am saying, let us have this maybe uncomfortable conversation with the openness and frankness that it deserves.

This is a book in which I ask, among other things, is South Africa already a failed state and when was the state captured? It is a book that seeks to make you, dear reader, ponder and pause while not only asking yourself, 'How did we get here?' but also thinking what the future might hold.

We need to think deeply about our country, and change course before it is too late.

PART I

They named it after *whom*?

'The beginning of wisdom is to call things by
their proper name.'
Confucius (c551 – c479 BCE),
Chinese philosopher

Chapter 1
THE DUTCH ADMINISTRATORS

On what must have been just another autumn day in 1652, Jan van Riebeeck, with a small fleet of three ships, dropped anchor in Table Bay. Life on the southern tip of the African continent, for better or for worse, was never the same again.

This was supposed to be a resupply station for the vessels of the Dutch East India Company but it rapidly expanded into a settler colony. Just short of a century later, the colony was so well established that the company proclaimed Swellendam a magisterial district, followed by Graaff-Reinet some forty years later, in 1786. By that stage, colonists had ventured so far from the Cape that the Great Fish River had been declared the eastern boundary of the colony.

Van Riebeeck was in the Cape for ten years. Over the next seventeen, from 1662, another eight Dutchmen took the reins, until Simon van der Stel in 1679. Other Dutch governors worth mentioning for the purposes of this book were Hendrik Swellengrebel (1739–1751), Ryk Tulbagh (1751–1771) and Joachim van Plettenberg (1771–1785). And then there were Pieter van Reede van Oudtshoorn, who never actually made it into the hot seat, as well as one of the Dutch East India Company's senior employees, Sebastiaan Nederburgh.

Being a speaker of parliament is one very senior position in government. It makes sense, therefore, that if you are on a naming spree, the wife of the speaker must be given her dues. (In those days, all the speakers were men.)

Christoffel Joseph Brand, who came from a long line of Dutch colonial administrators, was the first speaker of parliament in the Cape, in 1854. Ladybrand, a small town in the Free State, is named after his wife, Lady Catharina Brand.

Their son, Johannes, who became the president of the Orange Free State, followed in his father's footsteps by naming a town after his wife, but because Lady Brand was already taken, another had to be used; he opted for Zastron, the maiden name of his spouse, Johanna Sibella. The small town of Zastron lies in the northwest of the country, in the province that is also called – creatively – North West.

I have often wondered how the other madams felt when a man named a town after his wife. I can vividly imagine the late-night scene in a home where a wife felt she also deserved her own town: as the husband is suggestively getting closer to her, she brushes off his encroaching hand before cynically commenting, 'Johanna is so lucky to be married to an ambitious man who grew up to be a president. Now she even has a town named after her.' As she turns to give him the cold shoulder, with a heavy sigh, she mutters, 'What was I thinking?' Needless to say, that awkward moment is followed by days, although hopefully not a lifetime, of flaccidness.

Other couples took the marriage union to another level: towns named after both husband and wife. Swellendam, the country's third-oldest town after Cape Town and Stellenbosch, is a case in point. It is named after Governor Hendrik Swellengrebel and his wife Helena Wilhelmina ten Damme. And it just so happens that South Africa's fourth-oldest town, Graaff-Reinet, is also named after a couple: Governor Cornelis van de Graaff and his wife Reinet. This is what the young these days would call #CoupleGoals.

Van de Graaff was recalled by the Dutch East India Company in 1790, after just less than six years of governorship because – and this was the accusation – he'd caused inflation by allowing the money supply to increase about fivefold within five years. I must admit I did not know that governors also had the power to dictate the money supply, but it makes sense, for two reasons: one, they had absolute power over the colony they were administering; and, two, the South African Reserve Bank, which has the monopoly on the country's money supply, was only established in 1921. And from that moment, you had people who loved to believe they were in power (i.e., politicians), and yet had no control whatsoever over the monetary policy of the country which dictated, among other things, how much money was in circulation. This is but one of the reasons I do not take politicians seriously.

I might as well share an observation I have had for a while: a party is where people go in order to, among other things, loosen up, drink, get drunk, sing out loud, dance, flirt, pick up one-night stands and have a great time. Why, then, do we take politicians, people who are full-time members of a party, seriously?

Governor Van de Graaff's wife, Reinet, was born in Gouda in the Netherlands, where the famous Gouda cheese originates. And it just so happens that there is a village outside Paarl called Gouda. (As an aside, what is the difference between Gouda and Cheddar cheese? Just asking!)

A notable from Graaff-Reinet (besides Gerrit Ferreira, a co-founder of FirstRand Bank, which owns both FNB and Wesbank) is Dr Anton Rupert, founder of the Rembrandt Group, modern-day Remgro. Anton's son Johann still runs the family empire.

Coincidentally, one of the Rupert family's major investments is in a company called Reinet Investments, which includes a stake in British American Tobacco. The Ruperts are not the only South Africans to name a business after the area they come from: former president Jacob Zuma's son Duduzane, notwithstanding being born in Mozambique, named his company after a hill not far from Nkandla, Mabengela (Investments).

Thinking out loud: if – at this stage, a very big 'if' – I were to make it big in life one day and have my own business empire, maybe I should also name it after a mountain: Masenkomo in Qhudeni, where I spent the first eleven years of my life. The term 'masenkomo' actually consists of two words, 'amasi' (maas) and 'inkomo' (cow). There was a strong community belief that the grass on that particular hill was so special that it led to cows producing high-quality milk, which in turn led to outstanding maas. Taking this thought to its logical conclusion, when I eventually decide to list forty per cent of the company, the entity will then evolve from Masenkomo to Jou Ma Se Nkomo. Admittedly, that might not work, especially for sensitive investors because (i)nkomo in isiZulu is also a vagina.

Still on Graaff-Reinet, the founder of the Pan Africanist Congress (PAC), Robert Mangaliso Sobukwe, was born there in 1924, and raised there, and was buried there in 1978. A teacher turned lawyer, he was an eloquent leader who, after leaving the African National Congress (ANC), spearheaded a nationwide strike against the hated pass laws. It was exactly this strike that led to the Sharpeville massacre in March 1960, during which 69 of the thousands of people who marched on the Sharpeville police station were shot and killed by the police.

Sobukwe was arrested after the massacre and charged with incitement. After three years in prison, he spent an additional six years in jail on Robben Island, courtesy of the 1963 General Laws Amendment Act, known as the Sobukwe clause, which empowered the courts to renew a prisoner's period of confinement every year.

While we're on the PAC, it is worth mentioning that it identified itself as an Africanist organisation; its slogan was 'Africa for Africans', and the definition of 'African' in this context was black African. In fact, one of the key reasons for the split from the ANC was that white people, according to the Africanists, should not be allowed to join the party, as it was felt that colonisation and apartheid were mainly an Africanist problem, while white people were the beneficiaries of the very unjust system that black people were fighting against. Despite this, within four years of its formation, the PAC allowed a white person, Patrick Baker Duncan, not only to join the party but to take a key leadership role.

A few years after the PAC was banned, Duncan was appointed head of the party's Algeria office. This office oversaw and coordinated activities in all the north African countries, including the military training of PAC recruits. In other words, that same Africanist organisation not only allowed a white person to join it but he also coordinated its military activities.

The moral of the story: history, like life itself, is complicated.

Still on the PAC, its military wing, the Azanian People's Liberation Army (APLA), had the slogan 'one settler, one bullet', and it was in that context that it carried out a number of attacks targeting exclusively white people, mostly in the early 1990s, before it was disbanded in 1994. Its fighters were integrated into the new South African National Defence Force.

But let's go back to Patrick Duncan, the first white person (and the only one I know of) to join the PAC. In 1963, the same year that Duncan joined the PAC, he was chosen to represent the organisation and address the United Nations Special Committee on the Policies of Apartheid in New York.

It gets better (or worse). Duncan's father was Sir Patrick Duncan, the sixth governor-general of the Union of South Africa, who'd died in 1943, in his seventh year in office. He'd been cremated and his ashes interred in a monument at the then new Duncan Dock in Cape Town harbour, which is of course named after him. Besides street names dotted around the country, the suburb of Duncanville near Vereeniging, as well as the mostly informal township of Duncan Village outside East London, got their names from Sir Patrick.

You do not have to be a conspiracy theorist to, at the very least, question, first, how the PAC – a hardcore organisation that saw fit to split from the ANC, because of its strong Africanist stance – not only accepted a white person into its ranks, but also allowed this white person to occupy a very senior role within the organisation. How did Patrick Duncan manage to pull this one off? Something just does not add up. (See Part II: The power brokers.)

Another town besides Graaff-Reinet that punches way above its weight in terms of being a significant birthplace is Riebeek West in the Western Cape. Two boys were born there who went on to become successive South African prime ministers: Jan Christian Smuts (who served from 1919 to 1924, and then again from 1939 to 1948) and Daniël François 'DF' Malan (who was in power from 1948 to 1954).

Malan was born just outside the town on the farm Allesverloren. If the name looks and sounds familiar, there is a logical explanation: to this day, from the family-owned farm, the Malans produce wines that you can get at your local liquor shop. In fact, each and every bottle from Allesverloren states that 'present owner Danie Malan is the fifth generation on the farm, continuing the pioneering wine-making tradition of his forefathers, who acquired the farm in 1872'.

I would not be surprised if there are some leftist extremists who still hate 'DF Malan the racist' and yet who not only enjoy wines from Allesverloren but also highly recommend them to friends and family.

This reminds me of experiences I've had – and this is what I call the irony of our times – with people who by day swear at the Ruperts as pioneers of 'white monopoly capital' and by night swear by Rupert & Rothschild's blended wine, which they fondly call 'R&R'.

Still on the irony of our times, how do you explain that there is an informal settlement in this country named after a billionaire: Ramaphosa, in Ekurhuleni, Gauteng?

And lastly on the irony of our times, I am reminded of the heated debates I've had with different black individuals who refer to cricket and rugby as 'white sports', and proudly claim soccer as a 'black sport'. When I mention to them that soccer was, in fact, first played in Europe, specifically in modern-day Britain, they are first dismissive and then, after a simple fact-checking thanks to the internet, they remain inexplicably stuck on soccer being a black sport.

Contrary to popular belief, swimming is a black sport. At least this is my assertion. If you, like most people, subscribe to the narrative that the first human beings were born in Africa about three million years ago, it goes without saying, my assertion continues, that Africans must, at one stage or another, have learnt to swim. If they were terrified of water, how come, then, did they end up building rafts (or was it ships?) that made it all the way to Australia, the Americas and so on? Therefore, I conclude, swimming is a black African sport. I wonder what went wrong, and where?

There is a wine farm, by the way, that is also named after a senior employee of the Dutch East India Company: Sebastiaan Cornelis Nederburgh (who was, incidentally, a Freemason; see Part II: The power brokers). This farm was acquired by German immigrant Philippus Wolvaart a year before Nederburgh landed in the Cape in 1792. More than 250 years later, the Nederburg name (the 'h' was dropped long ago) still reigns supreme in some wine circles. And to think Sebastian Nederburgh was only in the Cape for fifteen months before heading to Batavia (modern-day Jakarta in Indonesia) ... It's enough to make me want to have a glass (or five) of Nederburg.

Allesverloren farm, which is, as mentioned before, now in the hands of the fifth Malan generation, is not the only farm where one generation inherited from previous ones. In fact, a simple stroll through your local liquor shop will reveal that some families – and this information is proudly displayed on the bottles of their produce – have owned wine farms for generations. As an example, Alvis Drift has been 'family owned since 1928', Diemersdal has been produced 'through six generations of the Louw family', and Meerlust has been 'owned by the Myburgh family for eight generations'.

At face value, you might be envious of people who inherit wine farms and take the baton from their forefathers. Another aspect to be considered, however, is to what extent the beneficiaries have a role in defining their own paths in life. Or is everything predetermined for them from the very first day? (Silent thought: maybe I am just consoling myself because I am never going to inherit any farm and, as things stand, my children will not inherit any farm – never mind a wine farm.)

The point, I insist, must still be made about children charting their own course based on their character, passion and so on.

I once had a very personal conversation with a white colleague. We were not even close but this whole thing must have been bugging him. A lot. We bumped into each other in the lift as we were on our way home. The ensuing conversation, in the parking lot, soon turned to his frustration with his father, who was cutting him off because he (the son, my colleague) had not chosen to be a lawyer, and had followed a different career path, and thus could not in future 'take over the old man's law firm'.

My colleague's biggest worry, besides that the old man was cutting him off, was that his sister had a boyfriend who was a lawyer, and the old man was so smitten (for lack of a better word) with this potential future son-in-law that he had already given him a partnership in his firm. This colleague of mine summed it up like this: 'This guy, I think, is in the relationship for one thing.'

I quipped, 'He is in there for two things.'

He ignored me for two weeks.

Moving swiftly along ...

Okay, maybe before we move on, let me give you another small town that, like Graaff-Reinet and Riebeek West, produced big hitters: Schweizer-Reneke. The Pahad brothers, Essop and Aziz, were born in this platteland town in North West province. They both went into exile in the 1960s, studied at Sussex University (where the future president Thabo Mbeki was also studying). The brothers went on to serve the new South Africa in different ministerial portfolios, and when Mbeki was recalled by the ANC, in 2008, they both resigned from their positions.

The late Ahmed Kathrada was also born in Schweizer-Reneke. 'Uncle Kathy', then aged 34, was sentenced as part of the Rivonia Trial to life imprisonment, and spent most of his sentence on Robben Island. He was only released 25 years later.

Schweizer-Reneke has something else in common with Graaff-Reinet: its double-barrel name. However, unlike Graaff-Reinet, which got its name from a husband and wife, the North West town was named after two soldiers, Captain Constantine Schweizer and Field Cornet Gerhardus Reneke, who died during the 1885 clash with the local Khoi-Khoi community that led to the seizure of their land and the establishment of the town.

Still on double-barrel names, there is another such-named town, this one honouring two wives of local farmers; the farmers donated the land on which the town was built.

These two ladies, Elizabeth and Alida, are remembered in the name of the town of Bethal in modern-day Mpumalanga. (Of course, you went back to double-check the names of the lucky women, right?)

It was an honourable thing that was done by the two farmers – nobody even remembers their names but those of their wives are cemented in the annals of history. There is something deep down in my soul that gives me a warm fuzzy feeling and makes me believe in love again when I read such a beautiful story.

About 65 kilometres from Bethal, however, another farmer had other ideas. Good old Adriaan Stander sold his farm, which lies on the banks of the Vaal River, to the government on one condition and one condition only: thou shalt keep my name! But then, we cannot blame Adriaan. And, come to think of it, his wife was also a Stander – who knows, maybe Standerton is named after Mrs and not Mr Stander.

In the Free State, meanwhile, one Mrs Steyn sold the family's farm to the government on condition that the town that was to be built there was named after her late husband Petrus Steyn. This town lies 275 kilometres northeast of Bloemfontein.

Then there's Pietermaritzburg which, depending on which narrative you subscribe to, also has a double-barrel name. One interpretation says the city was named after two Voortrekker leaders, Piet Retief and Gerrit Maritz; another says it was named after Retief alone. After all, Piet Retief's full name was Pieter Mauritz Retief. You be the judge.

Still in Pietermaritzburg, and as an aside, one of the streets in the central business district is Boshoff, named after a former Orange Free State president, Jacobus Nicolaas Boshoff (sometimes spelt Boshof). The farming town in the north of what is today the Free State bears his name. At one stage of his career, Boshoff was a magistrate in Pietermaritzburg (and he died in that town, in 1881) but it was in his capacity as the president of the Orange Free State that he laid the foundation stone for a school in Bloemfontein in 1856. That school was Grey College. (Interestingly, Boshoff was educated in those two husband-and-wife-named towns, Swellendam and Graaff-Reinet.)

Last on the double-barrel note is the town of Fauresmith, founded in 1850. The 'Smith' comes from Harry Smith (about whom more in Chapter 2), while 'Faure' makes reference to the Reverend Phillip Faure. Rev. Faure, who was educated in the Netherlands and England, was part of the executive council of the Groote Kerk, the mother Dutch Reformed church, in Cape Town in the early 1920s, and served on it for more than forty years. In mid-1850, Fauresmith lost out to Bloemfontein by a narrow margin as the capital of the then Boer republic of the Orange Free State. Fauresmith holds the record as the only town in South Africa, and one of only three in the world, with a rail track running down its main road. Is this a good or a bad record, or is there no such thing as a bad record?

Governor Hendrik Swellengrebel of Swellendam fame was succeeded in 1771 by Ryk Tulbagh, who held the position for twenty years, until 1791, when he died. I do not have to tell you that there is a town named after Tulbagh. It is a picturesque village about sixty kilometres north of Paarl. Ryk – just to keep it in the family, or perhaps to ensure continuity – married Swellengrebel's younger sister, Elizabeth.

Tulbagh was supposed to be succeeded by Pieter van Reede (also spelt Rheede) van Oudtshoorn. Unfortunately, Pieter died during the sea voyage to South Africa to start his new job. The fact that he never actually served as governor did not stop the ostrich capital of the world being named after him.

Sometimes – or maybe it's just me – there seems to be some confusion between Pieter van Reede van Oudtshoorn and Hendrik Adriaan van Rheede tot Drakenstein. In 1684, the latter was appointed by the Dutch East India Company to conduct an inspection in the Cape Colony, as well as in modern-day Sri Lanka and India, in order to, among other things, identify and combat corruption. Drakenstein was also a naturalist, and while he was in the Cape in 1685, he recommended wine growing and cultivation for the surrounding area to then governor Simon van der Stel. He also, importantly, granted land to Van der Stel in the modern-day southern suburbs of Cape Town, and Van der Stel wasted no time in planting vines there. Groot Constantia, although it's changed hands a number of times since then, is still operating, and is South Africa's oldest wine farm.

Drakenstein municipality, which is headquartered in Paarl, got its name from Hendrik. In 1687 Simon van der Stel handed out the first title deeds in the Paarl area to former Dutch East India Company employees known as 'free burghers'. The following year, Huguenots who were facing religious persecution in France arrived in the Cape. These new arrivals had experience in viniculture and, as they say in the documentaries, the rest is history.

The same Drakenstein municipality, together with five other local municipalities with their head offices in Ceres, Stellenbosch, Ashton and Worcester, form the Cape Winelands District Municipality – all courtesy of Hendrik Adriaan van Rheede tot Drakenstein. And, just to top it off, the mountain range east of Paarl is known as the Drakenstein mountains.

The arrival of the Huguenots in the Cape not only changed the demographics of the area, but some of their descendants went on to be, in one way or another, historical figures. Some of those Huguenot families included the Retiefs (the French version was 'Retif'), the De Klerks ('Le Clercq'), the Malans ('Mallan'), the Terblanches ('Terreblanque'), the Viljoens ('Villion'), the Cronjes ('Cronier'), the Nels ('Neel' and 'Niel'), the Labuschagnes ('la Buscagne'), the Rossouws ('Rousseau'), the Pienaars ('Pinard'), the Nortjes ('Nourtier') and the Therons ('Therond'). Some surnames, however, kept their original forms, like Du Toit, Meyer, Roux, Naudé, Du Plessis, Du Randt, Fourie and Le Roux.

One of the newcomers during that era was Jacques Mouton, 'a French Huguenot who arrived … on the 20th of July 1699 … in the hope of making a new life for himself and his family', according to the labels on the wine bottles bearing the Mouton name. In recent times, the Mouton name has been carried forward and upwards by JJ Mouton, the founder of investment holding company the PSG Group.

The company's website makes for a fascinating read. It all started in the 1995/96 financial year, when a personnel agency called PAG was bought for R7 million at 36c per share. By 2021, PSG had strategic investments in companies like Capitec and Curro, and its market capital was more than R20 billion. PJ Mouton, JJ's son, is now CEO of the group, while his father is a non-executive director. Jacques Mouton who arrived in the Cape in 1699 must be beaming with pride.

Imagine – yes, I am going there – if black people, soon after gaining political power in 1994, had had this type of mindset: creating, from scratch, their own companies and not depending on handouts/crumbs from established white companies. This reminds me of a quote by Palestinian poet Ghassan Kanafani: 'They steal your bread, then give you a crumb of it. Then they demand you to thank them for their generosity. O their audacity!'

Didn't BEE beneficiaries thank their benefactors for the crumbs that they had been given? Black people, almost all politically connected individuals, had their own stampede (comrades stabbing each other in the back) to be first in line to sign so-called BEE deals, and then thanked white people for their generosity. One day we as a country, but mostly as black people, need to have a frank conversation about the social value of those BEE deals. It is only a matter of time, part of me thinks, before black people who signed BEE deals are called sellouts.

As part of localising the Huguenots, one of the colony's policy directives was that instead of French, they had to speak Dutch. With Dutch evolving in time into Afrikaans, it was only natural that the descendants of the Huguenots spoke Afrikaans as their home language. That is how some people who know very well that they have French roots do not, even just a tiny bit, associate themselves with France and the French. Such is the power of language. Today, and for all these years, 'die taal' is part and parcel of Afrikaner heritage.

It was in that context that a decision was taken to erect a monument exclusively dedicated to 'die taal'. The Taal Monument in Paarl was officially opened on 10 October 1975, a public holiday back then because it was Paul Kruger's birthday. The year 1975 was not only the fiftieth celebration since Afrikaans had been declared an official language, but also the centenary of the founding of the Genootskap van Regte Afrikaners (Society of True Afrikaners), which had played a strategic role in bolstering the Afrikaans language as part of Afrikaner heritage.

But let's go back to Pieter van Reede van Oudtshoorn. As an employee of the Dutch East India Company, he was granted land by Governor Hendrik Swellengrebel. This is where, just a stone's throw from the Company's Gardens in Cape Town, the modern-day Mount Nelson Hotel is located.

When Ryk Tulbagh succeeded Swellengrebel, Pieter worked as Tulbagh's assistant, before heading back to the Netherlands in 1766 to assist in wrapping up his uncle's affairs in Europe, leaving his wife and children behind. It was in 1772, as previously mentioned, when he was on his way back via ship to take up the post of governor, that he died.

Nine years after his death, his then 61-year-old widow, Sophia Catharina, caused what must have been the scandal of the century when she tried, unsuccessfully, to withdraw all the inheritance and disappear into the sunset arm in arm with her lover, a 20-year-old soldier. (Of course, you went to double-check how old the lady was. Yes, there was a 41-year difference. I have often wondered if, in such cases, the 20-year-old were to call her 'Granny' during a steamy sex session, that would be a mood killer?)

In all of this I will reserve judgement except to state the obvious: love knows no boundaries. Love knows no colour. Love knows no age difference. Love, and sometimes lust, can make you take stupid decisions.

Many years later, a magistrate in George had a brilliant idea. This Egbertus Bergh, who happened to be married to Ernestina Johanna Geesje, one of Pieter's grandchildren, founded a town 65 kilometres from George, on the other side of the Outeniqua Mountains, and managed to convince everyone that it should be named after his wife's grandfather.

Let me state it again: love knows no boundaries. This Mr Bergh could have convinced all and sundry to name the town after his father or even his own grandfather. But nope, it had to be named after his wife's grandfather.

It comes as no surprise, I conclude, that, given the scandal of the century, there is no town called Lady Oudtshoorn.

Another story, which I read in June McKinnon's excellent book *Wine, Women & Good Hope: A history of scandalous behaviour in the Cape* (Penguin Random House, 2015), which must have overwhelmed the Cape Colony at the time, was that of a married woman named Maria Mouton who was, first, having an affair; second, it was with a slave, old Titus from Bengal; who, third (together with his friend Fortuyn from Angola), killed Maria's husband, the very unfortunate Franz Jooste. And, fourth, Maria helped her boyfriend by burying Franz's corpse in a shallow grave. All three were hanged for the crime. So dismayed was the community that Maria's father was forbidden from standing as a member of the church council.

But let's retrace our steps to where we were before being sidetracked by the stories of Hendrik Adriaan van Rheede tot Drakenstein and Pieter van Reede van Oudtshoorn – Ryk Tulbagh.

Ryk's eventual successor, after Oudtshoorn passed away before being able to take up the post, remained in office for fourteen years. It is not surprising, therefore, that the town that for almost two hundred years previously had borne the lyrical name Bahia Formosa ('beautiful bay' in Portuguese) was changed to Plettenberg Bay, in honour of governor Joachim Ammena van Plettenberg. The house that Van Plettenberg built in Cape Town, and which he subsequently used as his winter residence – coincidentally called The Residency – is still standing today; it is now the Simon's Town Museum.

Some governors, instead of (or in addition to) giving their name to a town, gave it to something else. As an example, a mental institution in Pietermaritzburg that started as a military base got its name from Sir George Thomas Napier, British governor of the Cape Colony from 1839 to 1843. But he does also, as expected, have his own town: Napier in the Western Cape.

The manner in which Napier got to be named after Sir George is interesting. Very interesting. It all began when Michiel van Breda, who was the first mayor of Cape Town, from 1840 to 1844 (and who was also a Freemason – see Part II), decided he wanted a church built on his farm, Zoetendals Vallei, in today's southern Overberg region of the Western Cape. But another prominent man of the time, Pieter Voltelyn van der Byl, strongly objected, because he wanted the church to be built on *his* farm, Klipdrift. Eventually, two churches were built, one on each farm, and in time you had two towns only nineteen kilometres apart. The one is Bredasdorp and the other Napier, named after Michiel van Breda and Governor Sir George Thomas Napier, respectively.

In retrospect, it was a good thing that Pieter Voltelyn van der Byl did not have the new town named after him, because years later another Van der Byl (but spelt Van der Bijl) would have his own town. This one lies on the banks of the Vaal River in Gauteng.

Dr Hendrik Johannes van der Bijl was not only the founding chairman of the Electricity Supply Commission (Escom, later Eskom, or – if you insist – Eishkom), he also established the Iron and Steel Corporation of South Africa, Iscor, and was its chair for many years. That explains why the city of Vanderbijlpark, where Iscor's major steelworks were built and still operate, is named after him.

As an aside, Klipdrift, South Africa's famous brandy, does not come from Pieter Voltelyn van der Byl's original farm of the same name. No, it does not. It comes from further north, and another farm, just outside Robertson. Jacobus Petrus 'Kosie' Marais, instead of focusing on wine, which is what almost all farmers were concentrating on at the time, decided to produce brandy. On 4 May 1938, at exactly o8ho2, the legend states, the first drop poured out; and to this day, the timestamp 'o8ho2' is still proudly displayed on each and every bottle of Klippies, as Klipdrift is affectionately known.

I have been reliably told that after eight double shots of Klippies, the clock starts ticking. Very fast.

Years later, the Van Loveren family from the same area put Robertson on the map again. But this time it was about wine. Hennie, Niel, Phillip and Bussel are cousins, and Four Cousins is one of South Africa's favourite sparkling wines. The Van Loverens' wide-ranging wines are enjoyed throughout our country and in more than sixty countries abroad.

Just thinking about my own cousins, and the prospect of us working together to literally take on the world, is enough for me to grab yet another bottle of Four Cousins red wine.

Is it not ironic that the town of Robertson, which gave us, and continues to give us, well-known alcohol brands, is named after a Scottish Dutch Reformed pastor? Is an alcohol-producing town great for Dr William Robertson's legacy, or does nobody care? Nobody cares, I am sure, but me. But then again, on a few occasions during ceremonies, I have found myself being ushered away from the crowds so that I can have alcohol with pastors in the bedroom.

The reason for being chosen as the one to share great whisky with the men of god is that, as one pastor told me when all of us were hopelessly drunk in one bedroom, I look like 'a good man who can keep great secrets'.

Back to George Napier. His mother, Lady Sarah Lennox, lived what I would call a colourful life. She almost married a future king, George III, but the prince was discouraged from closing that deal because she was considered a commoner, even though her father was one of King Charles II's eleven illegitimate children.

King George III, incidentally, married Charlotte of Mecklenburg-Strelitz of Germany, who was just 17 years old at the time. It was an arranged marriage, and the princess met her 22-year-old husband-to-be for the very first time on their wedding day. Just imagine! They went on to have 15 children. The marriage lasted 47 years.

Queen Charlotte died in 1818, and the king two years later, probably of a broken heart.

This reminds me of President Kwame Nkrumah, who also had an arranged marriage, at the age of 48, with Egyptian Fathia Halim Rizk, then aged 25. They had three children and their marriage had lasted 15 years when Nkrumah died in 1972. When Fathia passed on 35 years later in 2007, as per her request, she was buried next to her husband's remains at the Kwame Nkrumah Memorial Park in Accra, Ghana.

Maybe to curb the high divorce rate, I think we must ask our family members and/or very close friends to choose our spouses for us. After all, some people date for years, and after a few years (or, heaven forbid, months) of marriage, it is all over.

The moral of the story: marriage – I do not care who says what – has no formula.

Chapter 2
THE BRITISH ADMINISTRATORS

British governors must have been the gods, or, at the very least, the demigods, of their era. They were reigning lords in their respective colonies. Most of them started off as run-of-the-mill soldiers but after a battle or five they took on some administrative roles. Then it was often just a matter of time before, as part of being praised by their seniors, they were offered positions where they would hold sway over millions of hectares of land. No wonder they seemingly had a god complex.

Speaking of battles, the British occupied the Cape Colony after the Battle of Muizenberg in 1795. Eight years later the British, great global citizens that they were, gave the colony back to the Dutch. But three years later, in 1806, they changed their mind, and occupied the colony for a second time after the Battle of Blaauwberg.

If the governors did not have a god complex, then how do you explain the following? A 26-year-old soldier named Harry Smith got married to 14-year-old Juana María de Los Dolores de León during the Napoleonic wars of the early 1800s. Years later, Harry Smith, who served as a governor of the Cape Colony and a high commissioner in South Africa from 1847 to 1852, had a town in the Free State named after him (Harrismith); and, less than a hundred kilometres away, a town in KwaZulu-Natal is named after his wife, Lady Smith (Ladysmith). For good measure, there is another town, this one in the Western Cape, also named after Lady Smith (Ladismith). Talk about a formidable couple.

The year before being appointed governor, Smith had fought and vanquished the Sikh army in the Battle of Aliwal in India. Two towns in South Africa showcased Smith's victory: Aliwal South and Aliwal North. Aliwal South as a name did not stick. The inhabitants of the town were used to the original name, which had been used for centuries – more than 200 years, to be precise. Bartholomeu Dias, the Portuguese explorer, named the place Aguada de São Brás (Bay of St Blaise) in honour of the patron saint whose day was 3 February, the day he made landfall on these shores. It was only renamed in 1601, by Dutch navigator Paulus van Caerden, who was impressed by the abundance of mussels he saw there. Yep, that name was – and still is – Mossel Bay.

But there is yet another town named after Harry: Smithfield in the Free State. Yes, that means there are two towns less than 400 kilometres from each other, and in the same province, named after Lieutenant-General Sir Henry George Wakelyn Smith. This effectively means between Harry and Lady Smith, there are four and a half towns named after them (Harrismith, Smithfield, Ladysmith, Ladismith and Fauresmith); and if we include Aliwal North, that takes the number of towns named after Smith and his wife to five and a half.

When Lady Smith passed on, twelve years after her husband's death, her mortal remains were interred with him. English novelist Georgette Heyer's *The Spanish Bride* narrates this incredible love story in a novel that was published almost seventy years after Lady Smith's death, in 1940.

Another prime example of a power couple – at least, on the surface – is Sir George Grey and his wife, Elizabeth Lucy Grey (née Spencer). The story of Sir George and his wife is reminiscent of some of the modern couples who consistently post on social media highlighting, in fact advertising, how happy they are, when the reality is the exact opposite. But more about this disastrous relationship later. For now, dear reader, let me just say that Greytown, which is about 75 kilometres from Pietermaritzburg, is named after Sir George Grey. And just like Lady Smith, who gave her name to two towns, Sir George Grey is responsible for two: a village in the Western Cape that lies off the N2 between Swellendam and Caledon is called Greyton. As for his wife, there is a town between Aliwal North and Barkly East named after her, and it is called – yes – Lady Grey.

And, oh, Grey Hospital in the Eastern Cape and Grey's Hospital in KwaZulu-Natal got their names from this fine administrator. Even two of the oldest schools in the country, Grey College and Grey High School, got their names from Sir George. Both have a number of alumni who have contributed immensely to South Africa, especially in the sporting fraternity. Grey High School in Gqeberha produced cricketing legend Graeme Pollock, as well as Springbok captain Siya Kolisi, while Bloemfontein's Grey College is where former Proteas captain Hansie Cronje went to school and where his ashes are kept.

Speaking of ashes, I always thought – especially as a black African – that cremation was something far removed from me. Well, that was the case until I got married. My wife's maternal grandfather, David Cecil Oxford 'DCO' Matiwane, was cremated because – wait for it – he was worried that the white professors from the then University of Natal (Pietermaritzburg Campus) were so eager to understand his intellectual prowess that they would dig up his corpse in order to fully appreciate why he was so intelligent.

He was a political activist at the time, and I assume that is why he was so paranoid. Who in his right mind would think someone would dig up his decaying brain? Only DCO!

When, after being sick for a while, he passed on in 1982, aged 64, he was, as per his wishes, cremated. Since then, cremation is almost (for lack of a better term) a standing family tradition. In fact, since I met my wife, five of DCO's children (Thulasizwe, Barbara, Zanele, Themba and Ntsika) have passed on, and all of them were cremated. It is not so much, as far as I know, that they stated that they would like to be cremated. It is that, while in other families it is taken for granted that when you die you will be buried, for the Matiwanes, unless you state otherwise publicly while you are alive, the default setting is that you will be cremated.

I often used to quietly think to myself, *What type of black African people are these?* Now I am comfortable going to Umlazi, where my wife's aunt lives, and being in a house with not one but two sets of ashes. (Are they even called sets of ashes?) I have spent many nights in this township south of Durban at Aunt Sbongile's house and, unlike before, when I would consciously think of being in the company of two dead bodies, nowadays it no longer feels creepy. Now, I don't even think about it. That is how much I have accepted this cremation thing. In fact, I am even considering it for myself. The only thing that still bugs me is the actual burning of the body. But then, if I don't get cremated; the problem with being buried is that I am claustrophobic. The mere thought of my body being in a closed coffin six feet underground is enough to almost kill me.

Maybe that explains why I am an organ donor. It has less to do with me being a very nice person (which I am), and being selfless by helping the living (even when I am dead, I will still be a very nice person), and more to do with what you may call a death in-surance: knowing that as a fact of life under no circumstances will I ever wake up in the dark and realise that, eish …

Maybe I must get cremated and then get buried. Just to be dead sure.

The Smiths (Harry and the wife) and the Greys (George and the wife) were not the only power couple to grace these shores. Sir Henry Bartle Edward Frere and his wife Lady Catherine Frere (née Arthur) were also, and for quite some time, a power couple. These days, though, the town of Mount Frere is officially known as kwaBhaca, and Lady Frere has been renamed Cacadu.

Henry Frere had to face the consequences of being a shameless and overly ambitious imperialist: while serving as a high commissioner for Southern Africa, he was recalled and summoned back to England in 1880 to face a misconduct charge – he was accused of acting recklessly in his attempts to expand the British empire, both during his stint in India as governor of Bombay from 1862 to 1867, and in South Africa. At the time, he was at the forefront of trying to create a confederation of British states in South Africa, but was being met with resistance from all fronts: Basotho, Boers, Xhosas and Zulus.

The village that served as a British headquarters during the South African War of 1899–1902, just outside Estcourt in the KwaZulu-Natal Midlands, is called Frere. And further afield, the highest mountain in the state of Queensland in Australia is named Mount Bartle Frere – Frere was at one stage the president of the Royal Geographical Society.

Lord Charles Somerset, who was Cape governor from 1814 to 1826, has two towns almost 800 kilometres apart named after him: Somerset East and Somerset West, in the Eastern Cape and Western Cape, respectively. So influential was Lord Somerset that during his twelve years in office, not one, not two, but three towns were named after – wait for it – his father, Henry Somerset, the Fifth Earl of Beaufort. There are Port Beaufort and Fort Beaufort, both in the Eastern Cape; and Beaufort West in the Western Cape, where world-famous heart surgeon Christiaan Barnard grew up. (The Earl was also a prominent Freemason – see Part II: The power brokers.)

Just for control, as young people would say, another town in the Western Cape is named after Lord Charles's older brother, Henry Charles Somerset, the Sixth Duke of Beaufort and First Marquess of Worcester. So when Lord Charles named the town Worcester, I am sure he just thought, *What the heck, let me name this new establishment after, as the Afrikaners often put it, my boet.*

This means you have six towns in South Africa named after the father and his two sons. And, as far as I am aware, there is no record that Lord Charles's older brother and their father ever set foot in South Africa.

It was not only the Marquess of Worcester who had a geographical entity named after his title. The same thing happened to the governor of the Cape from 1807 to 1811, Du Pre Alexander, the Second Earl of Caledon. The Caledon River, with its source in Lesotho, flows to South Africa and eventually joins the Orange, our country's largest river.

And it was not only Harry Smith and Lord Charles Somerset who had two towns, or more, named after them. Sir Henry Barkly, who was governor of the Cape from 1870 until he was recalled in disgrace in 1877, is responsible for Barkly East in the Eastern Cape and Barkly West in the Northern Cape. On top of that, there is a Barkly mountain pass between Barkly East and Elliot. And it comes as no surprise, if one considers that Barkly, prior to coming to South Africa, was governor of Victoria in Australia, that the vast Barkly tableland of Queensland and the Northern Territory was named in his honour.

Henry's father, who was a merchant, owned more than four thousand – yep, four thousand – slaves for whom he was handsomely compensated when slavery was abolished in 1834. In 1836, Henry, aged only 20, inherited his father's estate – which was nothing to write home about, when you discover that some investors in the business of selling people in South America and the Caribbean lodged claims against the estate. Later, Henry, as a fully fledged adult, pursued a political career, during which he served as a governor of British Guiana, Jamaica, Mauritius and Victoria in Australia, before ending up in the Cape Colony.

The amount of money inherited by Henry is immaterial. What matters is that slavery was one of the biggest 'industries' (for want of a better term) in the history of humankind. Fortunes were made by slave traders, merchants and owners. The entire export market for some countries depended almost entirely on the slave trade. The Caribbean islands, for example, exported rum, sugar, cocoa and fruit, all of which would have been impossible to produce without slaves. Some of those fortunes, made two centuries ago, are still being passed down from one generation to the next to this day.

Although slavery was officially abolished in the 1800s, that did not stop the system treating black people here in South Africa effectively as slaves when they worked in the diamond fields of Kimberley, the gold mines of the Witwatersrand, or in the general economy in the 1800s and a large part of the 1900s.

One is tempted to conclude that slavery has just evolved. Modern-day slavery is much more subtle. It is more sophisticated. It is called credit. As that new saying goes, 'Modern slaves are not in chains; they are in debt.'

To return once again to the governors, a globetrotting Cape governor was Sir Charles Darling, who held the post from 1851 to 1854. Coincidentally, he succeeded Barkly in the Cape before also serving as a governor both in Jamaica and in Victoria in Australia. Pieter-Dirk Uys (aka Evita Bezuidenhout), a resident of the west coast town of Darling, has made that little place famous.

While governors such as Smith and Grey, and prominent men like Brand senior and his son, named towns after their wives, John Francis Cradock (who was a Freemason – see Part II) had other ideas. It was his father-in-law, Sir John Meade, First Earl of Clanwilliam, who was immortalised in the name of the town located on the Olifants River in the Western Cape.

Cradock was not, I might as well mention, the only governor to name a town after his father-in-law. Sir Galbraith Lowry Cole, who served a five-year stint, from 1828 to 1833, had a father-in-law who was a diplomat who worked in a number British embassies, including those in modern-day Russia, Germany, Spain and the

Netherlands. James Harris, First Earl of Malmesbury, is remembered today in the town that lies about sixty kilometres from Cape Town.

Of course, Cole himself had to have a town named after him. When driving between Bloemfontein and Cape Town, and you cannot wait to get to the Cape, the distance can be very discouraging. The road between Cape Town and Colesberg is a very long 780 kilometres. It was during Cole's governorship that a pass was built over the mountain range between the Elgin valley and Somerset West. Opened in 1830, it was named Sir Lowry's Pass.

A town in the Eastern Cape that was renamed Nxuba in the second half of 2022 (amidst the push-back by some local residents) had for decades carried the name of John Cradock, who is remembered for an order he gave during his three-year tenure as the Cape governor from 1811 to 1814: to drive the Xhosa off the land called the Zuurveld in what is today the Eastern Cape, which was seen as British territory. They were to be crushed by any means necessary, he said, including the burning of homes, destruction of crops and killing of men who resisted being moved.

Cradock gave the order to soldier Colonel John Graham, who delivered on the mandate. The town that was subsequently established on the site of his headquarters was naturally named after him. Cradock, once the locals had been defeated, reported back to England that the locals had been forced across the Fish River with 'a proper degree of terror'.

Does this mean that Clanwilliam, which is named after Cradock's father-in-law, will soon be renamed too?

Only recently was Grahamstown renamed Makhanda, after Makhanda kaNxele, a nineteenth-century Xhosa warrior. Makhanda, after surrendering, was sent to Robben Island where he attempted to escape by swimming across the ocean and drowned. Locals for generations have called this area Rhini and, notwithstanding there being different theories of where that name comes from, some would prefer to call the town Rhini, but the government insists on it being called Makhanda.

There is another town named after a Graham, but this one was Graham Barber, an explorer who discovered gold in 1884 in modern-day Mpumalanga. Soon thereafter, fortune-seekers flocked to Barberton, and there was so much commercial activity that the first stock exchange in the then Transvaal was established there. A few years later, when even more gold was discovered on the Witwaters-rand, the fortune-seekers left Barberton.

Sir Peregrine Maitland, governor of the Cape from 1844 to 1847, also honoured his father-in-law, Charles Lennox, the Fourth Duke of Richmond, in a South African naming spree. There are, in fact, three Richmonds in the country, one in KwaZulu-Natal, the second in the Northern Cape and another in Mpumalanga. They are so far apart, and so small, that even though they are spelt the same way, there is no confusion.

The Cape Town suburb of Maitland is named after the governor and, for good measure, so is a river in the Eastern Cape.

Sir Peregrine's father-in-law was appointed the governor-in-chief of British North America (today's Canada) in 1818. As any good father-in-law would do, he appointed his son-in-law as his assistant; officially, Sir Peregrine became the lieutenant-governor of Upper Canada. But then again, which father-in-law would not recruit his son-in-law when that very son-in-law had named not one, not two, but three towns after him? As young people often say, it must be nice.

Sir George Cathcart was another governor who got his own town. This one lies south of Komani (formerly Queenstown, where the prestigious Queens College is situated) in the Eastern Cape. Sir George Cathcart is not that well known, partly because he was in South Africa for such a short time, from 1852 to 1853. One thing that he did while in the Cape was succeed Harry Smith during the eighth Cape Frontier war (also known as the Eastern Cape Wars of Dispossession), which were fought over a full century, from 1779 to 1879.

Although the eighth war had by then already lasted about three years, within six months of Cathcart's taking the reins, Chief Sandile surrendered. Soon thereafter, Cathcart was promoted to adjutant-general to the British Armed Forces – basically, one of the top dogs.

A year after leaving the Cape, however, Cathcart was killed in the Crimean War in what is modern-day Russia after being shot in the heart. Or is it through the heart? Can a heart stop a bullet? If yes, then he was shot in the heart, if not, then through the heart. Or is it both? Shot in the heart and then the bullet went through the heart. Does it matter? Actually not, but that is just the pedantic me being, er, anal. Heartily so!

Another governor who got a promotion to adjutant-general was Sir Garnet Wolseley. As a soldier he'd fought in Burma, the Crimea and India. That was before donning the mantle of leadership, when he was appointed governor of various African west coast states, including Sierra Leone, Gambia, Gold Coast and Nigeria. It was during this time, in 1873, that he fought and beat the Ashanti in modern-day Ghana, and burnt to the ground the palace in the regional capital of Kumasi.

Years later, especially after the defeat of the British at the Battle of Isandlwana, Wolseley was called in to sort out the bloody Zulus. For good. But, officially appointed governor of Natal and the Transvaal and high commissioner of Southern Africa, by the time he landed in Natal in 1879, the war was effectively over: the British had reached King Cetshwayo's palace in Ondini and burnt it down, and the king was on the run.

Wolseley therefore took on another assignment: to defeat King Sekhukhune who, over the three-year period between 1876 and 1879, had successfully fought and won against both the Boers and the British. Sir Garnet, with the help of some ten thousand Swazis, delivered the Sekhukhune scalp. His palace, as had been the case in Ondini with the Zulus and the Ashanti in Ghana, was burnt to ashes.

Sekhukhune was imprisoned for three years before being released, soon after which he was killed by his half-brother, Mampuru II, who believed he was the rightful heir to the throne. Mampuru was captured and sentenced to death, and hanged in front of a crowd at the prison that today is a maximum-security facility and bears his name.

The Swazis (technically speaking, and in fact amaSwati) were not the only ethnic group who helped the European power against a rival tribal or ethnic group. The Tswanas supported Rhodes's private army, under the auspices of the British South Africa Company, when it not only attacked but annihilated the amaNdebele (back then called the Matebele) in modern-day Zimbabwe. And further north, slavery would not have thrived as it did for all those centuries had it not been for one tribe being used for hunting and transporting rival tribes to the coast where the Europeans were eagerly waiting.

Sir Garnet was so structured, efficient and methodical in his personality that soldiers, instead of saying 'everything is in good order' would say 'all Sir Garnet'. For all his efforts, at least in South Africa, he got a town, Wolseley, in today's Western Cape, named after him.

Most South Africans know Bell Pottinger as the public-relations company that, among other things, spearheaded the use of the term 'white monopoly capital', which purported to show that white South Africans were the ones owning the means of production while the majority of black people lived well below the poverty line. But it turns out that there was another Pottinger in South Africa, more than 150 years earlier. The reason why this Pottinger, also a governor, is not well known is because he was in South Africa for less than a year, in 1847, before heading to India. Prior to coming to South Africa, he was Hong Kong's first governor, appointed in 1843. It makes sense that not only a street but also a mountain are named after Sir Henry Pottinger – but in Hong Kong, not in South Africa.

And then just to illustrate how unfair life is, think about the two governors, Abraham Josias Sluysken and Sir Walter Hely-Hutchinson, who, notwithstanding being in South Africa for a while, are only remembered by historians, while there are two governors who never even set foot in South Africa but are extremely famous on these shores.

The first was the Dutch director-general for more 25 years in the then Colony of New Netherland, which covered part of the modern-day USA states of New York, New Jersey, Pennsylvania, Maryland, Connecticut and Delaware. There are a few places named after him in New York, including schools and apartment buildings, but it was not until the 1950s, when an international cigarette company named one of its brands after him, that he became a worldwide figure. His name was Peter Stuyvesant.

Then there was a Welshman who grew up to be not just an owner of hundreds of slaves but also the lieutenant-governor of Jamaica. Four years after his death, there was a major earthquake which resulted in part of the town of Port Royal, including the cemetery, sinking into the harbour. His body was, together with other corpses, washed away and never found. Sir Henry Morgan's name is today associated with a famous alcohol brand, Captain Morgan rum.

Is it fair, therefore, to conclude that Captain Morgan was lost at sea?

It was not only the governors of the Cape Colony whose names were etched into the annals of history through towns. Those in that other British colony, Natal, were also honoured accordingly and appropriately.

That naming spree started in earnest after the British annexed the Boer republic of Natalia in 1843. The first governor appointed was Martin Thomas West, in 1845. Thereafter, governors that interest us for the purposes of this book, all of whom served in the second half of the 1800s, include Benjamin Pine, John Scott and Anthony Musgrave; and two governors whose stints were cut short, George Colley and William Bellairs.

Lieutenant-General Benjamin D'Urban was the governor of the Cape when the British decided to also annex Natal in 1843 and make it – yep – a British colony. That explains why the biggest city in KwaZulu-Natal was named after him. And to show that he had roots in the Cape, a suburb in Cape Town, Durbanville, also bears his name.

During D'Urban's tenure, missionary Dr John Philip went all the way to England to attest to how the indigenous people were being ill-treated in the Cape Colony. That submission led to the dismissal of D'Urban just three years into his incumbency. Dr Philip, meanwhile, has a town in the Free State, Philippolis, named after him.

Philip's daughter, Eliza, married John Fairbairn, a financier, newspaper proprietor and educator. If the name 'Fairbairn' sounds familiar, it is because the investment arm of one of South Africa's biggest financial institutions, Old Mutual, is named after this gentleman. It was, after all, this high achiever who founded that company way back in 1845.

Whilst living in Durban in the 1990s and early 2000s, I, like other Durbanites, would pop in to the Martin West building, named after the lieutenant-governor of Natal from 1845 to 1849. We would go there now and then to deal with municipality-related queries such as electricity and rates. The building is now named after anti-apartheid activist Florence Mkhize. Florence's only daughter is Shauwn, the businesswoman who, among other things, owns the Premier League soccer team Royal AM.

West Street, also originally named after Sir Martin West, has been renamed Anton Lembede Street, after the founding president of the ANC Youth League.

In Durban, a road and a mall on the same road bear the name of a well-travelled governor: Sir Anthony Musgrave. Musgrave's career spanned many locations, including the British West Indies in the Caribbean, Newfoundland and British Columbia (in modern-day Canada), South Australia, Jamaica, and, of course, South Africa. His last posting was as governor of Queensland in Australia, and he died literally sitting at his desk nine days short of his sixtieth birthday.

I have, at times, wondered what the most appropriate way to die is. Surely, dying at your desk in the office creates, among other things, an administrative nightmare for your colleagues? Would such a death, as an example, be classified as work related? How do you even start recruiting a replacement for the deceased? Must you, as a prospective employer, declare during the interview, 'The person you will replace if successful died sitting in the chair that you will soon literally be occupying'?

I had always thought that dying of old age with your loved ones around you must be (for lack a better term) satisfying to most parties involved – until my mother passed away in June 2022, eleven days short of my 47th birthday. Although she had been sick for a few months, after seeing her on a video call I somehow knew that the end was nigh. In fact, the saddest search phrase I've ever typed into google, soon after that video call, was 'signs and symptoms that someone is slowly dying'. Admittedly, I had never thought before that moment of such a search.

Google took me to a number of hospice websites, and, one way or another, they confirmed my fear that my mother was dying: she was hardly eating or drinking, and thus had no bowel movements, she was withdrawn and could not speak, and her hands and forehead temperature were low (I was told – she was at home in Nquthu in KwaZulu-Natal, and I was in Johannesburg). The last sign, which was difficult to deal with, was seeing her having trouble breathing. It was like she was gasping for air.

Although she held on for the night, and my niece Ntokoe and

I were able to do the four-hour drive to Nquthu, it was clear that my mother's time on this planet was coming to an end. I had always thought it best for someone to die in the company of loved ones. But my sister Nontobeko and I, in consultation with other family members, decided to take her to the hospital, because we still believed against all the odds that she would pull through. Rebecca Duduzile 'RD' Sithole left these shores the following day, 8 June, at 06:15.

The moral of the story: nothing illustrates that life is a bitch like the fact that the best-case scenario is for you, over a period of time, to bury both your parents. Nothing illustrates that life is a bitch like the fact that, if you are lucky and you live a long life, you will in time bury all your siblings and cousins, and you will be the only one remaining of your generation. That is exactly what happened to my mother.

Personally, I would prefer to die either while reading a newspaper on the toilet (something I do now and then) or, even better, while sleeping in a bed on a private jet over the ocean with loved ones on board, on the return leg of a once-in-a-lifetime holiday during which I had ticked off the last item on my bucket list (i.e., finding out the meaning of life).

But enough about death and depressing stuff.

After an eight-year stint in South Africa, first as lieutenant-governor of Natal and then as governor, Sir Henry Bulwer became high commissioner in Cyprus. The town of Bulwer is about sixty kilometres from Ixopo, which is beautifully described in the opening line of Alan Paton's world-famous book, *Cry, The Beloved Country*: 'There is a lovely road which runs from Ixopo into the hills. These hills are grass covered and rolling, and they are lovely beyond any singing of it.'

Talking about books, English writer Sir Henry Rider Haggard posthumously became a global icon after his book *King Solomon's Mines*, which was published in 1885, was made into a movie in

1937. It was the first adventure novel set on the African continent. Henry's family seemingly were friends with, or at least acquaintances of, Sir Henry Bulwer's family. It was Bulwer who brought the young Rider Haggard to Africa as a member of his staff. As an adult, Haggard had a farm in Natal, and he must have appreciated Sir Henry Bulwer because he dedicated to him one of his books, *Marie*, written in 1912.

The criteria that dictated whether a governor was going to get a place name or not seem to have been very unscientific, subjective, arbitrary, sketchy and biased. Take, for example, a man who acted as governor for half a month before the powers that be decided that another person had to act. Major-General Sir William Bellairs, a military commander and civil administrator, was in the position for a mere fifteen days, and yet the Durban suburb to which he gave his name is – yep – Bellair. (Someone seemingly left off the 's' and no-one noticed. Or did someone think an 's' might cause other people to think of it as a plural? I have often noted how some South Africans, even educated ones, call the retail chain store 'Woolworth'.)

Years later, in the late 1800s, a man who served as attorney-general of Natal, and who completed an eight-month stint as prime minister of the colony, ensured that he would get his own suburb in Durban. His name was Harry Escombe, and the name of the suburb is – yep – Escombe.

Pinetown, on the outskirts of Durban, is named after Benjamin Pine. Pine had two stints as governor, the first from 1850 to 1855, and the second twenty years later, from 1873 to 1875. Besides Pinetown, until recently there was also Pine Street in Durban's central business district. Pine Street is now Monty Naicker Road, after Dr Gangathura Mohambry 'Monty' Naicker, who was the president of the Natal Indian Congress from 1945 to 1963.

It was Naicker who, together with Dr Alfred Bathini 'AB' Xuma, president of the ANC (1940–1949) and Dr Yusuf Mohamed Dadoo, president of the Transvaal Indian Congress from 1946, signed what became known as the 'Three Doctors' pact in 1947. The objective of the pact was to unite 'non-Europeans' against oppressive laws.

As far back as 1948, Naicker, who had studied medicine in Scotland, started calling for a 'united democratic front' to fight the apartheid system. It was 35 years later that the UDF was officially launched.

Dr Xuma studied medicine in America, and he had to do odd jobs, including being a waiter, in order to finance his studies. After almost thirteen years in the USA, he went to Hungary to specialise in gynaecology and obstetrics. Once back in South Africa, he served three terms as the president of the ANC, and it was under his leadership that the youth league was formed, after some young people within the ANC, including Ashby Peter 'AP' Mda, Nelson Mandela and Oliver Tambo, said that they felt the organisation was not effectively fighting the system. Xuma was ousted in 1949 when he failed to endorse the Youth League's 'programme of action'.

A primary school in Orlando East, Soweto, and streets in Durban and Soweto are also named after this former ANC president. Dr Xuma, by the way, was succeeded as ANC president by another medical practitioner, Dr James Sebe Moroka. He led the organisation for three years before pastor and chief/Inkosi Albert Luthuli was elected. Moroka in Soweto, home of soccer team Moroka Swallows, is named after the good doctor.

Interestingly, in 1949, when the ANC Youth League was looking for a candidate to challenge AB Xuma, Zachariah Keodirelang 'ZK' Matthews, then a professor at the University of Fort Hare, was the League's first choice. The professor was none too keen, however. Come to think of it, had Matthews accepted and won the post, maybe his granddaughter, Dr Naledi Pandor, could have followed in the old man's footsteps and became possibly the first female president of the ANC.

In 2020, another of ZK Matthews' grandchildren made the

headlines. Zolani Kgosietsile 'Kgosie' Matthews, aged 64, was appointed the CEO of the Passenger Rail Agency of South Africa (PRASA), notwithstanding that the company's age ceiling for the position was 63. His employment was soon terminated – not because of his age but because he could not get the required top security clearance due to an undeclared dual citizenship, which he had obtained when he'd lived in Britain in the 1980s during the exile of his father, struggle stalwart Joe Matthews.

Matthews challenged his dismissal and won. PRASA appealed. It is now only a matter of time before Matthews signs a multimillion-rand settlement. You can't make this stuff up – organisations sometimes just stuff up.

Dr Dadoo, meanwhile, was a prominent member of the Communist Party of South Africa (subsequently renamed the South African Communist Party); he was chair of the party for eleven years, from 1972 to his death from cancer in 1983. After the 1960 Sharpeville massacre, he was tasked with representing the South African Communist Party (SACP) outside the country. From his office in London, he travelled the world, championing, representing and fighting for the oppressed back in South Africa. He lived in exile for 23 years.

Three years after his death, the apartheid government banned Dr Dadoo for a further five years. And there are still those among us who believe that the pre-1994 government was an efficient, sleek, well-oiled machine. Here is the proof that sometimes politicians and public servants (like everybody else) can – and do – fuck up, badly.

Dadoo is buried a few metres from Karl Marx's grave in London. But this is not the only link between South Africa and Karl Marx, and it has absolutely nothing to do with Marxism. Louise and Jan Carel Juta moved from Europe to the Cape in 1853. The couple had seven children. (One of them, Henry Herbert Juta, grew up to be a judge and at one stage was the speaker of parliament for the Cape Colony.) In South Africa, Louise and Jan started a publishing company; Juta and Company, the oldest publishing house in the country, still focuses on legal and educational books. Who would have thought that (depending on your age) some of the books you read at school were published by a company started by Louise, Karl Marx's sister.

As an aside, there is this myth (I am tempted to say propaganda) that AB Xuma was the first black African doctor in South Africa. Nothing could be further from the truth. According to an article authored by Professor Bongani Mayosi (who died in 2018; may his soul rest in eternal peace) in the *South African Medical Journal*, the first two black African doctors were William Anderson Soga and John Mavuma Nembula, who qualified in 1883 in Glasgow and 1887 in Chicago, respectively. Dr Nembula's year of qualification means he became a doctor six years before AB Xuma was even born in 1893.

Prof Mayosi lays it bare by stating that 'Soga qualified in medicine from Glasgow in 1883 – about 30 years before the creation of the medical school in Cape Town, and 60 years before UCT and Wits considered black people fit for admission to their hallowed halls'. Boom!

Just south of Durban lies a town called Scottburgh; and about a hundred kilometres away, in Pietermaritzburg, lies the suburb of Scottsville. Both got their names from governor John Scott, who was in the position from 1856 to 1864. In recent years, KwaZulu-Natal had a provincial minister named Belinda Scott. Belinda, who became Durban's deputy mayor in 2019 (and resigned two years later), was appointed on an ANC ticket.

Sir George Colley is a special case. A small rural town in KwaZulu-Natal carries his middle name. He was a governor for only eight months, from 1880 to 1881. Aged 45, he was fatally shot through the head during the battle of Majuba in 1881. This battle was the deciding factor of the First Anglo-Boer War, when the British were beaten convincingly by the Afrikaners. Sir George's middle name was Pomeroy. He is the only governor I know who gave his middle name to a town.

George Pomeroy Colley had ten children. Just to prove how small the world is, one of the passengers who perished on the fateful day in April 1912 when the British transatlantic passenger cruise ship the *Titanic* sank after hitting an iceberg was one of Sir George's children, Edward Colley.

As I was finalising this book, the government officially changed the name of Pomeroy to Solomon Linda. Linda, who hailed from this area before moving to Johannesburg, is mostly known for composing the song 'Mbube' which, in time, was exported as 'The lion sleeps tonight'. It is long overdue, I say. Perhaps Ladysmith will one day be renamed Joseph Shabalala, after the late leader of isicathamiya group Ladysmith Black Mambazo.

Lady Susan Hamilton, the wife of British colonial secretary Henry Pelham Fiennes Pelham-Clinton, Fifth Duke of Newcastle, must have caused mayhem in British upper-crust society when she eloped in the mid-1850s with her lover Lord Horatio Walpole. ('Walpole' sounds too close to 'elope'; maybe it's just me.) Who knows, maybe, just maybe, KwaZulu-Natal's third-largest city, Newcastle, was named after Henry to console him in his misfortune.

Is it not strange, to say the least, that Christians sometimes refer to God as 'Lord', and yet there are people who have power to dish out the title 'Lord' as and when they want to? In essence, there are three ways in which one can become a lord in the UK: become a member of the House of Lords, or marry someone who is already a lord or a lady, or purchase land from an existing lord or lady and, as the new landowner, take over the title. How I wish I was making this up. Imagine buying land belonging to a professor and then – voilà – you in the process also become, er, a professor.

Henry Pelham-Clinton wasn't the only colonial secretary to have got his own town. The most influential town at the time, soon after the discovery of diamonds in the 1860s, struggled to get a 'decent and intelligible' name, according to then British colonial secretary John Wodehouse. At one stage it was called Vooruitzigt, before being renamed New Rush. It was eventually dubbed Kimberley – after John Wodehouse, First Earl of Kimberley, the very colonial secretary who had so bitterly complained about the first two names. Is it just me, or isn't this what sucking up to head office looks like?

Although Cape Town is known as the Mother City, Kimberley played a critical role in the economic transformation of what would become the Republic of South Africa. In fact, Kimberley achieved a number of firsts, including being the first city in the southern hemisphere to install electric street lighting in 1882. The following year, the first South African stock exchange was opened there. It comes as no surprise that the world's first diamond-cutting factory was also established in this city of diamonds.

While Kimberley was booming, the South African School of Mines was founded there in 1896. With the discovery of gold on the Witwatersrand, a strategic decision was taken to move the school to Johannesburg, two years after the end of the South African War, in 1904 … It was, by the way, only in 1922 that the then University College was granted a full university status, and was officially named the University of Witwatersrand. That explains why in 2022 Wits celebrated, with fanfare, its centenary. In any way you look at it, Wits University owes its existence to the city of Kimberley and its diamonds.

As part of consolidating British Empire interests in southern Africa, the secretary of state for the colonies, Henry Howard Molyneux Herbert, Fourth Earl of Carnarvon, who succeeded John Wodehouse, had to appoint a seasoned administrator. It was in this context that Theophilus Shepstone came to South Africa. Among other things, Shepstone annexed the Transvaal and dictated to the Zulus that ilobolo (dowry) must be fixed at eleven cows – a practice that still holds today. Before Shepstone regulated the number of cows to be paid, the figure was very flexible, depending on several factors, including how wealthy the boy's family was, the skills of the negotiating team representing the husband-to-be, the stubbornness and greed of the girl's father, and so on. Nowadays, money is used instead of cows.

As might be expected, like Wodehouse, Herbert also got his own town: Carnarvon in the Karoo.

To detour a little, Charles Grey, aka Lord Howick, another secretary of state for the colonies, continues to be honoured in Howick, a town outside Pietermaritzburg, which got its name from Grey's estate in England. Imagine a town named after your estate? It must be nice.

This issue of the name of an estate reminds me that former president Zuma's homestead is called KwaDakwadunuse, which means 'the place where you get drunk and then show your arse'. It was not abnormal for Zulu men – back in the day when they still had plenty of land, unlike now, when they live squashed up in unhygienic conditions in hostels and informal settlements – to give a name to their homesteads. My maternal grandfather, for example, who was a chief of the Sithole clan (in isiZulu, we say Inkosi yakwaSithole), named some of his homesteads – yes, he had more than one, because he had seven wives – KwaSongeluyise ('the place where you curse your father'), KwaKhethukuthula ('the place where you choose to be quiet') and KwaPhumelefile ('the place where you will only rest when you are dead').

I might as well mention in passing that my great-grandfather, Inkosi Matshane, had thirty wives. I know, right? We are all on the same page and, trust me, I am thinking exactly the same thing. But then again, Westerners have Viagra while Zulus (actually amaZulu) have (u)muthi called uqanduqandu.

One day I hope to have my own homestead (this is the second-last item on my bucket list), which I will call KwaFukul'abampofu ('the place where we uplift the poor'), KwaFukula for short. Don't we all want to make this world a better place? But for now, we are still chasing our selfish dreams in order to achieve big things and be seen as successful. Just a friendly reminder – as the old adage goes, even if you were to win the rat race, you would still be, er, a rat.

Grey's Howick estate was in the county of Northumberland in northern England, and Northumberland also happens to be a major arterial in the northwestern part of Johannesburg – again, thanks to Earl Grey.

North of the town of Howick is the town of Hilton, which at times is misty. There is an area in England that is sometimes misty and is green most of the year, and it is called – yes – Hilton. The most expensive school in South Africa is Hilton College, and that is where the children of the wealthy, including politicians, get their education, while poor parents still send their children, in this day and age, to muddy, cramped schools in rural parts of the country where there is a risk that they could fall into a pit latrine and die in human excrement.

Back to Carnarvon.

It was Henry Herbert, Fourth Earl of Carnarvon, who appointed Sir Henry Bartle Edward Frere governor of the Cape Colony in the late 1870s. Frere, who had spent more than a decade in India, was a seasoned administrator, was given one task and one task only: to create a confederation of British states in southern Africa. And for his troubles, he was promised the first British governor-generalship of those united states.

A year after landing in southern Africa, Frere issued an ultimatum to King Cetshwayo of the Zulus as the first part of a plan to usurp his kingdom. Ordering Cetshwayo to forsake his sovereignty and disarm his warriors, the ultimatum also demanded the payment of two fines with six hundred head of cattle. That was that, and with no response from the king, the British crossed into Zululand, and that is how the Anglo-Zulu War of 1879 began.

The following year, Frere decreed that all Basothos must be disarmed. The ensuing seven-month battle called the Basuto Gun War, also known as the Basutoland Rebellion, ended in a stalemate, which led to an armistice. Part of the deal was that the Basotho could keep their guns.

Three years later, thanks to the Disannexation Act of 1884, Basutoland became a colony ruled directly from Britain. This meant that in 1910, when South Africa became a union, Basutoland was already a standalone colony and thus could not be incorporated into the union. Lesotho eventually declared its independence from Britain in 1966.

In any case, Frere's superiors in London were not too happy about his poor success rate coupled with recklessness and recalled him in 1882. He died two years later in London.

And as an aside, it was Lord Carnarvon's eldest son, George Edward Stanhope Molyneux Herbert, the Fifth Earl of Carnarvon, who was the financial backer in 1922 of British archaeologist Howard Carter's expedition that made the most important archaeological discovery in history: the tomb of Tutankhamun, and in it thousands of artifacts, including a massive solid-gold coffin.

One of those artifacts was the king's dagger, which was reportedly forged from meteorites. Literally. The dagger was made from a piece of rock that the Egyptians sourced, not knowing it was a meteorite.

Only thousands of years later, when it was analysed, was it discovered that it was made from a meteorite. I repeat that it was a mere coincidence that a piece of rock that the Egyptians picked up in order to make a king's dagger out of all the other rocks in the veld just happened to be a meteorite. Talk about a one-in-a-trillion coincidence.

The question, at least to me, is whether the pharaohs, including

King Tut, were of this world or not? In simple terms, were we human beings once ruled by aliens? Or, even better (or worse), are we human beings currently ruled from a distance by aliens?

Chapter 3

THE AWE(FUL)SOME FOURSOME: JAN, PAUL, SIMON AND CECIL

Jan van Riebeeck, officially Commander Johan Anthoniszoon van Riebeeck, was the key implementer of the colonisation project in what we today call the Republic of South Africa. That explains why the day that he landed on our shores, 6 April 1652, was at one stage a public holiday known as Van Riebeeck's Day and later Founder's Day. It became a public holiday in 1952, during the Van Riebeeck Festival in honour of the 300th anniversary of the arrival of the Dutch in South Africa. It was scrapped as a public holiday in the early 1990s.

Van Riebeeck, who was in the Cape for ten years, has three towns named after him: Riebeek West and Riebeek Kasteel, which are five kilometres apart, both in the wine-producing Swartland region of the Western Cape; and Riebeek East, just outside Makhanda.

At one stage our currency, both coins and notes, had Jan van Riebeeck's mugshot on them. But, as it later turned out, it was a case of mistaken identity. All these years when the authorities thought they were immortalising old Jan, it turns out that the image was based on a painting of a man thought to be Bartholomeus Vermuyden. Bartholomeus who? Not Bartholomeu Dias, the Portuguese explorer. Bartholomeus Vermuyden. Bartholomeus Vermuyden had been immortalised because of exactly that – he was a man who was thought to be Jan van Riebeeck. What a costly mistake!

It turns out that Jan van Riebeek has something in common with Paul Kruger. Who would have thought? Can you guess what it is? Or, as some people say, can you connect the dots? Both gentlemen once had days linked to them proclaimed as public holidays. For Van Riebeeck, it was the day he landed in the Cape; for Oom Paul, it was his birthday: 10 October was a public holiday until the early 1990s. However, Kruger and his supporters cannot complain that much because, first, the biggest national park in the country is named after him. And then there is Krugersdorp in Gauteng. And don't forget Krugerrands. That is what I call a real legacy: a national park, a city and an investment class, all named after one individual – Stephanus Johannes Paulus Kruger.

The fact that Van Riebeeck and Kruger had public holidays dedicated to them shows how things have changed over time. This is what I call 'evolution of history': it is when yesterday's heroes become today's losers. Evolution of history occurs when a modern society looks back at history with a different perspective of the same event. For all we know, maybe one day South Africans in the distant future will march to the Union Buildings demanding that Mandela's statue be taken down (for whatever reason). One day, maybe some of today's prominent leaders will, like former president FW de Klerk, at one stage a globally respected leader, be buried in an undisclosed location, with the place of their last service never revealed. Who knows, maybe today's liberators will in future be seen as sellouts.

At one stage, especially during the 2015 #RhodesMustFall movement, which demanded the removal of statues of colonialists, Kruger's statue was one of those deemed to be inappropriate and thus to be taken down. The glaring irony is the fact that Mamelodi, a township east of Pretoria, is named for Paul Kruger, who was not only the Boer leader but also the president of the Zuid-Afrikaansche Republiek (South African Republic, later the Transvaal). Apparently Oom Paul, as he was affectionately known, was a great whistler, and could perfectly mimic birds' calls. So the black people named him Mamelodi, derived from the Sepedi for 'melody', and the township ended up being named after Kruger. So when people from Mamelodi marched to Pretoria demanding that Kruger's statue must fall, I often thought to myself in amazement, *Forget the statue, Mamelodi must fall first.*

Let me say it again: history, as life, is complicated.

Even the area where Kruger died, Clarens in Switzerland, ended up having a namesake in the Free State. Considering that during his last months Oom Paul also visited Germany, trying to get the Germans to join the South African War on the side of the Afrikaners, he could have died in Munich or Berlin or Frankfurt. But, hang on, we already have a Frankfort in the Free State, about 150 kilometres from Clarens. That Frankfort was established by a prominent German settler who was born in – yes – Frankfurt, Germany.

In fact, in South Africa, we have quite a few towns named after European counterparts. Sometimes they are spelt incorrectly or, shall we say, they are localised. One prime example is Parys in the Free State. A German surveyor who had taken part in the four-month Siege of Paris in 1870, during the Franco-Prussian War, was surveying this place along the Vaal River and said it reminded him of the River Seine in France's capital city.

One of Parys's well-known sons is Elias Sekgobelo 'Ace' Magashule, who at one stage was the premier of the province before hogging the national headlines for being charged with corruption, as well as for his fights (perceived or real) with President Cyril Ramaphosa.

Marseilles, France's second-largest city, also found its way all the way to the southern tip of the African continent. Both towns, which are about 300 kilometres apart, are located in the Free State.

Another European city that made its way to South Africa is

Amsterdam. The one-street town about eighty kilometres east of Ermelo in Mpumalanga was named in honour of Willem Eduard Bok, the state secretary of the Zuid-Afrikaansche Republiek from 1880 to 1889. Bok, who was born in Amsterdam in the Netherlands, must have been a remarkable administrator, because the mining town east of Johannesburg, Boksburg, also got its name from him. Boksburg was in the world news in April 1993 when Chris Hani, the SACP general-secretary, was gunned down in cold blood in front of his home there, by Polish immigrant Janusz Waluś.

Before that fateful Easter morning in 1993, Boksburg was known for something else. A boy who was born there in 1955 grew up to be not only the first South African but also the first African to win the boxing title in the World Boxing Association's heavyweight division. His fans called Gerhardus Christian Coetzee 'the Boksburg Bomber' but most South Africans knew him as Gerrie Coetzee (RIP).

It is not only towns that got their names from Europe, but also natural features. The highest waterfall in Mpumalanga, dropping 94 metres, is named after the capital city of Portugal. And not far from the Lisbon Falls are the Berlin Falls, so named in the 1870s after their country's capital city by German miners who were missing home. The Germans were in Mpumalanga (then the Eastern Transvaal) because of a short-lived gold rush there. And the Lisbon Falls were so named because of the Portuguese who ventured into this area and were clearly also dearly missing home.

Back to Paul Kruger, who died in Clarens in Switzerland.

Although Van Riebeeck and Kruger did not name any towns after their wives (and nobody saw fit to do exactly that), the madams were not completely forgotten. South Africa's first submarine, which was commissioned in 1970, got its name from Jan van Riebeeck's wife, Maria (née De la Queillerie). That name lasted for almost thirty years, when the submarine was renamed SAS *Spear*. It was scrapped in 2003 because of its age.

Paul Kruger's first wife was also called Maria; both she and their infant son died, probably of malaria, in 1846. His second wife, Gezina (which sounds very much like a Zulu name, but I am sure it is just me), has a suburb named after her, just outside Pretoria. During their marriage, which lasted from 1847 until Gezina's death in 1901, she and Paul had sixteen children.

During the South African War of 1899–1902, eight of Paul and Gezina's grandchildren were, like most Afrikaner children and women at the time, rounded up and forcibly moved to a concentration camp. Within nine days, five of them had died. Kruger, in exile in Europe, was not able to emotionally support his wife, who surely must have been traumatised and even overwhelmed by the circumstances. This could explain why she died soon afterwards.

This is but one of the thousands of stories which, through minute detail told from one generation to the next, have ensured that even younger Afrikaners, over time, are always aware of what the British did to their forefathers and foremothers, and their children. You might even say that some Afrikaners have been brought up and taught to, at best, tolerate the English.

The issue of the concentration camps of more than 110 years ago is a sin for which some – I am tempted to say most – Afrikaners will never forgive the English. The hatred of the British by some Afrikaners still rages after all these years. And yet when a black person talks about apartheid, which was declared by the United Nations to be a crime against humanity, and lasted officially until the 1990s, he often gets told very quickly to move on, to let the past remain where it belongs, in the past, and to focus on the future, blah, blah, blah.

I might as well just add that it is all well and good that history books extensively cover the fact that the Nazis put Jews in concentration camps; but how many history books mention that the Nazis were just imitating an art that had been perfected by the British?

Although things ended badly for Oom Paul, with the Boers losing the war and him dying overseas, things at one stage were great for him. For example, at the tender age of 16, the government gave him not one but two farms in the Magaliesberg area. This offer was not as a result of Paul's calibre, distinction and or excellence in anything; it was just normal for an ordinary Afrikaner boytjie aged 16 to get a farm or two. And there are some among us who still think of white privilege as some sort of theoretical abstract philosophical mumbo-jumbo. White privilege is a lived experience.

Incidentally, Paul took ownership of this land in the 1840s, way before the 1913 Land Act which apportioned only seven per cent of the total land in the country for black African people. Another illustration of the fact that Oom Paul, as the leader of ZAR, was at that stage, as young people would say, living large is that the state went out of its way to finance a road to his farm Boekenhoutfontein on the outskirts of modern-day Rustenburg.

To top it all, his annual salary during the gold-rush era was the equivalent of R24 million in today's money. To put things into perspective, the president of South Africa earned R2.99 million in 2021.

Of all the governors of the Cape Colony, the best known is Simon van der Stel, so it comes as no surprise that he would have his own town – Stellenbosch, which is Dutch for 'Stel's bush'. And South Africa's navy headquarters, Simon's Town, has his first name. His residence, which was at the Cape Town wine farm Groot Constantia, can still be visited today.

As an aside, here are two facts about Simon van der Stel that I personally find fascinating. First, he was born at sea. Van der Stel's father, Adriaan, and his wife were on their way to Mauritius, where Adriaan was to take up a governorship, when Simon was born. I have often wondered if he ever got seasick as an infant (or as an adult); and also what he would have written when filling in official forms for 'place of birth'. (Note to self: next time, when completing an immigration form, especially because they hardly read those forms before stamping you into the country, when answering the 'place of birth' question, consider responding with 'at sea'.)

Simon's eldest son, Willem Adriaan, succeeded him as governor of the Cape Colony. Talk about keeping it in the family. Willem, however, was removed from the position because of allegations of impropriety. In any case, that means you had three generations of Van der Stels who were governors.

The second fact about Simon I find fascinating is that he was of mixed race. Yes, his maternal grandmother was a freed Indian slave. I often wonder how other people feel about the fact that Stellenbosch, a town that has always been seen as the Afrikaner power base, is named after a coloured guy. Such is the economic muscle in this picturesque town that journalist Pieter du Toit wrote a bestselling book, *The Stellenbosch Mafia: Inside the Billionaires' Club* (Jonathan Ball, 2019) that tracks the wealth of the old money and the relatively new money.

To digress, what do Cyril Ramaphosa, Nelson Mandela and 1802 commissioner-general of the Cape Colony Jacob Abraham Uitenhage de Mist have in common? A clue is that it has to do with the number of marriages each had. That was a giveaway, right? All three gentlemen divorced twice and married three times. Hey, I am not judging anyone here. All I am saying, as mentioned before, is King George III and Kwame Nkrumah (and other people unknown to me) only met their wives on their wedding day and they lived happily ever after.

Uitenhage de Mist was in the Cape for nineteen months during the gap in government when the British were about to take over the Colony from the Dutch, and during that time, the town of Uitenhage was named after him. In 2021 it was renamed Kariega. Today it is known for, among other things, having the biggest car factory not only in the country but on the entire African continent.

Kariega has produced some formidable South Africans who have contributed to the nation we have today. One was Enoch Mankayi Sontonga, who composed the hymn 'Nkosi Sikelel'iAfrika', which the ANC adopted 28 years after its composition to be its official anthem. With the dawn of democracy in 1994, the song became the first part of the national anthem.

Another Kariega local was Allan Hendrickse, the coloured politician who made headlines in 1987 when he swam off a 'whites only' beach. At the time he was serving in the 'tricameral parliament', in which each of three races – white, Indian and coloured – had their own representation. After the swim, on President PW Botha's instruction, he apologised.

And both Smuts Ngonyama, one-time spokesperson for the ANC and later an ambassador, and Mcebisi Jonas, the former deputy minister of finance who was allegedly offered, but declined, a bribe of R600 million by the Gupta family, were born in Kariega. (As most South Africans know, the notorious Gupta brothers, Ajay, Atul and Rajesh, were implicated in state capture during the 2010s.)

Simon van der Stel might be the best-known governor but the most influential, I think, was Sir Alfred Milner. The Cape Town suburb of Milnerton, with its perfect view of Table Mountain, Lion's Head and Devil's Peak, bears his name, but considering his contribution to the British Empire, I would have thought a lot more would have been named after him. He was appointed governor of the Cape Colony two years before the British and the Boers were to fight again in what I would call the Anglo-Boer War Reloaded. It was called the Second Anglo-Boer War for a very long time before the name was changed to the South African War.

As an aside, one story that really touched me was that of Lieutenant Walter Oliphant Arnot. This Australian soldier who fought on the British side was, the story goes, so disturbed by the killing of black people in a white people's war that, after returning from a reconnaissance trip in the Karoo in 1902, he committed suicide on the outskirts of Merwewille, about 120 kilometres from Beaufort West. More than a century later, locals still tend and look after the 'Englishman's grave'.

The reason for the renaming of the South African War, we were told, was to acknowledge that all South Africans, white and black, were affected by the war and that many were participants. I must say that I have always struggled with calling the second Anglo-Boer War a 'South African' war. The war had absolutely nothing to do with black people. It was no coincidence that the war broke out three years after that huge pot of gold was discovered on the then Witwatersrand in 1886.

Notwithstanding the fact that black people fought on both sides, what happened eight years after the end of the war? In 1910, the Union of South Africa was formed and black people were nowhere to be found. As young people would say, dololo!

Then, just three years later, the very people who had created the Union promulgated the 1913 Land Act, which apportioned only seven per cent of land for black people. And yet, in 1914, seemingly still desperate to prove something (personally I am not sure what and to whom), black people decided to go and take part in the war in Europe. Another white men's war, if you insist.

The British in South Africa, ever calculating, were not too keen on militarily training the locals, who were mainly from the modern-day Eastern Cape. It was in that context that guns were not handed over to the black people, because the British were already thinking, *What will happen when all these black people are trained militarily and, even worse, have guns?* Therefore it was decided that all those heading to Europe would be mere 'support staff'. Unfortunately, on 21 February 1917, their ship, the SS *Mendi*, was rammed by another steam ship in thick fog. This resulted in the sinking of the *Mendi*, costing 616 souls, 607 of them black South Africans. Irrespective of who would win the Great War of 1914–1918, later called the First World War, nothing was going to change the third-class citizenship of black people on the southern tip of the African continent.

Armed Forces Day is now recognised every year on 21 February. Armed Forces Day, my black arse. The First World War had absolutely nothing to do with black people from South Africa. It is sad for me, and it really pains me, to write it, but here it is: black people who died on that fateful day died in vain.

Anyway, let's go back to Milner.

After the British won the South African War, partly as a result of the implementation of a ruthless 'scorched earth' policy that included poisoning wells, burning farms to the ground, and sending Afrikaner children and women to those concentration camps where thousands perished, Milner became the administrator of the Orange Free State and Transvaal. In short, he became the administrator of the entire damned country. He was in South Africa for eight years.

Later, during the second half of the First World War, he served as Britain's secretary of state for war. His last official position was that of secretary of state for the colonies, which included Australia, New Zealand, Canada, South Africa, Southern Rhodesia, Northern Rhodesia, Jamaica, India, Hong Kong … Those were the days when there was the saying, 'The sun never sets on the British Empire.'

The best-known prime minister of the Cape is none other than Cecil John Rhodes. Today a university and a hamlet, both in the Eastern Cape, bear his name.

Rhodes was at one time the only person in history to have two countries named after him. All that came to an abrupt end when Northern Rhodesia (Zambia) and Southern Rhodesia (Zimbabwe) got their independence, in 1964 and 1980, respectively.

Interestingly, Sir Charles Warren, who annexed Bechuanaland (modern-day Botswana) for Britain in 1885, got a town north of Kimberley named after him. It is surprising that Bechuanaland wasn't named after him, considering what happened in today's Zambia and Zimbabwe. Maybe that had to do with the fact that years later, during the South African War, Sir Charles was one of the commanders on the field at the Battle of Spion Kop in January 1900 where he was indecisive and his tactics were found somewhat wanting. The British lost almost 250 soldiers, compared to the Boers' 68.

One of Cecil John Rhodes's business partners was Alfred Beit (a Jew – see Part II: The power brokers). While Rhodes was busy with politics in the Cape, Beit was overseeing business in Kimberley. With the discovery of gold further north, on the Witwatersrand, he was quick to see potential, and invested heavily in gold-mining companies there.

Beit was one of Rhodes's key financial backers, especially with regard to expansion into modern-day Zimbabwe and Zambia. That could explain why the border post between South Africa and Zimbabwe is named Beitbridge.

Alfred's younger brother, Otto Beit, was the founder of the Royal Institute of International Affairs, often called Chatham House, headquartered in London. So influential is this think tank today that if you intend being a president of a strategic country, and the guys at Chatham House are lukewarm about your presidential ambitions, your chances of being citizen number one become negligible at best.

Yes, things in politics are complicated. Presidents get endorsed internationally first. It is called 'the international community'. If in doubt, read Simon Mann's book *Cry Havoc* (John Blake, 2011) in which he explains in detail how even if an election is stolen, or after a coup d'état, it does not matter as long as the international community accepts the new leader. The opposite is also true: you can win legitimately but if the international community does not recognise you, you are fucked.

Rhodes once boasted that his name would last for four thousand years. He was a strategic man who was concerned about his legacy. Two years after his death, in 1904, a grant from the Rhodes Trust provided capital for the founding of an institution of higher learning named – as expected – Rhodes University College. And while he was still alive, he donated the land on which the University of Cape Town currently stands. That explains why in 1934, more than three decades after his death, his statue was erected on the campus.

It must be mentioned that, also while he was still alive, Rhodes tried but failed to convince the powers-that-be that the institution should bear his name. Instead, it was decided that it would have the name of the city in which it was built, hence the University of Cape Town. The statue, incidentally, was removed in 2015 when students marched complaining about how such statues represented the colonial and apartheid past.

Just for good measure, Rhodes owned vast tracts of land where, now and then, he would go and reflect. Boschendal, now a wine farm owned by an array of international investors, was one of these. He also owned a cottage in Muizenberg on the Cape Town coast, and this is where he took his last breath in 1902.

The name Rhodes and the man behind it might, after all, last for four thousand years. He might just pull it off. After all, Rhodes is now standing on the shoulders of a giant, Nelson Mandela. Today we no longer have the Rhodes Trust but a politically correct name: the Mandela Rhodes Trust. Through this, after all these years, and albeit indirectly, Rhodes still sends young people who show leadership potential to study at his alma mater, Oxford University in England.

How Mandela agreed to add the gravitas of his name to Rhodes's remains a mystery, at least to me. The glaring irony is that some of the people who were fighting for Rhodes's statue to be removed from public view in the #RhodesMustFall protests were literally singing Mandela's praises. The fact is that Nelson Mandela wanted to be associated, and publicly so, with Cecil John Rhodes. I often ask myself, 'Why, Madiba, why?'

Chapter 4
THE ROYALS

The name Adelaide Frances Tshukudu is not well known in South Africa today. But Adelaide 'Mama' Tambo was once a household name in the country. The wife of Oliver Reginald 'OR' Tambo, the longest-serving ANC president, was a freedom fighter in her own right. A lesser-known fact about her is that she shared a birthday with Nelson Mandela: 18 July.

There is another Adelaide, who was born more than a hundred years before Miss Tshukudu, and who grew up to be Mrs Tambo. Adelaide Amelia Louise Theresa Caroline grew up to be Queen Adelaide after marrying King William IV in 1830, when the king was 65 years old and Adelaide herself was no spring chicken at 38.

Although the queen and her husband passed away more than 150 years ago, the towns named after them, Adelaide and King William's Town, stood proudly in the Eastern Cape until 2021, when King William's Town was renamed Qonce. Adelaide, by the way, also gave her name to Australia's fifth-largest city.

King William IV was succeeded by his niece, Victoria. Born in 1819, she was the only daughter of Edward, who died shortly after her birth, and she became heir to the throne because the three uncles who were ahead of her in the succession – George IV, Frederick Duke of York and William IV – had no surviving legitimate children. Although William IV had ten children, none of them were with his recognised wife. In fact, he had them all with one woman, an actress with whom he lived for twenty years. To be fair, when Queen Adelaide married him, he already had those kids. The queen had miscarriages and two of their children were stillborn. Therefore, against all the odds, Princess Victoria became the queen.

Victoria ruled the United Kingdom of Great Britain and Ireland for almost 64 years, until her death in 1901.

At face value, the queen was half British and half German. Her mother was the daughter of King Leopold I, who was the first king of the Belgians. That also explains why King Leopold II, who 'owned' modern-day Democratic Republic of Congo as his personal property, was the queen's cousin: their parents were siblings.

Queen Victoria, who married her first cousin, Prince Albert, spoke German fluently; after all, her mother, Princess Victoria of Saxe-Coburg-Saalfeld, was German. And the queen's father's mother – her paternal grandmother – was also a princess, Charlotte of Mecklen-burg-Strelitz, from Germany. Any way you look at it, the queen of the English was more German than English.

The market in Durban is named after Queen Victoria, and until recently two streets in the city were named after her: Victoria Street, now Bertha Mkhize Street, and Victoria Embankment, now Margaret Mncadi Avenue. And then there is Victoria West in the Northern Cape.

Queen Victoria's daughter, Alice, also has her own town in South Africa. So in one province, you have two towns named after members of one extended family: Adelaide and Alice. Locals call Alice 'Dikeni' but officially it is still Alice. And on the outskirts of Alice lies the biggest hospital in the region, Victoria Hospital, obviously named after the queen.

The University of Fort Hare, which has one of the most impressive alumni on the African continent, is located in the town of Alice. The names of former students who went on to achieve great

74

things include Robert Sobukwe, OR Tambo, Nelson Mandela, Chris Hani and ZK Matthews.

It looks like at the University of Fort Hare, however, there was an optional course called 'dictatorship', which some students not only took as their major but passed cum laude. Among those were Robert Mugabe, who spent 30 years in office in Zimbabwe; Julius Nyerere, who racked up 23 years as the president of Tanzania; Seretse Khama, who died in office after fourteen years in Botswana's prime position; and Kenneth Kaunda, Zambia's leader who spent 27 years in office. And that's to mention but a few. How can we forget Mangosuthu Buthelezi, who was Inkatha Freedom Party (IFP) leader for 44 years, and prime minister of the bantustan of Kwazulu for 22 years? Mangosuthu is also a chief of the Buthelezi clan and prime minister of the Zulu nation.

Two individuals – in fact, husband and wife – Griffiths and Victoria Mxenge were born in what was then King William's Town. Griffiths, a human-rights lawyer and activist, was banned many times and also incarcerated on Robben Island for his political beliefs. In 1981, aged 46, he was abducted by the apartheid death squad headed by Vlakplaas boss Dirk Coetzee, and stabbed more than 40 times and his throat was slit.

Four years later, Victoria, a trained nurse turned lawyer who had worked with her husband in his legal practice, was shot in her driveway in front of her children. She was 43 years old. Years later the assailant confessed to the murder, and that he was being handled by a known member of the apartheid death squad.

With King William's Town now being officially Qonce, I guess this town could never be renamed Mxengeville. Or, even better, the place of Mxenge in the vernacular: KwaMxenge. It is such a pity.

The irony is that one of the largest townships in the country is called 'Kwa-Marshall'. Marshall Campbell arrived in South Africa from Scotland with his family as a two-year-old and grew up to be a sugar baron in the then Natal province; he was also a politician and thus ended up as a parliamentarian. Black people, just to sound cool, call the township eSmashwini. Other darkies, to be extra cool, call it eS'nqawunqawini. The official name for it, a former sugar-cane plantation on the outskirts of Durban, is Kwa-Mashu, 'place of Marshall'.

Back to Mxenge. It gets worse. Another apartheid death-squad member and Vlakplaas operative was Eugene de Kock. After testifying at the Truth and Reconciliation Commission, whose mandate was to record atrocities committed during apartheid and also, where appropriate, to grant amnesty to perpetrators, De Kock was charged and eventually convicted for his role in kidnapping, torturing and murdering freedom fighters. He was sentenced to 212 years in prison but spent only nineteen years in jail before being paroled.

It looked a bit strange – why was he paroled so early, relative to the original sentence?

Now, this is where it gets worse. It came out in the Judicial Commission of Inquiry into State Capture (which we know as the Zondo Commission) that De Kock did not just get paroled, but that the state security agency (basically, the country's intelligence ministry) bankrolled his rented house and offered him a monthly allowance – you may call it a salary – of R40 000. Whoever said life is stranger than fiction was spot on.

This Eugene de Kok issue, I must admit, took me by huge surprise. And what made it still worse was when former minister of justice and correctional services Michael Masutha said the reason for financially taking care of De Kock was for fear that he could be recruited by extreme right-wingers. I have never heard such bullshit in my life. Why was he paroled, then, if there was a fear that he could commit the same crimes? I have yet to meet another parolee who is being financially taken care of by the government because there is fear that, for example, if he was a drug pusher, 'eish, he could be recruited by the mafia and the underworld'.

The De Kock matter made me realise, yet again, that sometimes I do not understand the ANC. Sometimes I do not understand the ANC government. Even more important, and you can quote me on this: sometimes I do not understand black people. This whole affair reminded me of the passage in Njabulo Ndebele's book *Fine Lines from the Box: Further thoughts about our country* (Umuzi, 2011) in which he describes a meeting he had with the former chair of the Truth and Reconciliation Commission, Archbishop Desmond Tutu (RIP).

> *There is a story, I tell the archbishop, of some Afrikaners who believe that black South Africans, oppressed for so long yet willing to reconcile instead of avenge, confirm in doing so that they are not human. A real human hits back ...*
>
> *And the arch responded partly by saying, 'There always has been the idea that only the weak forgive. In fact, it's the strong who are able to forgive. It's the strong, ultimately, who ask for forgiveness.'*

Well, that sums up why I am not an archbishop.

Qonce (former King William's Town) seemingly also punches above its weight. Besides the Mxenges, Steve Tshwete grew up there. As an adult, Tshwete was sentenced to fifteen years on Robben Island for being a member of a banned organisation. He was a minister in the administrations of both Nelson Mandela and Thabo Mbeki, before passing away, aged 63.

And Tengo Jabavu, a political activist who founded his own newspaper, *Imvo Zabantsundu* ('Black Opinion'), was also a native of Qonce.

The best-known local from Qonce is Bantu Stephen Biko. He grew up in Ginsberg, a stone's throw from the town. Aged 22, he was one of the founders of the South African Student Organisation, which aimed to coordinate black students in their fight against white supremacy. He also founded the Black People's Convention, which was to be used as a vehicle to raise awareness in the wider population about black consciousness. That explains why – rightfully so – he is regarded as the father of black consciousness. In September 1977, after being assaulted during a 22-hour-long interrogation, while shackled and naked, he was driven in the same state from Port Elizabeth (now Gqeberha) to Pretoria, a distance of more than a thousand kilometres. He died the following day, naked, in a police cell. He was 30 years old.

Although the University of Fort Hare has produced students who went on to be powerful leaders not only in this country but also throughout the southern Africa region, Stellenbosch University has been the powerhouse in this regard.

Five South African prime ministers, who succeeded one another, studied at this prestigious institution: Jan Smuts, DF Malan, Johannes Gerhardus 'JG' Strijdom, Hendrik Verwoerd and Balthazar Johannes 'BJ' Vorster. What are the odds? And depending on who you talk to, the number is not five but six. After Verwoerd's assassination in September 1966, Dr Theophilus Ebenhaezer 'Eben' Dönges, another Stellenbosch alumnus, acted as prime minister before BJ Vorster was officially sworn in. Dönges was subsequently elected to the ceremonial position of state president but died of a heart attack before he could be sworn in.

DF Malan, later on in life, became chancellor of Stellenbosch. He held the position for eighteen years, until his death in 1959. This means while he was prime minister, from 1948 to 1954, he was also chancellor.

Chancellor Malan was succeeded by Dönges, who served for nine years. Like his predecessor, he died while in office.

It was not only DF Malan who was a student at Stellenbosch and went on to be both prime minister of the country and chancellor of the university. BJ Vorster did exactly the same thing: during his twelve-year stint as prime minister, from 1966 to 1978, he was also chancellor for fifteen years, from 1968 to 1983. Vorster, too, died in office.

Okay, okay, okay, enough now about governance issues and conflicts of interest.

Stellenbosch has also produced four chief justices of South Africa (Nicolaas Jacobus de Wet, Henry Allan Fagan, Lucas Cornelius Steyn and Pieter Jacobus Rabie). Interestingly, the son of one of them, Quartus de Wet, became judge president of the Transvaal provincial division of the Supreme Court of South Africa, and presided over the infamous 1963 Rivonia Treason Trial.

At the time of writing, the chancellor at Stellenbosch is Edwin Cameron, who served for 25 years as a judge of the High Court, the Supreme Court of Appeal and the Constitutional Court of South Africa. Cameron, who possesses a very progressive legal mind, was instrumental in drafting the first HIV/Aids agreement between unions and the Chamber of Mines in the 1980s. And, seemingly, Stellenbosch is moving away from its Afrikaner image: Cameron is the first English chancellor. Surely that must upset some hardcore Afrikaner folks? And the fact that Cameron is openly gay must, surely, irk some conservatives too. A lot.

Notwithstanding the progress at Stellenbosch, the university was in the news for race/racism-related incidents so much that retired Constitutional Court Judge Khampepe was asked to 'investigate incidents of racism …' Her conclusion, amongst others was, 'Although the university appears to have in its arsenal a formidable transformation apparatus, black students and staff members still feel unwelcome and excluded at the university.'

Phew, what a detour! How did we end up here? Ah, yes. We were distracted by Fort Hare, which is located in Alice, and I could not help but deal with the issue of another university – Stellenbosch.

Back to the royals.

Queen Victoria's husband, Prince Albert, has a town named after him in the Western Cape. And then there is Prince Alfred Hamlet, also in the Western Cape, which got its name when, coincidentally, its founder, Johannes Cornelis Goosen, was busy converting his farm and selling the plots in 1861, and Queen Victoria's son Prince Alfred was visiting the Cape Colony. Goosen decided to name the new town after the prince.

The picturesque small town of Port Alfred in the Eastern Cape also got its name from him. And just for good measure, the queen and her second son's names were used in one South Africa's top property developments, the Victoria & Alfred (v&a) Waterfront in Cape Town.

Queen Victoria was succeeded by her first son, Edward, who became King Edward VII – not to be confused with the later king, Edward VIII. The biggest hospital in KwaZulu-Natal got its name from King Edward VIII. This hospital opened its doors in 1936, the year of the latter Edward's ascendance to the throne as king of the United Kingdom and the Dominions of the British Empire and Emperor of India. This was the same year that he abdicated after there was a huge public outcry, and especially when he was condemned by the Church of England for marrying an American divorcée, Wallis Warfield Simpson.

Ms Simpson actually had two living ex-husbands. It is stories like this that make me craugh (i.e., cry and laugh at the same time). This is what I call true love, real love. If Ms Simpson had been black, most of my people would have reached a very simple conclusion: that woman bewitched the king.

One fact that is known mostly by only historians is that Queen Victoria's grandson, full name Prince Arthur Frederick Patrick Albert Windsor, served as a governor for more than three years. His father was Queen Victoria's third son, Prince Arthur. He was employed officially as the governor-general of the Union of South Africa from 1920 to 1924.

Given how many royals, even the ones who never set foot in this country, ended up with town names and all, it is a bit strange that nothing is named after Prince Arthur. His successor, Alexander Augustus Frederick William Alfred George, got a suburb named him. Alexander's title was the First Earl of Athlone, and that is where the Cape Town suburb of Athlone got its name.

There are some local (read black) royals who bestowed their names on places. King Shaka kaSenzangakhona is one prime example. Somehow it was felt necessary to give the Zulu king an airport – the country's third largest and busiest. And in 2021, East London Airport was renamed King Phalo Airport, while Port Elizabeth International Airport was changed to Chief Dawid Stuurman International Airport.

Why do other traditional leaders not even get an airstrip named after them? What are the odds of a King Mphephu airport in Polokwane or a King Hintsa airport in Mthatha? Why not?

It gets better for King Shaka, however. Even Shaka's date of death (or what was thought to be his date of death), 24 September, is a national holiday. Seemingly, all kings are equal but some are more equal than others. Or is it all ethnic groups are equal but some are more equal than others?

At least I can raise this issue because I am Zulu (actually um'Zulu). If someone else raises these issues, he would quickly be told, in isiZulu by Zulus (amaZulu), to back off. Except that the language and tone used would be much stronger. No wonder that no-one – at least publicly – raises such issues. Zulus, rightfully so, are very protective and sensitive when it comes to King Shaka kaSenzangakhona.

The national holiday on 24 September was negotiated into being by the IFP. Even the fact that you have the name of a bantustan (or ethnic group) as part of the province's name shows how some Zulus have pushed to somehow restore their heritage and history. Maybe, who knows, Zulus are domineering and even overbearing at times ...

The founder and president emeritus of the IFP is the only leader of a bantustan with a technikon (now 'university of technology') named after him. Even leaders of the TBVC states (the four bantustans, Transkei, Bophuthatswana, Venda and Ciskei, which were declared nominally independent by the government between 1948 and 1994) like Lucas Mangope, never, even in their prime, had an institution of higher learning named after them. But Buthelezi managed to organise the funds to build an institution in his homeland. You might not like his politics but, you've got to give it him, he had foresight. Buthelezi has an airport named after him, in Ulundi. And there is also a road named after him in, yep, Ulundi. Even the stadium in KwaMashu is named after his mother, Princess Magogo. (The late King Zwelithini kaBhekuzulu has a stadium in Umlazi.)

Another chief who in recent times got a city named after him is Mokopane. Originally called Potgietersrus after Boer leader Andries Potgieter, it was renamed Mokopane. Potgieter cannot complain that much: he retained Potchefstroom.

Venda King Makhado wa Ramabulana was unlucky when it came to renaming the town Louis Trichardt after him. The government did at one stage change the name to Makhado, but thanks to a lack of consultation, and the fact that Makhado was a Venda king and yet the area also has other ethnic groups like Pedis and Tsongas, they were forced to change it back. The government then started the process afresh, and renamed it Makhado for a second time. And again the citizens were able to successfully launch a challenge. In 2014, after losing twice, the government quietly backed off and the supporters of Voortrekker leader Louis Trichardt must be smiling from ear to ear.

Another local chief who got his own town was Adam Kok (officially Adam Kok III). In the 1860s, after trekking for two years across the country with his people from Griqualand West (in the modern-day Northern Cape), they eventually settled in Griqualand East, which now straddles the Eastern Cape and KwaZulu-Natal.

Kok was deposed as the leader of his people by the British in 1874, and died a year later from injuries sustained in a wagon accident. The state officially took over his land by passing the Griqualand East Annexation Act, and subdivided it into four magisterial areas: Kokstad, Matatiele, Mount Frere (now KwaBhaca) and Umzim-khulu.

If, as a country, we were genuinely serious about land restitution, the Griquas could claim not just these four areas but also large parts of the Northern Cape, including Kimberley.

But then one of the questions that would have to be answered is, who is a modern-day Griqua? Maybe, just maybe, putting everyone in a big box called mixed race/coloured was a scam from the very onset …

Let's go back to those other royals – the ones from Europe.

For a long time in the Eastern Cape there was a town named Queenstown, for Her Majesty Queen Victoria. Now it is called Komani. In the bigger scheme of things that should not matter because cities, towns, streets, lakes and waterfalls in a number of countries, including but not limited to Tanzania, Zimbabwe, New Zealand, Australia, Jamaica, Malta, Malaysia and Canada, still bear the queen's name. It was and still is true: the sun never sets on the British Empire.

Among the places named after Queen Victoria are two natural phenomena, the largest lake in Africa and the biggest curtain of falling water, Lake Victoria and the Victoria Falls, respectively. The Organisation of African Unity and subsequently the African Union has never seen a reason to rectify this anomaly. Remember what I said earlier about the international community and elections? It is small things like the names of lakes and waterfalls that are enough to get your African arse deposed. The thinking seems to be clear among African leaders, both democrats and dictators: whatever you do, don't piss off the royals.

Victoria's biggest legacy, however, is the white wedding dress. To this day women all over the world aspire to and dream of walking down the aisle in a white dress and being a princess for a day. It is all well and good, I say, to be a princess for a day, but just know that this institution or social compact called marriage is, thanks to our patriarchal system, weighted in favour of men. Therefore: a princess for a day, fucked for life.

This reminds me of a post I saw a few years ago on Facebook. A woman who was a feminist was about to get married, so she asked her Facebook friends whether she should keep her own surname or take her husband's. Different friends offered different opinions; some suggested a double-barrel surname. It was all to and fro until one friend ended the debate with a simple observation: whether she kept her own surname or used her husband's, she still would have the surname of a man. It was this very notion, I believe, that made James Brown write and perform the song 'It's a Man's World'.

The royals left other legacies besides place names and dresses – they gave us food names. According to folklore, King James I was so dazzled by a juicy piece of steak in 1617 that, there and then, he took out his sword and knighted the cut of meat 'Sir Loin'. That is how, the legend concludes, we have sirloin today. And when Victoria's son Alfred was about to get married to Russia's grand duchess Maria Alexandrovna in 1874, a London bakery decided to commemorate the marriage by creating the Marie biscuit.

Lastly, on the legacy of the royals, when King Charles II died without an heir (notwithstanding having eleven children, but all illegitimate), he was succeeded by his brother, who became King James II. It was this very King James II (not to be confused with King James I, who sponsored the first translation of the Bible into English) who was the major shareholder in the Royal African Company. This company, according to William Andrew Pettigrew's *Freedom's Debt: The Royal African Company and the politics of the Atlantic slave trade, 1672–1752* (UNC Press Books, 2013), transported more African slaves to the Americas than any other company in the history of the entire Atlantic slave trade. In the process, as we know, the demographics of the Americas were changed forever.

Chapter 5
GREATER EUROPE AND THE AMERICAS

It was not just the Dutch and the English who, through governors and colonial secretaries, as well as royals, ensured that so many places in South Africa were named after Europeans that you could be forgiven for thinking our country is actually in Europe. Other European countries have also jumped on the bandwagon.

Although the British monarch reigned over England, Scotland, Wales and Ireland (latterly Northern Ireland), for the purposes of this book and as far as naming sprees go, I will look at these individually.

Aberdeen, Scotland's third-largest city, after Glasgow and Edinburgh, was the birthplace of Rev. Andrew Murray. The Reverend, who was based in Graaff-Reinet, would regularly travel about fifty kilometres to the settlement of Brakkefontein to minister to the flock there, and saw fit to rename it after his hometown. And if that weren't enough, the same Reverend also gave another town his name: Murraysburg, about a hundred kilometres from Aberdeen.

Murray was also a teacher. In fact, he was the first headmaster of Grey College, the first school north of the Orange River, and named, as we have already discovered, after Cape governor George Grey.

Another Scot, Thomas Smith, settled on a farm in what was then Natal in 1855, and named it Dundee after his hometown. He was later joined by his brother Peter and his wife. Peter found an abundance of coal on the farm – so abundant that by the late 1870s he was employing staff and sending coal for sale to Pietermaritzburg. That is how Dundee became a thriving town.

It was only a matter of time before this coal made it to the Johannesburg-to-Durban railway line, which was only eight kilometres away. Naturally, a village sprang up there, too, and in 1934 it was named Glencoe after a mountain valley in Scotland.

In this country, we also have our own Edinburgh. There is, however, a small difference. Ours, which lies south of Bloemfontein in the Free State, is spelt Edenburg. I have often wondered, in cases like this, if indeed it was deliberate to misspell the original name as part of hiding something in plain sight? Or was it a genuine mistake that was never corrected?

In the 1860s, William Murray (not to be confused with Andrew) established a mission station, and because he had been born in one of the settlements along the Ugie River in Scotland, he decided to call the mission station after the river.

Even a chain of islands north of Scotland is recognised here in Mzansi. Orkney, a gold-mining town in the North West province, is named after these Scottish islands. What is the connection? Simon Fraser, a mining pioneer who was instrumental in the development of our Orkney, was born in, yep, Orkney in Scotland.

The Irish, not to be outdone by the Scots, also contributed to the naming spree. As was the case with Dundee, immigrant Richard Charles O'Neil acquired a farm that he called Belfast, the town from which he hailed in Ireland. Like Dundee, the town developed as a mining town but these days it is mainly agricultural. And as was the case with Dundee, one of the battles of the South African War was fought in the vicinity of Belfast.

The Welsh, not to be outdone by the Irish and the Scots, named an area that in time would be one of the most expensive suburbs not only in the Western Cape but in the entire country. Named after a Welsh seaside resort in 1903, our Llandudno lies on South

Africa's Atlantic seaboard, and most South Africans can only dream of owning property there.

Llandudno is next to Sandy Bay beach, which is mostly frequented by nudists. I must admit that one of the things I wish I had done when I was younger (I am still young – at heart) is take a stroll on that nudist beach. I definitely cannot do it now. I am one of those people who by nature tend to stare and giggle. It is small things like that, especially among men, that lead to fights.

Considering that South Africa was a colony of the Dutch for more than 200 years, it is only fair to assume that some places in the country will have their roots in the Netherlands. The cattle-ranching and coal-mining town of Utrecht in the northwestern corner of KwaZulu-Natal was established in the mid-1850s by Dutch settlers who 'traded' land for cattle with King Mpande of the Zulus. There is still a dispute over whether the king genuinely understood that he was selling land to them as their sole property because, back then in the Zulu culture, it was unheard of that land could be a commodity that could be sold and bought.

In the province of Utrecht in the Netherlands lies a town called Amersfoort. In Mpumalanga in South Africa, too, lies a small town called Amersfoort.

The Germans also contributed to some of the names we use in this country.

While on their way to engage in the Crimean War of 1853 to 1856, which was fought between Russia and an alliance of other European countries, a large group of German soldiers were overtaken by events when a truce was called. These soldiers had joined the British-German Legion to, among other things, look for adventure and potential financial rewards, so it wasn't a surprise when 2 400 of them decided to take the offer of not returning to their home country and instead moving to Africa.

The following year, 1857, another gathering of German settlers made their way to the Eastern Cape. This group was made up mainly of peasant farmers who had thought it worth the risk to move to another continent and start over. Together with their families, they were sent to South Africa, specifically East London. That explains why in the Eastern Cape there are places with names like Hamburg and Berlin.

It does not end there. What we today refer to as Xhosa culture, especially what women wear, has been greatly influenced by the German women who arrived with their husbands back in the day. A traditional Xhosa dress is called 'isijalimali' which loosely interpreted means 'from Germany' or 'of Germany'.

The Germans who landed in the Eastern Cape were not the first group to make it to South Africa. Some years previously, in 1848, there was a German settlement scheme that saw Germans settling around then Port Natal (modern-day Durban). To this day there is a suburb in Pinetown, just outside Durban, called New Germany.

Some of these newcomers established the settlement of Wartburg, now a small town about thirty kilometres from Pietermaritzburg. The name comes from Wartburg Castle in Germany, where Martin Luther, the German professor of theology and reformer who steadfastly questioned the Roman Catholic Church, translated the Bible from Greek and Latin into German.

Within a decade of settling in Natal, the Germans had founded a school about sixty kilometres from Wartburg and called it the Deutsche Schule Hermannsburg. It is the oldest private school in KwaZulu-Natal and is still thriving today.

While some Germans settled in what were then Natal and the Cape, another prominent German decided to settle in the Orange Free State. While he was at it, he established a settlement that in time grew to be a town, and of course he named it after his place of birth. Albert von Gordon was born in Frankfurt, but we South Africans call the place Frankfort.

Local man Sam Tshabalala (RIP) made most people from Frankfort, and all black people, very happy when in 1989 he made history by becoming the first black man to win the Comrades Marathon. Personally, I was so touched by Tshabalala's win that I made a commitment to myself on that eventful winter day that I would also one day win the Comrades. A week later I came to my senses and acknowledged that winning the Comrades was physically and mentally beyond me (I have always been a practical guy). Eleven years later, on 16 June 2000, three days short of my 25th birthday (you can stop counting, I was born on 19 June 1975), I surprised myself and my family by finishing the Comrades with about 1 200 seconds in hand (which, to spare my Zulu people this arithmetic quagmire, was twenty minutes).

The moral of the story: it is extremely important for young people to be exposed to a winning person or persons that they can relate to or identify with, because it inspires and motivates them to work hard in this game of life.

There is another Frankfort in South Africa. It is a village in the Eastern Cape.

There is one German guy, Heinrich Julius Ueckermann, who settled further north. He was an entrepreneur, and to that end in 1862 he started a trading station. A town grew around his store. Ueckermann was from Heidelberg, and voilà, today, on the drive from Durban to Johannesburg, you know you have arrived in Gauteng when you pass Heidelberg.

Before this Heidelberg was established, another one was already in existence in the Cape Colony. The Dutch Reformed Church bought some land in the mid-1850s and, as was often the case, a town grew around the church. They called their new town Heidelberg because – wait for it – they practised a confessional doctrine that had its roots in, ahem, Heidelberg in Germany.

Of all the Europeans who made an impact on South Africa, the Portuguese are in the top three (after – in random order, I repeat, in random order – the Dutch and the British). For starters, the

Portuguese were the first Europeans, in the late 1480s, to round the Cape during a sea voyage. Bartolomeu Dias called it the Cape of Storms, although the Portuguese king, João II, who was Dias's key financial sponsor, called it the Cape of Good Hope. This was mainly because the king saw the importance of the identification of a route to India around Africa, and Dias's 'discovery' gave him, and the Portuguese people, hope. South Africa's first town, Cape Town, therefore, got its name from the Portuguese.

About a decade later, in 1497, another Portuguese explorer, Vasco da Gama, landed in what is today Durban on Christmas Day, and called it Terra Natalis – Portuguese for 'Land of Christmas'. And to this day we have a province called KwaZulu-Christmas.

Then there is Machadodorp in Mpumalanga, which is named after a Portuguese engineer who surveyed the land there for the proposed Nelspruit-to-Delagoa Bay railway line. His name was Joachim Machado.

France and the French played their role in the country we call South Africa today. As mentioned before, some descendants of the original Huguenot families became prominent figures in South African society, including the late FW de Klerk, the last president of apartheid South Africa.

FW caused a media frenzy by leaving a 'final message' on a video in which he said, among other things, 'I, without qualification, apologise for the pain and hurt and the indignity and the damage that apartheid has done.' Some – I am tempted to say most – black South Africans felt that FW was not sincere at all in his 'so-called' apology. It was felt that the video was just a last PR act to salvage whatever was left of his legacy. Filmmaker, writer and political commentator David Forbes summed it up perfectly when he wrote in the *Daily Maverick* on 23 November 2021, 'De Klerk was an unrepentant liar, an apologist for apartheid, and a murderer. He left life without answering for his role in apartheid-era crimes.' I could not have said it better myself.

The FW de Klerk video, admittedly, spurred me to one day re-cord my own final message. The difference between FW's and mine is that I will spill all the beans. All the shenanigans I got up to in my day will be laid bare for all to hear about. My only misgiving about making the video in which I will spill all the beans is, what if the video leaks while I am still alive? As they say in the movies, then I will be fucked.

Still on making videos and leaving final messages, American engineer Boyd Bushman, who passed on in 2014 aged 78, made one as well. In his video, Bushman, who worked at aerospace company Lockheed Martin, stated as a matter of fact – and this was the whole point of making the video – that the company was getting help from highly advanced extraterrestrials in developing the technology and products that helped them win multimillion-dollar contracts from mainly the US Department of Defense and the National Aeronautics and Space Administration (NASA). In the video, he even shows a photo of an 'alien'.

Needless to say, besides some small community-based media outlets, this story did not make global headlines because – come to think of it – an average person would lose their mind if there were proof not only that aliens do exist, but some among us are working with them in order, thanks to highly advanced weaponry, to bully other children into perpetual submission. I sometimes think some people can never handle the truth, and must therefore, for their own sanity, continually be told lies.

Although South Africa has never been colonised by the United States, Americans have played a role not only in the names of South African places but also in the history of our beautiful, wonderful, picturesque and culturally diverse but racially and tribally complex country. And none have shaped the history of this country more than Newton Adams and Daniel Lindley, together with their wives.

But before I delve into these two missionaries' legacies, let me

touch on one Aldin Grout, who was born in Pelham, Massachusetts. Grout was sent to Zululand to spread the word of God in
1835. The town where Chief Albert Luthuli had a house (which is
now a museum), Groutville, is named after this American missionary.
He was not the last missionary to have a settlement named after
him.

Newton Adams, a doctor by profession, was a missionary by
calling. He was sent to South Africa in the 1830s with, among
others, Daniel Lindley. Adams established a mission south of Durban
which, years later, became a school. Therefore Adams was basically
doing three jobs – he was a medical doctor, a teacher and a pastor.

Adams's school would produce a large array of notable people.
Adams College's impressive alumni include writers such as Herbert
Isaac Ernest Dhlomo and Es'kia Mphahlele, and Zimbabwe's Stanlake
John William Thompson Samkange; jurists including chief justices
Pius Langa (South Africa) and Enoch Dumbutshena (Zimbabwe);
and politicians John Dube, Pixley ka Isaka Seme, Inkosi Mangosuthu
Buthelezi, Ellen Khuzwayo, Anton Lembede and Nkosazana Dlamini
Zuma.

One of the founder members of the PAC, Zephania Mothopeng,
was a teacher at Adams College. ZK Matthews was also an educator there; later in life he became Botswana's ambassador to the
USA. Albert Luthuli was a learner here, and later returned to teach
at the same institution. Luthuli made international headlines when he
became the first African to win a Nobel peace prize.

Students who grew up to be presidents include Ian Khama of
Botswana, Julius Nyerere of Tanzania, Kenneth Kaunda of Zambia
and Robert Mugabe of Zimbabwe; and Joshua Nkomo, the future
vice-president of Zimbabwe, was educated at Adams.

Herbert Chitepo, who became a barrister and leader of the Zimbabwe African National Union (Zanu), before being assassinated
with a car bomb in 1975 aged 52, also went to this prestigious school.

This list is definitely not exhaustive. However, it highlights the impact that Dr Newton Adams had on the history of not only South Africa but southern Africa.

Just imagine if this one person, who'd been sponsored by an American missionary society, had not come to South Africa.

Just imagine.

It would mean that Pixley would not have studied in the US and come back to convince his fellow men to elect his uncle, John Langalibalele Dube, as the first president of the ANC (then called the South African Native National Congress), even though Dube was not even at the conference. According to Heather Hughes's book *The First President: A life of John L Dube, founding president of the* ANC (Jacana Media, 2011), Dube did not attend the conference because he was afraid of losing the vital financial support of white people both locally and abroad for the school that he and his wife had tirelessly worked to build, and he may have hoped that his election in absentia would be treated as 'greatness thrust upon him' rather than actively sought.

If Adams had not come to South Africa, that would mean that the first African to win a Nobel peace prize, rather than Chief Albert Luthuli, would have been somebody else.

It would mean that, if Nkosazana had not studied here, she probably would have been just another village girl who grew up to marry just another village boy. Instead, she married Jacob Zuma, the village boy who became the president of the country. And Dlamini Zuma herself almost became the president. Twice. (See Part III, Chapter 16, 'Pondering the ANC elective conferences of 2007, 2012 and 2017'.) (Thinking silently: I wonder if a person ever gets over such setbacks in life?) Nkosazana, again, availed herself for the ANC Presidency for the 2022 elective conference but this time her campaign never really took off.

Dr Adams died in 1851, sixteen years after arriving in South Africa, and is buried at Adams Mission. So he was in the country for less than twenty years. Such is the power of education …

It is worth mentioning that missionary James McCord, also a medical doctor, also worked at Adams Mission, having been sent there with his wife Margaret in 1899, but felt it was way too far from the city of Durban. Although only thirty kilometres away, in those days, prior to the laying of tarred roads and even the invention of cars, the journey was obviously much more difficult than it is today. Hence he and Margaret lobbied authorities for a hospital to be built in Durban. In May 1909, McCord Hospital opened its doors.

Daniel Lindley, mentioned earlier, also had a huge impact on this country. He'd studied at the University of Ohio, which was founded by his father. After landing in South Africa, his original aim was to preach to the Matebele (amaNdebele) in what was then Southern Rhodesia (now Zimbabwe) but it was not to be, mainly due to wars at the time. He tried Plan B: to preach to the Zulus. This was negatively affected by the fighting between the Zulus and the Boers. So he ended up – and this was Plan C – preaching to the Boers. In appreciation of his contributions, the Boers named a town in the Free State after him.

Lindley ended up settling in Inanda, just north of Durban, and this is where, together with his wife and their eleven children, he founded the Inanda seminary school for girls. This institution, just like Adams College, is historic, and its alumni are luminaries.

Nokutela Dube was one of the very first learners at Inanda. She was bright and excelled in her studies. Later, after she married John Langalibalele Dube in 1894, she co-founded with her husband the newspaper *Ilanga lase Natali* ('The Natal Sun') and their school, the Ohlange Institute (which is in walking distance of the Inanda Seminary). She accompanied her husband abroad and worked hard raising funds for the school. During their time abroad, she was featured, in 1898, in the *Los Angeles Times* as a 'woman of note'.

Her inability to have children led to a strain in the marriage, and ultimately she left her husband and went to live in the then Transvaal.

She died a few years later, probably of a broken heart. She was buried in Johannesburg, and her headstone referred to her only as 'CK' and a number. CK stood for 'Christian Kaffir'.

It took an academic, Mali-born Professor Chérif Keita, to investigate the whole Nokutela Dube story and in the process raise her profile. The prof even made a documentary about her. Thanks to Keita, in 2017, a hundred years after her death, Nokutela was awarded South Africa's highest honour, the Order of the Baobab. Better late than never.

John Dube, meanwhile, went on to marry Angeline Khumalo and live happily ever after; the couple had six children who survived to adulthood.

Other than Nokutela, the Inanda Seminary produced many important women. One of these is Baleka Mbete, who was at one stage the chair of the ANC and the speaker of parliament, before reaching her career zenith as deputy president of South Africa for eight months, after President Mbeki resigned in 2008. Coincidentally, when Mbete became deputy president, she succeeded Phumzile Mlambo Ngcuka, who matriculated from the Ohlange Institute – the very school co-founded by Nokutela Dube.

Another girl who matriculated from Inanda Seminary would grow up to lead the country's health ministry. Edmie Mantombazana 'Manto' Tshabalala-Msimang (née Mali) was minister of health from 1999 to 2008, under President Mbeki. When he was recalled by the ANC, she served as minister in the presidency under President Kgalema Motlanthe. She died a year later.

Inanda has also produced luminaries in business, such as Noluthando 'Thandi' Orleyn, co-founder of investment holdings company Peoton and chair of BP Southern Africa, as well as Nonkululeko 'Nku' Nyembezi, former CEO of ArcelorMittal South Africa who in 2022 was appointed board chair of the Standard Bank Group – the biggest bank, in terms of assets, not only in South Africa but on the continent.

The most prominent person who was once a learner at Inanda Seminary is Nonkululeko 'Lulu' Khumalo (née Matiwane). You may not have heard of her, but she is my wife, and that is what makes her the most prominent of them all.

The Lindleys were in South Africa for 38 years, and when Daniel retired, they moved back to the USA.

Two other Americans can claim to have contributed to this country. They were surveyors from Virginia in the USA. After surveying a particular area following the discovery of gold there, it was named Virginia. It is located in the Free State, and the railway line between Johannesburg and Cape Town passes through this town. It was here in 1994 that heavy rains caused a tailings dam to collapse, resulting in flooding that killed seventeen people. A similar thing happened in September 2022 at Jagersfontein: a tailings dam of a mothballed diamond mine burst, and the resulting deluge of mud swept away houses and cars in a nearby residential area, killing at least three people and putting several in hospital.

On mining-related incidents, South Africa had its worst mining disaster in 1960 about 200 kilometres from Virginia. In the Coalbrook accident, 437 miners lost their lives when parts of a mine caved in: many were crushed by rockfall and others suffocated by methane gas. Six of the deceased miners were white men. Due to the rules of the game at the time, a black widow was granted a once-off payment for her loss, while a white widow was entitled to her deceased husband's full pension.

Back to the Americans.

It appears that they did not only influence us through missionaries and later through music and movies. In the 1930s, long before we were hooked on McDonald's, KFC, Pizza Hut and Starbucks, three American Mormon missionaries-turned-entrepreneurs, Layton Alldredge, Clarence Randall and Evan Wright, brought a family recipe for ice cream to South Africa. They built a roadhouse, then an unknown concept in the country, in what was effectively wild bushveld: at the time, Louis Botha Avenue was basically a small two-lane road running through the veld between Johannesburg and Pretoria.

The Doll House closed down in 2017 but the memories live on …

Chapter 6
PROFESSIONALS, PAGANS AND PATRONISERS

Members of the legal fraternity were not left out of the naming spree. As an example, Sir Henry Elliot, who, following a 25-year career in the British army, retired to Natal in 1870, and was appointed the chief magistrate for the Transkei territories in 1891, got the nod in Elliot, as well as Elliotdale.

A famous son of Elliotdale is one Samson Gwede Mantashe, former trade unionist and current politician. Gwede served two terms as the secretary-general of the ANC between 2007 and 2017. He ran a very tight ship and ensured that everyone, including MPs, toed the line; and he defended Zuma in parliament to the very end. Gwede, shrewd politician that he is, was in the winning faction at the 2017 ANC conference, where he became the ANCs national chair. Two months later, he was appointed minister of mineral resources and energy.

Another chief magistrate who had a town named after him was Sir Melmoth Osborn, the British commissioner for Zululand in the 1880s. Although Sir Melmoth was officially based in Eshowe at the time, it was decided his name would be bestowed on this other town about fifty kilometres distant.

Not to be outdone, another magistrate who was based in one town but gave his name to another was Charles Frederick Warden, magistrate of Harrismith from 1884 to 1900. Today, travellers between Durban and Johannesburg on the N3 use Warden, which is about halfway, as a gauge to see how far they've come and how much road still lies ahead.

Further north, the first capital of the Zuid-Afrikaansche Republiek (later the Transvaal) also got its name from a magistrate. So influential was Klerksdorp in its heyday after the discovery of gold in the area that it even opened its own stock exchange in 1888. But with more gold reserves discovered further east, on the Witwatersrand, the prospectors soon left.

Klerksdorp is the birthplace of a boy who grew up to be, among other things, a human-rights activist, the Archbishop of Cape Town and a Nobel Prize winner – Desmond Mpilo Tutu (RIP). So, while the town was named after magistrate Jacob le Clercq (remember that some of the French Huguenots' surnames were South Africanised), why can't it, as part of honouring and treasuring The Arch's legacy, be renamed Kwa-Tutu (or Tutuville)?

If magistrates could lend their names to towns, it goes without saying that senior legal eagles could be similarly honoured. One of them was the first chief justice of Natal, in 1858, Walter Harding. The town that owes its name to him is on the province's South Coast. So what are the odds of this town being renamed Mogoeng Mogoeng? Some Zulus might be lukewarm about this idea because Mogoeng is not from this province. Okay, so how about renaming it after Raymond Zondo? Forget it: some Zulus will be pissed off because, they'll say, Zondo allowed himself to be used by white monopoly capital, and, because he was obsessed about becoming chief justice, he threw Zuma under the bus.

The Northern Cape's second-largest city (after Kimberley) got its name from an Irishman who arrived in the region in 1874, aged 30. Notwithstanding being an elected member of parliament, he also served as the attorney-general for the Cape Colony. I know, right? How was that even possible? Isn't that a glaring conflict of interest? Well, if your name was Thomas Upington, anything was possible.

Upington, by the way, made a strategic blunder and had to resign from the government in 1881, having sided in a dispute with Sir Bartle Frere, the British high commissioner who had been recalled in 1880, and had to be content with being the leader of the opposition in the Cape parliament. That, however, did not affect his influence, because when the Boers established their own republic in modern-day northern Namibia, they called it Upingtonia. But they also had an ulterior motive for this flattery: they wanted the Cape Colony's protection from the Portuguese further north in modern-day Angola. Upingtonia lasted for only two years before being incorporated, in 1887, into German South West Africa, which in time became South West Africa and then Namibia.

During the Great Trek, and the resulting Boer-Sotho battles between 1858 and 1868 in what is now the Free State, one soldier, General Johan Fick, fought gallantly and gained some land for the volk from the Sothos (actually Basotho). He later subdivided the land and sold erven to some of his travel buddies. The town that arose from this would, a couple of decades later, be called Ficksburg.

In 2011 the very same town was in the news when local resident Andries Tatane was shot and killed by police officers during a service-delivery protest. And there we'd thought that shooting and killing protestors happened only in the pre-1994 era. It sounds like a cliché but it is true: the more things change, the more they stay the same.

All the police officers who were charged for Tatane's murder were eventually acquitted because at the time of the shooting all of them were wearing helmets that partly covered their faces. Therefore, it was difficult for witnesses to identify exactly which of the officers had shot Tatane.

Nine years after Tatane's tragic death, another town in the eastern Free State, Senekal, was in the news. This was after the murder of 21-year-old Brendin Horner, a manager on one of the local farms.

The white farmers descended on the local magistrate's offices on the day the two suspects – both black – were supposed to appear in court. During the subsequent protest, a police van was rolled over and set alight.

With the next court appearance of the accused, police reinforcements from nearby provinces were called in to separate two groups: one exclusively white and the other exclusively black. All of this was done in order to prevent denting our perfect-from-a-distance-but-very-structurally-shaky rainbow nation.

But, hey, we as a country will never deal with such glaring racially tense events, despite our public singing as a united nation 'Shosholoza' every twelve years when the Springboks win the World Cup, because – and you can quote me on this – if sweeping things under the carpet was a sport, South Africa would be guaranteed an Olympic gold medal.

On the same sport-related note, although I don't have a crystal ball, it is clear that it is only a matter of time before there is, like we had with cricket, a social-justice and nation-building project of some sort that will investigate racial discrimination in the sport of rugby. And, just like we had with cricket, black rugby players will come out in their droves, shedding tears about how they were racially discriminated against by the system and by their employers. The thing I often want to say when such things happen is, 'Bru! Why did you not speak up when you were still a sports star raking in millions through your salary and endorsements? Please, shut the fuck up!'

Another soldier who, like General Fick, established a town was Helgaardt Theunissen. He also named the town after himself and, just for control, was its mayor for a number of years.

Talking of war heroes, Boer general Koos de la Rey of guerrilla-tactics fame during the South African War has also got a town named for him: Delareyville. And it just so happens that De la Rey married one Jacoba Elizabeth 'Nonnie' Greeff, whose father, Hendrik Adriaan Greeff, was the founder of Lichtenburg, which is about a hundred kilometres from Delareyville. De la Rey is buried in Lichtenburg.

Another well-known Boer commander was Louis Botha (who was also a Freemason – see Part II). He rose through the ranks during the South African War, and after the death of leader of forces Piet Joubert (also a Freemason) in 1900, he became the commandant-general of the Zuid-Afrikaansche Republiek troops. Botha fought to the bitter end, using guerrilla tactics, even when the British were implementing their merciless scorched-earth policy, and sending women and children to concentration camps.

Botha was one of the signatories of the Treaty of Vereeniging, which ended the war. Eight years later, in 1910, he became the first prime minister of the Union of South Africa. It was in that context that, in June 1919, he was one of the signatories of the Treaty of Versailles, which brought an end to the First World War. He died two months later.

Durban international airport was at one stage named after this soldier turned politician. And people who have taken part in the Comrades Marathon would all agree that rather than being called Botha's Hill, that geographic entity should be called Botha's Colossal Mountain. And then there is Bothaville in the Free State.

Louis Botha's statue stands – proudly so – outside parliament in Cape Town.

Naval officers also got in on the naming of South African places. Frederick William Richards of the Royal Navy during the South African War has the honour of having the town with the deepest port in the country, and today KwaZulu-Natal's second-largest port, named after him. It was his ship, HMS *Forester*, that surveyed that stretch of coast in 1879, and his map is the earliest to record Mhlathuze Lagoon as 'Richards Bay'.

Captain Matthew Nolloth got a piece on the northwest coast. In 1854, shortly after the start of copper mining in Namaqualand, Nolloth was ordered to investigate the west coast between the Olifants and Orange rivers in order to find a suitable harbour to service the copper fields. He suggested Robbe Bay, about eighty kilometres south of the Orange River mouth, because it was deep and sheltered, and there was drinking water nearby. The Cape government renamed it Port Nolloth in his honour.

The adventurous Admiral Robert Lambert gave us Lambert's Bay. The commander of the Cape Town naval station in the early 1820s, he sailed up the west coast to map out the furthest reaches of this rugged coastline.

Even Muizenberg, a seaside suburb of Cape Town, is named after the man who was commander of what at the time, in 1844, was an outlying post. His name was Wynand Willem Muijs.

Back to the war theme.

There was a fight that raged thousands of miles from South Africa on 18 June 1815. The Battle of Waterloo was the clash that ended the Napoleonic Wars, which had been going on for twelve years by then. French commander and politician Napoleon Bonaparte was defeated by two units on that day, one of which was led by Arthur Wellesley, the First Duke of Wellington, aka the Iron Duke for his hardline leadership style.

The implication of the Napoleonic Wars is that, had Napoleon won and taken over Britain, maybe, just maybe, this book would be written in – oui – French. In fact, all the British colonies would in time have become French colonies, and with colonisation comes the superiority of the language of the coloniser. Then maybe all the French Huguenots who South Africanised their surnames and referred to themselves as Boers and/or Afrikaners would have gone back to using their original surnames and also started speaking French as their home language.

But, as you know, none of that happened. And the Duke of Wellington got, among other things, a town near Paarl in the Western Cape called, yes, Wellington.

*

We started with legal eagles. Let us now deal with religious eagles.

Politics and religion seemingly go hand in hand. One of the most influential people in the history of our country was a reverend. I am talking about Dr DF Malan. He studied theology and had a doctorate in divinity. Often, and understandably so, because he had a PhD and is mostly referred to as 'Dr Malan', we forget – maybe conveniently – that he was also 'Rev. Malan'. He became prime minister when his Gesuiwerde Nasionale Party (Purified National Party) gained power in the 1948 elections. It was the preacher Malan who laid the solid and almost unshakeable foundation of the apartheid policy whose effects are still felt today, more than sixty years after his death.

On the other side, you had pastors who were fighting white supremacy, like Dr John Langalibalele Dube. By the way, the first two Africans ever to receive the Nobel peace prize for, among other things, fighting a crime against humanity through peaceful means, Chief Albert Luthuli and Desmond Tutu, were preachers. But no towns are named after Dube, Luthuli or Tutu. The best the ruling party could do in this regard was to name its headquarters in Johannesburg Luthuli House.

Seemingly, some pastors have throughout the ages found it in their hearts to fight the system. This includes the youngest person at the time ever to win the Nobel peace prize, Martin Luther King Jr. He won it at the tender age of 35, and he died – assassinated by a gunman – just four years later, nine months short of his 40th birthday.

It's almost surreal to think about that. As an aside, how old are you now and, besides reading my book, what important things have you done with your life?

John William Colenso, the first bishop of Natal, caused a stir when he publicly declared that he was a polygenist – someone who believes that people were created separately, and that there was no way all races could have come from the same source.

(Note to self – write a book one day illustrating that indeed the bishop may have had a point.) Colenso worked closely with the Zulus, especially with regard to how the British authorities were undermining long-observed institutions such as the Zulu royal family and the role of the king in society.

He caused another stir when he published *Remarks on the Proper Treatment of Cases of Polygamy* (May & Davis, 1855), which seemed to accept, or at least tolerate, polygamy. That was unheard of – a bishop tolerating polygamy!

He also put his foot in it when, thanks to questions from his African Bible students, with whom he spent a lot of time engaging (and who called him 'Sobantu', meaning 'Father of the People'), he started questioning if everything in the Bible was factual and an absolute historic account, or if part of it could be fable and story. That was it: he was – in simple terms – fired as the bishop.

One of the young Zulu men with whom Colenso engaged and whom he took under his wing grew up to be the first isiZulu speaker, in 1922, to publish a book. Magema Magwaza Fuze wrote *Abantu Abamnyama Lapa Bavela Ngakona* ('The Black People and Whence They Came'). I might as well mention that six years later, in 1928, Rolfes Robert Reginald 'RRR' Dhlomo published his novella, *An African Tragedy*, the first fiction work written by a black South African to appear in book form. Two years later, notwithstanding that he had completed writing the book nine years earlier, Solomon Tshekisho Plaatje, a founder general-secretary of the ANC, published *Mhudi: An epic of South African native life a hundred years ago*.

Colenso's legacy includes a town on the banks of the uThukela River, where one of the key battles of the South African War took place. And black people, especially the Zulus, loved and appreciated him so much that in 1947 they renamed a township, which had been built on his farm near Pietermaritzburg in 1927, Sobantu.

While Colenso was focused on the Zulus, in another part of the country, what was then the Eastern Transvaal, Rev. Frans Lion

Cachet was focused primarily on preaching to the Jews. Rev. Lion Cachet of the Dutch Reformed Church had Jewish roots, and as a preacher he had been heavily influenced by Pastor Willem Witteveen of Ermelo in the Netherlands. Lion Cachet named the settlement where the church had been built in honour of the man who had inspired him. Black people sometimes refer to Ermelo as Mlomo, because 'Ermelo' and 'mlomo' rhyme. And oh, mlomo, or umlomo, is an Nguni term for mouth.

Rev. Alexander Smith gave his name to the small farming town of Alexandria (not to be confused with Alexandria in Egypt, which is named after Alexander the Great), which is about a hundred kilometres from Gqeberha. The settlement started, as did so many others, as a church, and because of its age, the local Dutch Reformed church is now a provincial heritage site.

Like Sir Melmoth Osborn in KwaZulu-Natal, who was based in Eshowe but who, as the British resident commissioner of Zululand's 'reserve territory' was able to give his name to another town about fifty kilometres away, so Rev. Johannes Albertyn gave us Albertinia, a settlement fifty kilometres from Riversdale on the N2 between Cape Town and George. The name Albertinia is, at least to me, a low-hanging fruit. If this government was serious about renaming cities and towns, why hasn't this town been renamed Albertina, after Albertina Sisulu? But hey, Rev. Albertyn started as a pastor in Riversdale and subsequently fought for the establishment of a church in what eventually became a settlement named after him. Therefore, the odds of Albertinia being renamed Albertina (who has no link to the place) are almost zero.

Like the Duke of Wellington – and many others – who never made it to South Africa and yet whose influence was so great that it was decided that a town must be named after him, the same applies to the religious reformer John Calvin. A lawyer by profession, Calvin – born Jehan Cauvin, in France – rebelled against the Catholic Church. It is no wonder that when a Dutch Reformed church was built in a remote place in modern-day Northern Cape, the local reverend recommended that it be named after this man. And that is how we ended up with Calvinia.

About 160 kilometres from Calvinia lies a town that not only has amazingly clear skies but also holds the record as the coldest place in the country: Sutherland, named after Rev. Henry Sutherland. This reverend, by the way, did not even live in this place, but travelled to it once a year to conduct a service for the local sheep farmers. In 1899, a church was built there and finally the town emerged. The number of tourists visiting Sutherland has increased in recent years, thanks to the nearby Southern African Large Telescope (SALT), the largest single optical telescope in the southern hemisphere, which is part of the South African Astronomical Observatory.

Rev. Andrew McGregor, meanwhile, is remembered in the name of a winelands town in the Western Cape. The original name of that settlement was Lady Grey. Yep, the one and only. It gets better. McGregor is only twenty kilometres as the crow flies from Greyton, which was named after Lady Grey's husband, Sir George Grey.

If you look at all the places named after George Grey and his wife, you could easily conclude that theirs must have been a fairy-tale love story. But it was the exact opposite. In fact, these two must hold the record for the longest separation in history.

In 1854 Sir George arrived in the Cape as governor of the colony. After a nervous breakdown in 1858, Lady Grey returned to England, and Grey followed in 1859. On their return voyage to Cape Town from England in 1860, via South America, Sir George caught his wife flirting outrageously with the captain, and he kicked up such a storm that the captain turned the ship around and returned to Rio de Janeiro, where he gave the couple time to cool off and possibly rekindle their relationship. The fuming George would have none of it. He left his wife in Brazil, and they only saw each other again – are you ready? – 37 years later, when they both were old and, er, grey.

There's an incredible story behind the name of a settlement very close to Postmasburg (by Northern Cape standards – it's only 75 kilometres away). Officially the town got its name from a six-metre-deep cone-shaped depression in the limestone, a pit or 'kuil' in Afrikaans. But I prefer the legend. Remember the story of Daniel in the Bible, who was thrown into the lions' den but survived? Well, in this part of the country, locals had exactly that idea: suspected criminals were thrown into this pit, which, instead of lions, held venomous snakes. If the suspect survived the ordeal, then it meant he was not guilty. If he did not survive it, it did not matter because – besides being guilty – he would be dead. (Or is it the other way round? It did not matter because – besides being dead – he would be deemed guilty.)

Boom. That is how the settlement got its name – Danielskuil.

Lastly, let's talk about other professionals.

One who got the nod was a teacher. Hermanus Pieters was appreciated by the community of a Western Cape seaside settlement because at the time, in the early 1800s, there were only English teachers in the area. So the Dutch parents loved him dearly, because it meant their children could be taught in their mother tongue. Pieters lived on a farm near Caledon, but travelled to various surrounding settlements to teach. In summer he would often bring his flock of sheep to a spring in the area to graze, and it became known as 'Hermanus Pieters se Fonteyn'. The postmaster shortened it to Hermanus in 1902 and, voilà, the name stuck.

It gets better. The community about sixty kilometres south of Lichtenburg in today's North West province were so appreciative of the role played by the postmaster in the distribution of the post that they named a town after his wife. Yes, after his wife. That is how Sannieshof came about. And nobody even remembers the postmaster's name. Just kidding – he was John Voorendijk. But you've still never heard of him, have you? My point exactly.

A manager – not even a city manager or a mayor – also got recognised. TJ Chester, a manager in the 'native department' of a local municipality in 1946, gave his name to the township down the road from The Pavilion shopping centre outside Durban. The city's Heroes' Acre, where prominent figures are buried, is in the Chesterville cemetery.

If a departmental manager can get a township named after him, surely it must be a given for a railway engineer? And, indeed, that is the case. Ashton in the Western Cape is named after this engineer who was also a director of the New Cape Central Railways (Ltd) whose name was, yep, Job Ashton.

While the naming of cities and towns after professionals was a straightforward affair, there are names whose history either re-mains a mystery or was the result of the butchering of the original name.

Legend has it – and remember that most of black history is oral – that when King Shaka kaSenzangakhona tasted water in a stream just south of modern-day Durban, he declared, 'Lamanzi amtoti,' meaning 'this water is sweet'. And that is how the name for Amanzimtoti, often shortened to Toti, came about.

Years later, on the opposite side of the country, the Afrikaners during the South African War declared the drinking water along the west coast to be bitter. And that is how we ended up with Bitterfontein.

Still on King Shaka, another legend says that he once asked a woman to go and check how deep the water was north of kwaDukuza on what is today the KwaZulu-Natal north coast. She returned with very simple feedback: 'Kumanzigolo', which literally translates as 'the vagina is wet'. And that is how the river got its name. However, as you can imagine, it was not socially correct to have such a name. Therefore, the legend concludes, the name changed to Matigulu.

I cannot confirm how true this legend is. What I can confirm, however, as someone whose home language is isiZulu, that 'ma-tigulu' is not a Zulu word, and as such it is impossible to decipher what exactly it means. So maybe there is an element of truth to the 'kumanzigolo' legend.

Maybe – and I am thinking out loud here – the woman who told the king about her wet private parts had other ideas. But the king, forever thinking about fighting and wars, completely missed that open invitation …

There is another legend about an area just outside Durban. This one needs a bit of context. Cheating in isiZulu is called, among other words, ukuphinga. The same word is used when referring to mating of dogs. The theory is that Isiphingo got its name because sex – loads of it – happened in this area. And, to cut even closer to the bone, and if the theory is to be believed, loads of perversion and prostitution also happened here. However, officially, Isiphingo got its name from a certain type of shrub called cat-thorn (scientific name *Scutia myrtina*, and isiphingo in isiZulu), which is found along the river in this particular area.

There are some names which, although indigenous, are, from my perspective, very patronising. Take Gugulethu in Cape Town, for instance. It means 'our pride'. While other children lived in the leafy suburbs of Constantia, Rondebosch or Durbanville, or in the winelands of Paarl, Stellenbosch and Franschhoek, darkies got to take 'pride' in a cramped shanty-town with no running water and few toilet facilities, which was stiflingly hot in summer and turned into a mudbath in winter, and where the vulnerable were – and still are – never safe. Our pride, my black arse.

And there's a township outside Dundee called Sibongile, which means 'we are thankful'. I have always wondered if this ridiculous name was genuinely given by black people, or if it was white municipal council members who came up with it, because, they reasoned, black people had to be thankful because, after all, the small township houses were much more solid than, say, the huts in the village they had left behind.

Then there is the township I lived in for five years, from 1987 to 1991, when I went to boarding school there. It translates as 'flower'. Flower, my black arse. Imbali township, like so many townships in South Africa, had (and still has) 'matchbox' houses consisting of four rooms (two bedrooms, a kitchen and a lounge) under an asbestos roof.

Years later, black professionals (mostly teachers, nurses and police officers) could build 'subsidy' houses, which were better than those in the old sections of the townships. The subsidy houses were so called because these professionals received a subsidy from the government to build better houses with tiled roofs. Almost all townships had (and still have) the class phenomenon where those living in the subsidy section would look down on those living in the 'matchboxes'.

As if 'flower' wasn't bad enough, there is eMbalenhle in Secunda. Technically speaking two words, 'imbali' and 'enhle', it means 'beautiful flower'. Then there is Kwa-Nobuhle, 'place of beauty', on the outskirts of Kariega in the Eastern Cape. I have never been to eMbalenhle and Kwa-Nobuhle, and I am in no hurry to visit either.

Talking of Secunda, it stems from the word 'second'. This also needs a bit of context. The energy and chemical company Sasol is the only firm I know of that has not one but two towns named after it. (As an aside, Sasol is an acronym for Suid-Afrikaanse Steenkool-, Olie- en Gasmaatskappy, which translates to South African Coal, Oil and Gas Company.) The first Sasol operations were, and still are, in a town called Sasolburg. When the second operation was established, naturally, in keeping with tradition, the town that grew around it had to be called after the company as well. Sasolburg Two would have been a silly name, to say the least. And that is how Secunda came about.

Enough about the patronising names like eMbalenhle. Let's go to the butchered indigenous names. There are quite a few but I will mention just a handful.

First, there is 'ezimbokodweni', 'place of boulders', but it was felt by some among us (side-eyeing white people) that it had to be simplified. So it was simplified to Umbongintwini, which is a suburb of Durban.

The same happened when the locals referred to a railway siding and called it 'ezinqoleni', loosely meaning 'place of (railway) carts', and that is how we ended up with Ezingolweni.

And black people, generally speaking, have accepted that Nqura is now called Coega. And life goes on …

The one that takes the cake for me, though, is a small town in the eastern Free State. When two tribes fought over the harvest there, the message from one of the tribes was 'stand up and fight' in the local language. That is how Hlohla-o-lwane came about. However, years later, when this local tribe was defeated in a battle during the Great Trek, the new inhabitants found it impossible to pronounce Hlohla-o-lwane. I am sure they tried very, very hard for five seconds before deciding, 'Fuck it, there has to be a better way.' So since the early 1900s, it has been officially known as Clocolan.

Even the founder of the Zulu nation was not spared. King Shaka, oral history tells us, had a specific rock that he enjoyed sitting on while appreciating the views over his land. There is another version that says he used this area, where there is piece of land that extends to the sea, to throw his enemies into the raging waters below. Zulus called it Itshe lika Shaka, 'Shaka's rock'. At one stage a simple typo became an official name but thank goodness Chaka's Rock has gone back to Shaka's Rock, even if it will never go back to its original name, Itshe lika Shaka.

It is not only white people, by the way, who mess up black names. Black people also find ways to make names simpler. It is just that the black versions have never made it as official names.

Ermelo, as noted previously, is referred to as Mlomo, Cradock is called Khaladokwe, and Charlestown Shalastoni. Charlestown is outside Volksrust, which some of us call Vagros. And Camperdown just outside Pietermaritzburg is sometimes called Mkhambathini.

At one stage or another in our lives we are bound to enjoy produce from a town named after the Roman goddess of agriculture – Ceres. The Ceres Beverage Company, which makes fruit juices, has its headquarters in Paarl, and its products are exported to the rest of the world.

If you're wondering how we ended up celebrating a Roman goddess, well, just look into history. The Roman Empire at its peak spanned Europe, North Africa and Asia. As night follows day, by the time the British – who were Christianised – came to colonise natives at the southern tip of the African continent, they were carrying with them the beliefs and religion of their former colonisers, the Romans, who had started out as pagans. Basically, Christians co-opted the various pagan festivals (like Easter and Christmas) and made them into Christian festivals.

Still on goddesses, every year we set aside a day, actually four days, to celebrate the goddess of war, sexual love, fertility and desire. We call it Easter. The Easter Weekend. The pagan communities of the Roman Empire celebrated Ishtar, the goddess of fertility and sex, at the start of the northern-hemisphere spring because, as you can imagine, farmers would begin planting and people would start mingling more thanks to the warmer weather.

The relevance to this day of the goddess of sex and fertility becomes clearer when you consider rabbits – the most sexually active animals of them all. But I can't say what bunnies have to do with the death and resurrection of a messiah.

So the next time you are washing down an Easter bunny with a fruit juice from Ceres, know that you are celebrating two goddesses, the one of agriculture and the other of sexual love.

The Roman emperors gave us the names of two months: July

and August. Octavian Augustus (meaning Octavian the Great), Rome's first emperor, was Julius Caesar's great-nephew and adopted son. As part of ensuring that his legacy was bigger and better than that of his great-uncle, Augustus decided that the month named after his uncle must be followed by a month named after him. That is how we ended up with July, then August. But over and above that, Augustus could also not accept that 'his' month had only 30 days, and that's why both July and August now have 31 days.

Talking of days, the internationally accepted calendar that we use today, called the Gregorian calendar, was commissioned and adopted by a man who was born Ugo Boncompagni. He grew up to be Pope Gregory XIII.

Let's move on from emperors, pagan goddesses and rabbits, and deal with a horse.

This particular horse, called Kroon, belonged to Boer leader Sarel Cilliers. And some time in the 1850s, this particular horse fell into a stream and drowned. When this unfortunate incident happened, a surveyor happened to be laying out a new town. He witnessed the incident and decided to name the town after the animal.

Kroonstad, the third-largest city in the Free State, is named after a horse. A dead horse.

It makes me want to scream until I am hoarse.

PART II

The power brokers

'You've got to find some way of saying it without saying it.'
Edward 'Duke' Ellington (1899–1974),
pianist and composer

Chapter 7

THE BROEDERBOND: THE ROLEPLAYERS AND THEIR INFLUENCE

In 1918, a handful of staunch Afrikaners decided to form a secret organisation. They called it the Broederbond, the League of Brothers.

This needs some background.

From the start of the colonisation project, some non-British settlers – including the French Huguenots, the Dutch and the Germans – had felt that the English were dominating them not only politically but also economically and socially. After the English took over the Cape Colony in 1814, the Dutch started leaving in order to found their own independent country. That culminated in the 1838 Great Trek, as more Dutch families started trekking north. The British did not object.

The Great Trek was an event that had an everlasting political, social and economic impact, not only in South Africa but throughout the southern Africa region.

As the Afrikaners travelled inland, they faced resistance from the natives. That led to land disputes which, as would be expected, in time culminated in battles with different ethnic groups throughout the region. One of the most famous is the battle of eNcome (Blood River) of 16 December 1838. The Zulus were convincingly defeated and 16 December during the 'good old days' was a public holiday called the Day of the Vow.

It is still a public holiday and because, apparently, we have reconciled, it is now called Reconciliation Day. If we are really serious about reconciliation, we as a nation should – in fact, must – ask ourselves a question: was the battle of eNcome really such an important event in our history? If the general consensus is yes, then we should rename the holiday Battle of eNcome Day. But due to our obsession with the 'rainbow nation', 'social cohesion', 'nation-building' and all those fluffy terms, we lose endless opportunities for having genuine national conversations and instead end up putting lipstick on a pig.

In time, the Boers established three major territories: the Zuid-Afrikaansche Republiek, the Orange Free State and the Natalia Republic. The British now changed their minds about how they felt about the Boers leaving, and decided they should get more territory as well. The Boers were aggrieved but, as young people would say, they let it slide.

Then, after defeating the Zulus and Pedis in 1879, the British set their eyes on the Zuid-Afrikaansche Republiek – what would become the Transvaal. That led to even more animosity by the Boers. It all spilt over when, on 16 December 1880 – 42 years to the day after the Boers had defeated the Zulus at eNcome River – a Boer revolt started in Potchefstroom. That was the start of the First Anglo-Boer War, sometimes called the First Transvaal War of Independence.

The war lasted three months, and the Afrikaners won it convincingly. The decider was the Battle of Majuba, where the British lost almost a hundred soldiers – including Major General George Pomeroy Colley – while the Afrikaners' dead numbered just one.

Peace was restored, but it did not last.

After gold was discovered on the Witwatersrand, the British Empire just had to lay their hands on the richest and biggest gold discovery in the world at the time. Therefore, all resources had to be consolidated in order for the British to claim, literally, the pot of gold. It was in that context that soldiers from as far afield as Australia and Canada found themselves fighting a war on the southern tip of the African continent. The Boers had to be defeated at all costs. The Empire had to prove not only to the Boers but to other budding empires that whatever you did, you didn't mess with the Brits.

Although the Afrikaners initially did well, the longer the war dragged on, the more the British – thanks to reinforcements from abroad – got the upper hand. One of the key battles took place on a hill called Spion Kop less than forty kilometres from Lady-smith in KwaZulu-Natal. The British lost more than 240 soldiers, compared to the Boers' seventy-odd. (Some of the British soldiers killed in that battle were from Liverpool, which is why one of the stands at Anfield Stadium, Liverpool's home ground, is called The Kop.)

A key strategic weakness of the Boers was the fact that they did not have an international partner. That was one of the main reasons why Paul Kruger, accompanied by the Transvaal's attorney-general, Dr Eduard Jorissen, went to Europe: to galvanise support, mainly in Germany. (As an aside, Jorissen Street in Braamfontein, Johannesburg is named after this legal eagle.)

Kruger and his entourage were turned down by Germany, which at the time was becoming a global power, thanks to the unification of different states under Otto von Bismarck, who would become chancellor of the German Empire.

It was only a matter of time before the Afrikaners, notwithstanding their desire to fight to the bitter end, had to surrender, especially after the British implemented its cruel scorched-earth policy.

Relations, in time, started to thaw. And eight years later, a Union of South Africa was formed.

Some Afrikaners still felt strongly that they were being marginalised. Hence the formation of the secret organisation.

As in many such organisations, those at the very bottom were not exactly aware of the true nature and objectives of the Afrikaner Broederbond. As such, some of those truly and genuinely believed that, as per the narrative at the time, it was nothing more than a cultural organisation concerned with Afrikaner heritage, including language, customs and traditions.

The First and Second World Wars proved to be polarising among white South Africans. The English, for obvious reasons, wanted the country to join on the side of the Allied powers, which included Britain and France. There were some who wanted the country to remain neutral. And there were those – Afrikaners – who proposed fighting on the side of the Axis powers, which included Germany.

In the Second World War, South Africa, with Jan Smuts serving his second stint as prime minister, ended up fighting on the side of the Allied forces. That decision – to fight on the side of the British – pissed off some Afrikaners.

This must be read in the context of renewed Afrikaner nationalism, especially after the 1938 Battle of Blood River centenary celebrations and the laying of the foundation stone of the Voortrekker Monument in Pretoria. The ground was fertile for an Afrikaner resurgence.

Exactly ten years later, in 1948, the National Party became the governing party. And that is when apartheid – the crime against humanity – officially started.

That was also the turning point, not only politically but economically, in the lives of the Afrikaner volk. It was the beginning of the boom years.

That was when the Broederbond, the inner circle, the state within the state, took control of the true levers of power. So influential was the organisation that it has been constantly rumoured that all the Afrikaner presidents were members of the Afrikaner Broederbond.

In 1979 the American *Washington Post* ran an article headlined 'Secret power behind apartheid' in which it was mentioned that the Broederbond was 'probably the most powerful secret society in the world'. 'The Broederbond winds its grip around South Africa like an octopus,' the article revealed. 'Its 12 000 carefully chosen members, grouped in about 800 cells, hold key positions in almost every walk of life.' During initiation, participants apparently swore vows to keep Broederbond secrets until death.

Four years after the watershed 1948 South African elections, Daniël Hendrik Celliers du Plessis, a co-founder of the Broederbond, was appointed head of South African Railways. He held this position from 1952 to 1961, when he retired.

In 1943, 25 years after the establishment of the Broederbond, another co-founder, HJ Klopper, became a member of parliament and later, from 1961, served his country as the speaker of parliament for 13 years. In fact, it was Klopper who was the speaker when Hendrik Verwoerd was stabbed to death by Dimitri Tsafendas in 1966. Hendrik Verwoerd was, by the way, also a member of the Afrikaner Broederbond.

Just to digress a little, there are three things that I struggle to comprehend regarding the assassination of Verwoerd. The first one is that Tsafendas had been imprisoned a couple of times, in Portugal and Mozambique, for being a known communist. He had also been refused entry to South Africa a number of times for exactly that reason. The man was known to be insane – he believed he was St Peter – and that is why he was released from prison. So how did a person with such a background end up as a parliamentary messenger? I find it extremely strange that no-one picked up on his communist background and/or mental-health problems. I concede that the systems, including the internet of things, were not as sophisticated back then as they are today, but even then, didn't any elementary and basic background checks reveal anything?

The second strange thing is that a few months before the assassination, Tsafendas had applied to be reclassified from white to mixed race/coloured (his mother was mixed race), but he was turned down. If he had been reclassified, he would have lost his job, because at the time parliamentary messenger positions were reserved for white people. That means Verwoerd would not have been assassinated, or at least not by stabbing by Tsafendas in parliament.

The third and final strange thing (okay, maybe this one is just a coincidence) is that *Time* magazine did an extensive feature on Hendrik Verwoerd and his pet project, apartheid, in its issue of 26 August 1966. The cover even had Verwoerd's big mug on it, with the strapline 'South Africa: The delusions of apartheid'. Hendrik Frensch Verwoerd was killed eleven days later, on 6 September 1966.

Moving swiftly along ...

Rumours have always circulated about how influential the Broederbond truly was. We will never know the full picture because it was a secret organisation. However, the chairmen of this secret organisation in time became known, thanks mainly to a series of scoops by Hennie Serfontein, under the byline JHP Serfontein, which appeared in the *Sunday Times* over the twelve-year period between 1963 and 1975. Serfontein consolidated his findings in a book, *Brotherhood of Power: An exposé of the secret Afrikaner Broederbond* (Indiana University Press, 1978).

In the same year, journalists Ivor Wilkins and Hans Strydom caused a scandal when they published their book *The Super-Afrikaners: Inside the Afrikaner Broederbond* (Jonathan Ball Publishers, 1978), which similarly highlighted the networks and power of the brotherhood.

Let's have a look at the known chairmen – they were all men – of the Broederbond, and especially the positions they occupied during and/or after their appointment as chair.

As mentioned, Klopper became the speaker of parliament. He was succeeded by William Nicol. If that name sounds familiar, it's because one of the busiest roads in the northwest of Johannesburg is named after this former Broederbond chair.

Nicol, by the way, was also a pastor. His full title was Rev. Dr William Nicol. And he was a governor of the Transvaal – modern-day Gauteng, Mpumalanga, Limpopo and North West provinces – for ten years, from 1948 to 1958. Just imagine the power he had! Of course, it is a mere coincidence that the very year the National Party became the ruling party is the same year that the former Broederbond chair was appointed governor of the Transvaal.

Would Nicol have been governor had he not been part of the brotherhood?

Nicol was succeeded as Broederbond chair by Johan Hendrik Greijbe, a teacher by profession, who was a strong advocate for a whites-only education system. Greijbe also served as a director for Volkskas Bank, one of the four banks that merged to form modern-day Absa (more about this later).

By the time the National Party won the elections in 1948, Johannes Cornelis 'Joon' van Rooy, who had succeeded Greijbe, had been chair for six years. When he stepped down in 1952, he was immediately appointed as the rector (modern-day vice-chancellor) of Potchefstroom University. He occupied that position for three years, after which he was appointed chancellor. He died in office the following year.

Van Rooy was succeeded by Nico Diederichs, a National Party heavyweight. Diederichs served as a member of parliament for 22 years, from 1953 to 1975. During that time, he was minister in three different portfolios; as minister of finance, he was known as 'Dr Gold', because he strongly believed in that precious metal. And he still had time to offer his services as the first chancellor of the newly established Randse Afrikaanse Universiteit (Rand Afrikaans University, today's University of Johannesburg).

He was appointed state president in 1975, a position he held for three years, until his death.

Diederichs was rumoured to have had an offshore account in Switzerland. The rumour spread like wildfire after the editor of an influential newspaper at the time, the *Rand Daily Mail*, went to Switzerland and deposited money into said account.

The government eventually instituted a commission of inquiry into these allegations. It was found that the account, which had a balance of about R20 million in 1980 (about R570 million in today's money), belonged to somebody else. And that was the end of the story. Except for, that is, what was not in the findings of the commission – that that 'somebody else' was actually a friend of Diederichs.

Still on offshore accounts, besides this Diederichs episode, there have always been rumours about how wealthy white families (including politicians and businesspeople) not only siphoned money from the fiscus (in the case of politicians), but also illegally took their ill-gotten gains and hid them in various offshore accounts. With the dawn of democracy, more rumours and reports started surfacing about even more money stashed offshore.

In order to try to remedy this, taxpayers were given the opportunity, through a special voluntary disclosure programme that ran from October 2016 to August 2017, to voluntarily disclose tax and exchange-control 'defaults specifically in relation to offshore assets'. It didn't work, as evidenced by the screaming headline in the online International Adviser, 'South African tax amnesty on undeclared offshore assets flops'. According to that source, while the South African government had hoped to rake in as much R40 billion, by the end of the amnesty period only R4 billion had been recovered. And we all moved on.

Hendrik Bernardus Thom was the next chair of the Broederbond. He had started his career as a lecturer at Stellenbosch University and, aged 32, was appointed professor of history there. It was only a matter of time before Thom was appointed the vice-chancellor, a position he held for fifteen years, until his retirement in 1969. Fourteen years later, he was back at Stellenbosch, this time as chancellor. He died in office nine months later.

Pieter Meyer, who succeeded Thom, was one of the most influential Afrikaners of his era. He started his career as a public relations officer at the Rembrandt Group. A year after being appointed director-general of the South African Broadcasting Corporation

(SABC), in 1960, he began his twelve-year tenure as chair of the Broederbond. He was at the helm of the SABC for 21 years. Amid all this busyness, Meyer also chaired a committee that decided that it was strategically important to have an Afrikaans university in Johannesburg. After all the groundwork, with Meyer in the driving seat, the government agreed, and that is how Randse Afrikaanse Universiteit was established in 1966.

Someone, if I may add, who also studied at Randse Afrikaanse Universiteit was one Marthinus van Schalkwyk, who as a student belonged to the Ruiterwag (Horse Guard), the youth wing of the Broederbond. He went on to hold a number of positions, including premier of the Western Cape, leader of the opposition in parliament and leader of the New National Party.

Van Schalkwyk was exposed years later as having been a leader, in the 1980s, of a shortlived youth organisation called Jeugkrag (Youth Power), which publicly pretended to fight the Afrikaner establishment; after slight digging, it was discovered, however, that it was receiving funds from the apartheid government's military intelligence division.

But back to Meyer, who started his career at the Rembrandt Group – which was founded by Dr Anton Rupert. Rupert was also, at least for a time, a member of the Broederbond. The Rembrandt Group is Remgro today, with strategic investments in banking, insurance, healthcare, infrastructure and media.

The man who took over from Meyer (and served for just two years, from 1972 to 1974) was known to most South Africans of my generation. He was Andries Petrus Treurnicht. Besides being minister of education during the 1976 Soweto uprising, when the government attempted to implement a 50/50 split between English and Afrikaans as mediums of instruction, he is mostly remembered as the founder of the Conservative Party. At the time, in the early 1980s, the National Party, as part of not only pacifying some black people (Indians and coloureds) but also delaying the inevitable, introduced a so-called tricameral parliament. The Conservative Party was totally against this proposition, and Treurnicht's staunch views on this struck such a chord with so many white voters that he was the leader of the opposition from 1987 until his death in 1993.

What complicated Treurnicht's life even more was the arrest of his friend and political ally Clive Derby-Lewis. Derby-Lewis was charged with conspiracy to murder after it emerged, a week after the fact, that he had provided the gun used to assassinate Chris Hani. Derby-Lewis, the government alleged at the time, was working with the man who pulled the trigger, Janusz Waluś. All the signs, many thought, pointed to the involvement of the right wing, and especially the Conservative Party.

On that fateful weekend, by the way, when Hani was gunned down, all his bodyguards had been given time off. This reminds me of what US president Franklin D Roosevelt once said: 'In politics, nothing happens by accident. If it happens, you can bet it was planned that way.' But surely, in Hani's case, it was not planned that way?

In life, I am tempted to say, nothing happens by accident. This reminds me, just to detour for a second, of a 24-year-old University of Cape Town student who created a grey-water system aimed at households, and with the potential to alleviate the water crisis in Cape Town during the record-breaking drought of 2015–2017. As his company was starting to make some money, Nkosinathi Nkomo, a third-year civil-engineering student, fell to his death from a multistorey building in Cape Town. Three months later, Helen Zille, then Western Cape premier, tweeted congratulations to an 'industrial designer' who had created a 'quick and easy way of using your shower water to flush your loo'. Sure, that one was a genuine one-in-a-billion coincidence!

Treurnicht died twelve days after Hani's assassination, during a heart operation. Of course, it was a mere coincidence. There is no need to get a sworn statement from the cardiologists who were operating on him at the time.

By the time Treurnicht died, it was clear to all and sundry that it was not a matter of *if* black people took over political power, but *when*. That fact to some spelt disaster. In their heart of hearts, they could not wrap their heads around the imminent change.

After Treurnicht as chair came Gerrit van Niekerk Viljoen who, during his last year of his six at the helm of the Broederbond, was appointed administrator-general of what was then South West Africa. He then got a nine-year nod as minister of education in South Africa, followed by a three-year tenure as minister of constitutional development, from 1989 to 1992.

Before all these powerful positions, it just so happens, Viljoen had been the vice-chancellor of Randse Afrikaanse Universiteit for twelve years, from 1967 to 1979 – a tenure that substantially overlapped with his chairmanship of the Broederbond.

Another sheer coincidence when it came to Viljoen is that FW de Klerk appointed a former Afrikaner Broederbond chair to deal with constitutional matters during a critical period in South Africa's history: just before the unbanning of political organisations, the freeing of political prisoners, and the laying of the foundation for a new South Africa.

Next up was Carel Willem Hendrik Boshoff, Hendrick Verwoerd's son-in-law, who also was the founder of Orania, the Afrikaner fiefdom in the Northern Cape. This may explain why there is a Verwoerd museum in that town: it was just the son-in-law paying homage to the old man.

Boshoff, like DF Malan, had a PhD in theology. These men, and all other proponents of 'separate development', read the same Bible and were able to justify, through the word of God, that they were the chosen ones.

After Boshoff's death, his son (Verwoerd's grandson) took over as mayor of Orania. And now the new generation sustains Verwoerd's legacy.

One thing not often mentioned about Boshoff is the fact that, besides being the Broederbond chair, he was also the chair of the South African Bureau of Racial Affairs for 27 years, from 1972 to 1999. Based at Stellenbosch University, this was an Afrikaner think tank, founded in 1948 (the year the National Party won the elections) as the brainchild of the Afrikaner Broederbond, and it had one overarching mission: to offer a sophisticated and intellectual justification for the National Party's apartheid policy and how to optimally implement it. It was thanks to this think tank that, as an example, the government adopted the homelands system.

Thinking out loud: I wonder what think tank(s) the ANC used before and after the 1994 elections? Or was it a matter of 'we will make a plan as we go along'? No wonder black people, for all practical purposes, are on the fringes of society. You can quote me on this: black people in South Africa are like a moon on a sunny day – they are there but not there.

The use of think tanks during negotiations reminds me of a book, *Shadow of Liberation: Contestation and compromise in the economic and social policy of the African National Congress, 1943–1996* (Wits University Press, 2019) by Robert van Niekerk and Vishnu Padayachee. These scholars dissect, among other things, what happened during the policy discussions that preceded the founding of the new South Africa. Apparently, the ANC cadres were 'vastly outgunned' by the well-resourced National Party government and its think tanks. (Talk about bringing a knife to a gunfight.) Well, the evidence thereof can be seen and felt, here and now.

Boshoff was succeeded as Broederbond chair by Pieter de Lange, who was in the hot seat for a decade, from 1984 to 1994. And he succeeded former Broederbond chair Gerrit Viljoen as vice-chancellor at Randse Afrikaanse Universiteit. Therefore, both Viljoen and De Lange, while filling the role of vice-chancellor, were also filling the role of chair of the Broederbond.

The intellectual power of the Broederbond is truly amazing.

Senior people at universities were senior leaders of a secret organisation. Randse Afrikaanse Universiteit and Stellenbosch University were truly in the thick of things.

The last chair of the Broederbond and first chair of the more inclusive Afrikanerbond (which allowed women and people from other races to join) was Tom de Beer. A qualified chartered accountant who had joined the Broederbond at the age of 25, De Beer grew up to be the CFO of Gencor. Gencor was the first mining conglomerate bought by Afrikaners. It was one of the economic pillars that gave Afrikaners the financial muscle they still have today. (More about this later.)

This all raises serious suspicion about how Broederbond chairs ended up in very senior positions in the public sector and, in the case of Tom de Beer, in the private sector. Of course, it may just be a coincidence that the Broederbond leadership occupied such important positions, especially in academia.

Today it is strange to see, as an outsider looking in, how what was then Randse Afrikaanse Universiteit, as well as – to an extent – Stellenbosch University, have cast aside their Afrikaner origins. Surely there must be some volk out there who are pissed off with the latest developments of not having 'proper' Afrikaner universities? Maybe, just maybe, one day there will be a Universiteit van Orania.

What Afrikaners in general and the Broederbond in particular were able to do was seamlessly fuse religion and politics.

There has always been this underlying belief for certain Afrikaners of being the chosen ones. Well, in the Bible, the Israelites were the chosen ones; in the South African context, seemingly, the Afrikaners are the chosen ones. Even the fact that the Israelites escaped from Egypt to journey to the promised land was equated to that historical event when Afrikaners left the Cape in the well-documented Great Trek. So pushed is this Great Trek narrative that during the 'good old days' most towns in the country had a

Voortrekker Road as their main street. The difference, however, between the Israelites and the Afrikaners is that the Afrikaners were not lost in the (Kalahari) desert for forty years.

Of all the books written about the Afrikaner Broederbond, Wilkins and Strydom's *The Super-Afrikaners* is arguably the most in-depth and comprehensive. At the time of the first publishing, it was a bomb-shell. It was not just some heresy stuff; it was real concrete material, with secret memos that had been sent from head office to the members over a period of time. To top it all, it even had a compre-hensive list of the members together with – wait for it – their physical addresses. It shook the establishment to the core.

Another book, written by a former insider, although not strictly about the Broederbond, highlighted how powerful white people in this country managed to dictate the whats and hows of the economic transformation that would play out during the new dispensation. *Lost in Transformation: South Africa's search for a new future since 1986* by the late Sampie Terreblanche (KMM Review Publishing Com-pany, 2012) gives a blow-by-blow account of the secret economic talks that were going on at the same time as the political talks at the Conventions for a Democratic South Africa (Codesa I and II).

Those secret talks were held first at the offices of the then Chamber of Mines (now the Mining Council) in Johannesburg but were later moved to the premises of the Development Bank of Southern Africa in Midrand, which at the time was isolated, and the area around the offices was not as built up as it is now.

These powerful individuals and institutions, which Terreblanche calls the MEC, the 'minerals energy complex', were concerned mainly with two things: how the apartheid debt would be paid, and by whom; and how their monies could legally be taken out of the country.

What happened next is well known.

I wonder how many people know about Prof Terreblanche's book. It should be read by anyone who wants to understand the economic transformation (or lack thereof) of South Africa. I am reminded of that adage, 'If you want to hide something from a black person, put it in a book.' But then, even those who do know about this – that some secret economic deal was signed before the 1994 historic elections – are very subdued and not angry about it. After all these years, I have come to one conclusion: black people were bewitched.

In any case ...

It is a historic matter that after the elections in 1994, the ANC, the ruling party, decided that it would inherit one hundred per cent of the apartheid debt, no questions asked. In 1998, the Truth and Reconciliation Commission recommended a wealth tax and a once-off levy on corporate and private income as ways of compensating those who had suffered under apartheid. The commission also proposed that companies listed on the Johannesburg Stock Exchange (JSE) make a one per cent donation of their market capitalisation. Other suggestions included a retrospective surcharge on corporate profits extending back to a specific date, a surcharge on golden handshakes given to senior public servants since 1990, and the suspension of tax on all land occupied by previously disadvantaged communities.

All these recommendations went into file 13 and were never followed through. This means that white people who handsomely benefitted materially from apartheid got off scot free. (I must admit that sometimes I quietly wonder when white South Africans will produce a hard-hitting documentary titled *How We Got Away with It, Suckers*.)

Still on the issue of tax, in 2003, a new tax incentive policy paper was launched by father and son Nicky and Jonathan Oppenheimer, whose family empire included both gold-mining company Anglo American and diamond mine De Beers. That same year the government had finally woken up to the fact that there was no legal framework dealing exclusively with black economic empowerment (BEE), and quickly promulgated an Act. This piece of legislation was seen by some captains of industry as a stick; the Oppenheimer's policy paper was proposed as a carrot. Basically, it suggested that companies that transferred part of their shareholding to their black employees would get tax breaks. The following year, 2004, the South African Revenue Service (SARS) duly announced tax breaks for companies that signed BEE deals. Except only a few politically connected individuals actually signed almost all the BEE deals. (More about this later.)

As night follows day, five years into the new dispensation, exchange controls were relaxed so much that, first, big companies were allowed to list offshore. These companies, which had made their loot thanks to the conducive environment that had been created by an oppressive regime, felt that the JSE was too small and/or South Africa (all of a sudden, and ironically) was too risky for them. And with the relaxation of exchange controls, wealthy individuals were also legally able to take their money offshore. Even now, rich people can take R11 million per year out of South Africa. And some still complain that this is way too little. They want to take out more. It must be nice.

Sampie Terreblanche, for the record, was a true insider. Besides being professor of economics for 27 years at – wait for it – Stellenbosch University, he was a member of the Broederbond for decades; at one stage he was the deputy national chairperson. Then he had a Damascus moment, and to that end he became one of the founders of the liberal Democratic Party.

This matter of secret talks, as described in Terreblanche's book, leads me to another issue: could it be that the lacklustre movement and transformation in South Africa's workplaces, especially in the private sector, was one of those items discussed away from the public and the media? Could it be that the agreement was simple, and went something like this: 'We white people will not interfere with the public service, and you can let us do almost as we please in the private sector'? That could explain why every year, without fail, we have the Commission for Employment Equity telling us what we all know: executive and senior management positions in the private sector are still dominated by white males. Every year. If it wanted to, the commission could just change the dates and issue exactly the same report annually because, in the bigger scheme of things, nothing changes.

And as soon the commission publishes its report, there is an immediate response from the minister of employment and labour, also saying exactly the same thing, year after year after year: 'Things must change.' Blah, blah, blah. And then the train leaves the station, only to appear the following year with exactly the same narrative: the commission says white men are at the top and black women are at the bottom, and the minister says things must change.

This annual game has been playing out right in front of our eyes since the promulgation of the Employment Equity Act in 1998.

Could this, as stated before, have been part of the secret agreements between the old and the new government signed in the early 1990s? In fact – thinking out loud again – could there be other agreements which, for example, include justice and prosecution issues? (More about this later too.)

One of the best-known members of the Broederbond who had a Damascus moment was Beyers Naudé, known fondly as Oom Bey. What made Naudé's 1963 public dumping of the Broederbond hurt even more was that his own father, Jozua Naudé, was one of the founders. And he didn't only leave the organisation, he also publicly spoke out and preached about the ills of the Broederbond.

After 21 years as an ordained pastor, Oom Bey took a firm decision to stop using the Bible to justify the unjustifiable. He was such a nuisance to the apartheid government that he was banned – his movements were severely restricted, which effectively meant he was a prisoner in his own home.

Yet another Broederbond member who had a Damascus moment was Nico Smith. At the pinnacle of his career as a professor of theology at Stellenbosch University, in 1981, he left it all behind (the perks, the lifestyle, the security) and, while he was at it, he stopped being a pastor in the Dutch Reformed Church. He moved to Mamelodi where, after the first democratic elections in 1994, he opened a multiracial church. His criticism of the Afrikaner Broederbond led him to write a book, *Die Afrikaner Broederbond: Belewinge van die binnekant* (Experiences from the inside). (Lapa Publishers, 2009). He died in 2010, aged 81.

Another person who jumped off the Broederbond train was professor emeritus Willem Petrus 'Willie' Esterhuyse. Age 28, he got his PhD at, yup, Stellenbosch. After lecturing at a number of universities, he was appointed professor of philosophy at his alma mater in 1974 at the age of 38. He is the author of the book *Endgame: Secret talks and the end of apartheid* (NB Publishers, 2012), which chronicles the secret talks, mostly in Europe, between ANC leaders and government representatives, which were coordinated by the National Intelligence Service. It is an eye-opening account of the amount of work that went into laying the foundation – behind closed doors and far away from home – of the country we have today.

In recent times ANC veterans Mac Maharaj and Pallo Jordan have also written a book, *Breakthrough: The struggles and secret talks that brought apartheid South Africa to the negotiating table* (Penguin Random House, 2021), about those events, including the 'skirmishes' from 1984 to 1990 that led to the relatively peaceful transfer of political power in 1994.

Esterhuyse says in his book that he resigned from the Broederbond in 1987. He also mentions that the society's headquarters were in a building called Einke in Auckland Park, the same neighbourhood where the SABC's headquarters are located.

The Broederbond had another facility, away from everyone, in what is now North West province, next to Hartbeespoort dam. This one was used for strategy meetings, workshops and training.

In his book, Esterhuyse mentions that the ANC, after being unbanned, sometimes held its caucus meetings at Vergelegen, a wine estate owned by Anglo American. Coincidentally, this is the very estate where Mandela had lunch on 12 February 1990 – his second day as a free man. The entire world saw pictures of Mandela, thanks to the local and international media following him around, on the manicured lawn with, in the background, camphor trees that had been planted by Simon van der Stel's son.

It would be a stretch of the imagination, however, to link these two facts (Mandela's lunch and the ANC caucus meetings being hosted on the wine farm) with the fact that Anglo was given the green light not only to move its primary listing from Johannesburg to London but also to buy the mining division of Iscor, a strategic asset that had been owned by the apartheid government for decades. It is now called Kumba Iron Ore, and is the biggest iron-ore producer on the entire African continent and the fourth-largest in the world.

As I was drafting this book in mid-2021, Kumba's interim results reported earnings of R12.6 billion. Imagine if all those billions were accruing to the state! Imagine what the government could accomplish with such a windfall! But then again, the question that must be asked is, would the ANC government have been able to run such sophisticated operations, given its heavily tainted cadre-deployment policy, underpinned by nepotism and characterised by short-sightedness?

Even when cadre deployment is discounted, the ANC government has struggled with running some state-owned enterprises. Nothing proves this case like South African Airways (SAA). An American, Coleman Andrews, came to this country and, as CEO of SAA, and under the leadership of the enterprise's board, decided to – among other things – sell SAA aircraft, and then lease back the very same aircraft at a higher fee. In thirty months, he was paid R200 million in salary; and his contract stated that his employer – effectively the government but essentially we taxpayers – would pay his personal tax. This translated to about R6.6 million per month. And I am aware that he got a big chunk when his contract was cut short.

SAA also paid R300 million in one financial year (2000/2001) to consultants Bain & Company and McKinsey, who were 'advising' Andrews on the strategic approach to turning the ship, er, fleet around. Almost twenty years later, the same two consulting firms were implicated in Zondo's State Capture Commission. They had also been 'advising' other state entities, and eventually agreed to pay back millions of the fees they had made from mainly Eskom, Transnet and SAA. (Thinking out loud: I wonder what would have been discovered if the terms of reference of the Zondo Commission had covered other administrations, over and above Zuma's? In fact, now that we know the advantages of having a judicial commission of enquiry looking into the affairs of an administration, why don't we have it – as a standard – that every time the president leaves the office *thou shall be investigated to determine whether you were captured, or not?*)

Chapter 8

THE BROEDERBOND: THE PRIVATE SECTOR AND INTELLIGENCE

It just so happens that in the very year that the Afrikaner Broeder-bond was formed, 1918, an assurance company that grew up to be Africa's biggest was also formed.

(Note to self: maybe this book should have been called *A Country of Coincidences*.)

The Suid-Afrikaanse Nasionale Trust en Assuransie Maatskappij Beperk (South African National Trust and Assurance Company Limited), Santam, was registered in March 1918. It was then decided to convert the life assurance department into a separate company, and that is how the Suid-Afrikaanse Nasionale Lewens Assuransie Maatskappij Beperk (South African National Life Assurance Company Limited), Sanlam, came into being. It was registered three months later, in June 1918.

And another company was founded in that great Afrikaner year of 1918. It was the Co-operative Winemakers Union of South Africa. It may not look familiar until you see the Afrikaans version, Koo-peratiewe Wijnbouwers Vereeniging van Suid-Afrika, which – and this is the familiar part – is abbreviated as KWV. It produces various wines and an assortment of brandies.

Although the year 1918, with the formation of the Afrikaner Broederbond, KWV, Santam and Sanlam, was a great year for the Afri-kaner volk, it was in 1914 that the volk had organised themselves and taken strategic decisions on how to move the Afrikaners to the country's economic, social and political pinnacle.

First was the creation of a political vehicle, and the National Party was formed in 1914.

That same year, prominent volk met in December and spoke about the importance of creating a publishing company. One of those gentlemen was Johannes 'Jannie' Henoch Marais, a wealthy local farmer who'd made his money from diamond prospecting in Kimberley. The following year, Jannie donated £100 000 (about R167 million in 2022 money; South Africa didn't use rands until 1961) for the creation of the modern-day Stellenbosch University. The university celebrated its centenary in 2018. Jannie died, aged 63, in 1915 and his statue stands – proudly so – on the main campus. Hey, why not? The man laid the foundation, right?

In 1915, De Nasionale Pers Beperkt (The National Press Ltd) was founded. The first product produced by this company, which today is known as Naspers, was the newspaper *Die Burger* (The Citizen, but not to be confused with the modern-day *Citizen* newspaper). And it just so happened that the first editor of *Die Burger*, who left being a pastor to oversee this venture, was none other than DF Malan. More than three decades later, Malan, who was by then the leader of the National Party, became the prime minister of South Africa and officially launched apartheid policy.

This is what long-term planning is all about. This shows without a doubt that the Afrikaners had strategy and tactics. They were not just blowing hot air on the podium.

While those other children were thinking far, far ahead, some were stuck on 'A' ... 'A' for 'Amandla'.

There is a gentleman who, for whatever reason, is not well captured in the records with regard to the role he played in the empowerment of the Afrikaner. He was William 'Willie' Angus Hofmeyr (not to be confused with advocate William Andrew 'Willie' Hofmeyr, the modern political activist who has served as the deputy national director of public prosecutions, the head of the Asset Forfeiture Unit and the head of the Special Investigating Unit). Hofmeyr was one of the fourteen men who co-founded *Die Burger*. In 1915, a year after the National Party was formed, he was appointed as the organiser for the new party. In 1918, he was one of the co-founders of Santam and Sanlam, and he served as the first chairperson of both companies, a position he held for 35 years, until his death in 1953.

Hofmeyr was also the co-founder, with Jannie Marais, of Naspers.

The first copy of *Die Burger* hit the shelves in June 1915, and the following year the first magazine, *Die Huisgenoot* (The Home Companion), made its appearance. Two years later they started publishing books.

In the 1980s, Naspers realised that more and more South Africans were watching TV, and that therefore they as a media company had to play in that space as well. That is how MNET began. South Africa's first pay television, it started operating in 1986. The following year, cabinet approved a resolution that allowed (or, depending on how you look at it, forced) the SABC to show MNET shows free of charge, initially for an hour. And then that increased to two hours. It was during that 'open time', which ran for twenty years, until 2007, that MNET showcased to all South Africans what they were missing by only watching SABC. The show that really did the trick, when it was launched in 1988, was *Carte Blanche*, which went on to win numerous awards for investigating and exposing the ills in our society. It is South Africa's longest-running current-affairs TV show.

Still in the 1980s, MNET launched SuperSport. The public soon wanted to access these premier shows and – boom – MNET was, as young people say, rolling in the dough. Through subscriptions they were making handsome profits. It was only a matter of time before they started operating in other African countries.

In 1994, the parent company MultiChoice was formed. And in

1995, digital satellite television, or DSTV, a direct-broadcast satellite service owned by MultiChoice, began operating. It provides multiple channels and services to subscribers.

So next time you are watching sport on SuperSport, or any channel on DSTV (besides SABC and etv), think about those men, those visionaries, in Stellenbosch back in December 1914 who created the media company we call Naspers today. Their legacy lives on.

Naspers played a strategic role in talking to the hearts and minds of Afrikaners. It therefore came as no surprise to discover that Naspers had supported the National Party through, among other things, donating handsomely before elections.

It also emerged that in the 1980s the National Party had a minority stake in Naspers through ownership of shares in the company. The obvious conflict of interest is glaring. How can a political party – the governing party at that – own shares in a private company, especially a media group? That could explain how and why MNET got the first pay-TV licence in the country. It could also explain why the SABC ended up showing 'open time'. Effectively, the SABC was advertising its competitor's product.

Talking about glaring conflicts of interest, the National Party seemingly taught the ANC a thing or three. The ANC did exactly the same thing – owning shares in a private company. The investment arm of the ANC, Chancellor House, was reported in 2007 to partly own Hitachi Power Africa, the local subsidiary of the Japanese multinational conglomerate. And Hitachi Power Africa, as might be expected in such circumstances, won a tender to do some work on one of the power stations that Eskom was building.

Here we are, almost twenty years later, complaining how corrupt some of the senior employees at Eskom were (and are), when actually they learnt from their leaders. The more things change, the more they stay the same.

Back to Naspers.

When the information eventually came out how Naspers had

been in bed with the Nats, the leadership of Naspers was invited to appear at the Truth and Reconciliation Commission. But Naspers's leadership staunchly refused. Yes, Naspers's executives said no, we are not going there. Same as PW Botha, who, when invited to the commission, said, 'Go fuck yourselves.' Okay, he did not say that, but to my ears it sounded like that. He just called the commission a circus. Botha was fined, and he appealed. He was cleared, and all was forgiven and/or forgotten. Life continued as if nothing had happened.

When Jacob Zuma tried the same stunt, however, he was sent to jail for fifteen months. Okay, maybe it was not exactly the same, because PW Botha appealed his fine, whereas Zuma did not even appear in court where he could have stated his case. Books, I hope, will be written in the future that will dissect whether the Constitutional Court erred in its handling of the Zuma/Zondo debacle (see Part III).

Some Naspers employees did appear before the commission, and apologised for the role played by the organisation in supporting the National Party and thus helping sustain apartheid. But it was almost twenty years later that Naspers officially apologised. And, after that, all was forgiven.

Actually, nothing was forgiven, because no-one was holding a grudge against Naspers. No-one. Certainly not me. We have, from day one, been paying our DStv subscriptions. Before and after an apology, we continued paying our subscriptions – and we would not have stopped if Naspers had not apologised. In fact, Naspers could even retract the apology here and now, and we would still pay our subscriptions because, among other things, and truth be told, most people cannot live without TV. That is how much we are addicted to it. If not, try living without it for a few days; and if indeed you pull it off, you will probably share the wonderful news with friends and family as if it were one massive achievement.

One person who must take credit for ultra-boosting Naspers,

especially when he acquired a significant stake in the then un-known Chinese technology and internet company Tencent, is Koos Bekker. So bullish about the future of the company he head-ed was he that for about fifteen years he wasn't paid a salary. Not a cent. His only compensation was through shares. And that paid off – spectacularly. In 2022, Bekker, the chair of Naspers, had a net worth of US$2.3 billion (about R40 billion). TJ Strydom's book *Koos Bekker's Billions* (Penguin Random House, 2022) explores the master plan that made Bekker a billionaire.

It is quite clear that Afrikaners had a proper strategy and formidable tactics: they formed a political platform, created a mouthpiece and built economic muscle. And it makes sense that a man like Hofmeyr ended up playing a part in three things: as an organiser for the National Party, as chair of Naspers, and as chair of both Santam and Sanlam. Everything was interrelated. And it makes sense why, as an example, DF Malan the editor ended up being a minister and eventually a prime minister. In retrospect, it is quite clear why a university started operating in 1918 – future leaders had to be groomed, coached and mentored.

The Afrikaners did it between 1914 and 1918. A true, solid foundation was laid within those four years. Although it took years to achieve some of their objectives, it is clear, with the ben-efit of hindsight, that the Afrikaners – who are sometimes viewed by their English counterparts as intellectually inferior – always had a vision for the country, with them in the pound seats.

Notwithstanding the political platform, the mouthpiece and the economic muscle, something was still missing, however. Something very important.

One Joseph Jacobus 'JJ' Bosman had been toying with the idea since 1921 but it took him more than a decade to bring it to fruition. That thing was a savings bank. Bosman finally presented his idea to the upper echelons of the Broederbond in 1933. The

Broederbond, in turn, formed a committee to investigate the matter, with JJ as the chair. And in July 1934, a savings bank was registered. And that is how the 'people's bank', Volkskas, came into being. By the time it opened its first branch in Pretoria in 1935, JJ Bosman was one of the managers at head office.

By the mid-1940s Volkskas had evolved into a fully fledged commercial bank. And with the National Party winning the 1948 elections, Volkskas was soon in prime position. Thanks to the Nats being in power, Afrikaners in their numbers could be appointed to senior positions, not only in government but also at state-owned enterprises such as Iscor and South African Railways and Harbours. And those state-owned enterprises could have their primary accounts with the people's bank.

The expansion was so immense that in 1952, Volkskas opened its hundredth branch. It was by then the third-largest bank in the country (after Barclays and Standard), with a forex department dealing with foreign currency. As accountants would say, the balance sheet was healthy – so much so, that the bank ended up buying stakes in non-banking assets. As an example, in the 1960s, it bought into mining (the General Mining and Finance Corporation) and agriculture (the Transvaal Sugar Corporation). The times, they were good.

In the 1980s Volkskas sold its merchant bank, Bankorp, to Sanlam. Within a decade, Bankorp had to get a bailout from the South African Reserve Bank. It was that bailout, of R1.125 billion, that led to the public protector, Absa and the Reserve Bank slugging it out in court thirty years later.

Amalgamated Banks of South Africa, officially known as Absa since 1998, was formed in 1991 following the merger of four banks: United, Allied, Volkskas and parts of the Sage Group. Absa acquired Bankorp in April 1992, while the bailout money was still flowing to the latter.

The 2017 report of advocate Busisiwe Mkhwebane, the public

protector, into the apartheid-era bailout ordered Absa to pay more than R2 billion (capital plus interest) back to the Reserve Bank. Mkhwebane, besides losing when her report was taken on review, was asked to pay some legal costs in her personal capacity – the first time this had ever happened to the head of a Chapter 9 institution, which are organisations whose specific purpose is to guard our democracy.

Mkhwebane subsequently lost other court cases … and it was becoming clearer and clearer that the end was nigh. But, still, a point has to be made about the personal costs issue.

I must say, as an outsider looking in, the court order for Mkhwebane to pay in her personal capacity did not sit well with me. Just imagine if the judges were also ordered to pay in their personal capacity if a matter they had handled was overruled or successfully appealed by a higher court? Let me ask it differently: why aren't judges ordered to pay in their personal capacity if the matter they handled is successfully appealed?

Anyway, the key issue was, how come, after getting a loan at an interest rate of just one per cent, did Bankorp use the loan to buy government bonds at sixteen per cent, thus garnering a neat fifteen per cent profit? The bank insisted in its submissions to the public protector and during the review application process that the fifteen per cent interest (which generated more than R225 million) was used to write off the debts of customers who could not pay back the bank's money.

This bailout matter, by the way, was first investigated by Judge Dennis Davis and his team of experts between 2000 and 2002. Their conclusion was that the benefit of the bailout went to the shareholders of Bankorp. And Bankorp was 88 per cent owned by Sanlam.

Given the abovementioned public knowledge, dear reader, we can easily conclude that the Broederbond laid the foundation for the launching and eventual success of Volkskas. It therefore comes as no surprise that Volkskas employees, especially at a senior level, would be Broederbond members. This is confirmed by former Absa banker Bob Aldworth's book *The Infernal Tower: The damage to people, careers and reputations in corporate South Africa* (Contra Press, 1996), in which he states that former Volkskas CEO Hennie Diedericks told him that 'it was a prerequisite to be a Broederbonder if one sought to rise to the top'.

Another high flyer, Danie Cronjé, who held various positions at Volkskas from 1975 (and who had previously lectured in money and banking at Potchefstroom University), and who became the bank's group chief executive in 1988, and chairperson of Absa in 1997, a position he held for ten years, is referred to as a 'former Broederbonder' in a 2007 IOL article.

In his book, Aldworth noted, 'At board meetings, Broederbond matters were openly discussed and the ethos of Afrikaners sustaining other Afrikaners was paramount.'

Let's go back to Sanlam, which was the majority shareholder when Bankorp got the bailout from the South African Reserve Bank.

It just so happens that in 1985, Sanlam had established a subsidiary called Sankorp, a strategic investment vehicle that was going to be involved in large-scale development projects. Four years later, in 1989, Sanlam made R2 billion available to Sankorp as part of dealing with job creation in the country. And it was during that very year that the first corporate report in South Africa, that of Sankorp, referred to the concept of black economic empowerment – BEE.

Four years later, in 1993, before we voted in the country's first democratic elections, Sanlam, the very organisation created to empower Afrikaners, signed the first BEE deal when it sold a stake in one of its divisions, Metropolitan, to an entity called New Africa Investments Limited (NAIL).

So the multibillion-rand question is: did Sanlam create BEE?

One Cyril Ramaphosa, by the way, was part of the Sanlam/NAIL deal, which lasted ten years, until 2003. The following year,

2004, Sanlam signed another BEE deal. This time, it was with Ubuntu-Botho Investments. The major shareholder there was, and still is, Patrice Motsepe (through his family trust). That explains why the main sponsor of Premier League football team Sundowns is, as depicted in their kit, Ubuntu-Botho. Sundowns is owned by Patrice Motsepe.

The deal saw the Ubuntu-Botho consortium take an initial eight per cent stake in Sanlam. This shareholding was extended to include broad-based groups consisting of trade union companies, religious organisations, women and youth groups, representing about 700 shareholders.

By 2014, ten years later, Motsepe had made R8 billion out of the total R14 billion raked in by the broader consortium. The value created, crowed Sanlam's media statement at the time, 'makes the transaction ... one of the most successful transactions of its kind in the financial services sector and in South African history'.

The Sanlam deal was not Motsepe's only mega deal. In 2014, the twenty-year anniversary of the new South Africa, timeslive journalist Ann Crotty wrote, 'Presumably Motsepe's relationship with long-serving cabinet minister Jeff Radebe helped persuade the Sacco family, who may have had an eye on mineral rights, that Motsepe was the ideal partner.' Radebe is married to Motsepe's sister, Bridgette. Cyril, by the way, is also married to a sister of Patrice – Tshepo.

Crotty was referring to the 2006 joint venture agreement between Motsepe's African Rainbow Minerals and Assore. The Sacco family, at the time of the deal, controlled Assore – a mining, processing and marketing company. Assore in turn owned fifty per cent of Assmang, which is in the mining and alloys businesses.

In 2016, Motsepe joined forces with Johan van Zyl, former Sanlam CEO, and Johan van der Merwe, former Sanlam head of investments, to form African Rainbow Capital (ARC). ARC, through the ARC Fund, has two divisions: diversified investments (telecom-munications, property, agriculture, mining, construction, energy, etc.) and diversified financial investments (insurance, banking, etc.). Some of the companies/brands that the ARC Fund has invested in include TymeBank and Rain.

Bear in mind that the Black Economic Empowerment Act was only passed in 2003. This means that for nine years into the new dispensation, there was no legal framework exclusively dealing with the economic empowerment of black people.

As black people, in retrospect, it becomes clear that the exclusive focus was on political power, political power and more political power. It seems as if there was no plan looking further down the road. We were like a boy who pursues a beautiful girl for years, and then one day the girl, out of the blue, finally says, 'Yes, I love you too,' and the guy is so stunned that he does not know what to do with the love that is now in his lap.

How did we end up dealing with BEE in this chapter, I hear you ask. Because, first, the Broederbond was not just about political power; it was also about the economic (and social and cultural) empowerment of the Afrikaner volk. And second, and even more important, BEE as a term and concept seemingly was not conceived by black people but by, eish, white people. If this assertion is indeed true, it means black people have been passengers, from day one, on the bus they are supposed to be driving.

According to Esterhuyse's 2012 book *Endgame*, Johannes 'Jan' de Klerk was a member of the Broederbond. And his son, Frederik Willem 'FW' de Klerk, was also a Broederbonder. Jan was at one stage the minister of education (1961 to 1969) and FW later occupied the same position (1984 to 1989). This phenomenon of a father and son occupying the same position at different times also happened at the Reserve Bank (more about that later).

One thing not often mentioned about FW is that he was Hans Strijdom's nephew: JG Strijdom, leader of the National Party and prime minister of South Africa from 1954 to 1958, was married to FW de Klerk's aunt, Susan, the sister of FW's father, Jan.

Another Broederbond member who played a critical role in the country we have today is one Niël Barnard. In his book, *Secret Revolution: Memoirs of a spy boss* (Tafelberg, 2015), he states clearly that he was part of the Ruiterwag (as mentioned, the youth wing of the Broederbond). Before turning 30, armed with a PhD, he was appointed professor at the University of the Orange Free State. And in 1980, aged 30, he was appointed director-general of the National Intelligence Service, a position he held for twelve years. During that time, he – among other things – played a key role behind the scenes as the apartheid government started conversations with the ANC leadership in exile and inside the country.

Barnard gives the finer details of secret conversations between Nelson Mandela and the state. These talks started, according to him, while Mandela was still in Pollsmoor Prison, and continued later when he had been moved to what was then Victor Verster prison in Paarl. 'PW Botha and Nelson Mandela were in continuous, indirect contact with each other for more than two years before it was announced to the world,' according to Barnard.

What is clear is that there was a lot of manoeuvring behind the scenes from about the mid-1980s.

Besides the fact that there were almost fifty discussions between Mandela and the government, represented by the National Intelligence Service, there is another surprising thing – in fact, jaw-dropping stuff – that Barnard mentions in his book. That is that Winnie Mandela refused to go and live with her husband in the house in which Mandela was staying on the Victor Verster property. Which wife, I think to myself, would refuse an opportunity to (secretly) live with her husband, especially when he has been in prison for almost three decades?

Barnard also mentions – and this is to be expected – that the house in which Mandela stayed was bugged. There were listening devices that captured all conversations that Mandela had with his visitors. Maybe – just thinking out loud – that is why Winnie refused to move into that house. It can never be fun, I imagine, being blackmailed by people who have your sex tape (even if you were having sex with your spouse, in prison).

Still on the issue of blackmail, I have often wondered what the apartheid government had on Mandela. In other words, what secrets did the National Party have that at any given moment they could have unleashed against Madiba? I am talking about insurance of some sort. Just in case. Just in case he did not play ball.

You really have to be very naive to think that, after having imprisoned a known communist (a swear word at the time), who had been instrumental in the formation of an armed wing, for almost thirty years, and knowing full well – it was almost a given – that he would be the head of state within a few years of his release, you would just fold your arms and believe he would do the right thing (read: preach peace, nation-building and reconciliation). The pragmatic side of me tells me that the real world does not work on some fuzzy mumbo-jumbo pie-in-the-sky live-in-hope scenario. The real world works on, among other things, insurance. Just In Case.

There are two things Barnard wrote about that I fully expected from him. First, he mentioned that the ANC was infiltrated. There are some books that have mentioned this same issue over and over again. I was not even surprised when he mentioned that the late Kenneth Kaunda, former president of Zambia, where the ANC had its head-quarters in exile, was giving information to the National Intelligence Service about liberation movements, including the ANC. The reason why this claim did not shock me is because, before reading Barnard's book, I had read one by another intelligence operative, Riaan Labuschagne, *On South Africa's Secret Service: An undercover agent's story* (Galago Publishing, 2003), which claims that the National Intelligence Service recruited and handled Kaunda as 'an agent of influence' (more about this later).

The second thing that did not surprise me was Barnard's admiration and love for PW Botha. 'Botha was a doer who made things happen: roads, schools and hospitals were built,' he wrote. 'Above all, he was driven by the desire to help people – to serve.' Barnard believed that, 'taking everything into account, PW will still be given his rightful and well-earned place in the history of South Africa'.

I suppose when someone gives you the opportunity of a lifetime, and in the process you have numerous secret meetings with Nelson Mandela and play a role in changing the course of a country's history, you are bound to have a soft spot for that individual, irrespective of how much he messed up not just countrywide but at a regional scale. It is just human nature.

My major memory of PW Botha is all the songs we used to sing about him when toyi-toying in black areas, and, trust me, you don't want to read those expletives.

There is, however, something that Barnard mentioned that made my mind go into a spin. Young people call it a mind fuck. The first meeting between PW Botha and Mandela was secretly recorded. This is public knowledge. The tape was, after some time, destroyed – by none other than the head of the National Intelligence Service, Niël Barnard. Again, this is public knowledge. The tapes were destroyed, he tells us. I repeat: the tapes were destroyed, he tells us. Imagine – just imagine – had they not been destroyed, what their true value would be today. Priceless! You can keep your cryptocurrency; I will keep the tapes, thank you very much.

On a serious note, surely the tapes were destroyed because – and this is public knowledge – in 1992 the then minister of justice and national intelligence, Kobie Coetsee, approved the destruction of 'sensitive' state records. The following year, all ministers were authorised to rubber-stamp the destruction of any state secrets in their departments. (If you thought Iscor furnaces were exclusively used to make steel, think again.)

Back to the Afrikaner Broederbond.

A question that could be asked is how Barnard, for example, ended up in such a senior position. The way he tells it is that, after getting the offer to head the National Intelligence Service, he went and consulted with a certain professor at the University of the Free State who was – yes, you have guessed it – a Broederbond member.

Another coincidence is the fact that a former chair of the South African Reserve Bank, Gerhard de Kock, just happens to be the son of Michiel Hendrik de Kock, who was the third governor of the Reserve Bank, from 1945 to 1962. What are the odds of former governor of the Reserve Bank Tito Mboweni's son one day being the governor of the Reserve Bank? I ask again, what are the odds?

In his well-researched 2006 report for a national anti-corruption forum, 'Apartheid Grand Corruption', author Hennie van Vuuren wrote, 'At the helm of the institution from the early 1980s until after 1994 were two alleged members of the Broederbond, Gerhard de Kock (1981–89) and Dr Chris Stals (1989–99). These two leaders' membership of the Broederbond and their positions at the Reserve Bank may, of course, have been purely coincidental, but it was clear that the Broederbond had friends in high places.'

This seems to be confirmed by Labuschagne in his book, which spells it out: 'Most of those who made it had the right connections – membership of the Broederbond – regardless of their operational successes or lack of them ... It was not necessarily the right man for the job, but rather the best job for the man ... This tendency was undoubtedly multiplied in the stratospheric levels of the security forces, National Intelligence and in the National Party cabinet itself.'

The year 1968, when they celebrated their fiftieth anniversary, was a massive milestone for the Broederbond. They had by then, indirectly, been running the country for two decades, since the watershed elections of 1948. At what must have been joyous and jovial occasion, first chair HJ Klopper said (according to *The Super-Afrikaners*), 'Do you realise what a powerful force is gathered here tonight between these walls? Show me a greater power on the whole continent of Africa! Show me a greater power anywhere, even in your so-called civilised countries.'

Certainly, ten years later, authors Wilkins and Strydom stated as a matter of fact in *The Super-Afrikaners*, 'Mr PW Botha, the current prime minister, is a member [of the Broederbond], as were his four predecessors, Dr DF Malan, Advocate JG Strijdom, Dr HF Verwoerd and Mr John Vorster.' At the time, they noted, 'the South African government today is the Broederbond and the Broederbond is the government ... Through its network of more than 800 cells in the villages and cities of South Africa, the organisation has infiltrated members into town and city councils, school boards, agricultural unions, the state-controlled radio and television networks, industry and commerce, banks, building societies ...'

I must admit that, as a black African, especially after researching the history of the Broederbond and how multifaceted it was, I can see that we black people were never ready to govern. Never! Ever! And it explains why, after decades of so-called black power, nothing fundamentally has changed.

I must confess, as a black African, that I do not think – although I hope I am proved wrong – we black people will ever be ready to govern, that is, to ensure that our own black people are at the centre and core of all meaningful economic, social and cultural activity, even a hundred years from now.

Chapter 9
THE COMMUNISTS

The ANC had not even celebrated the first decade of its existence when the Communist Party of South Africa, the forerunner of the current South African Communist Party (SACP), was launched.

In July 1921, more than two thousand people, mainly from working-class communities, gathered in Cape Town to form the new party. Central to the formation of the party were white workers who had been heavily influenced by the 1917 Bolshevik Revolution, in which members of the Bolshevik party seized power in the capital of Russia, Petrograd (now St Petersburg).

The Bolsheviks believed that the working classes would at some point liberate themselves from the economic and political control of the ruling elite. Led by Bolshevik party leader Vladimir Lenin, this Revolution resulted not only in the storming and capture of the Winter Palace, the official residence of the Russian Emperor since 1732, but also the formation of a new government, which led to the establishment of the Soviet Union in 1922. (This 'October Revolution' was, by the way, in November – but it was October according to the Julian calendar, which was still in use in the Soviet Union at the time.)

During the 1921 three-day conference, not only was the Communist Party of South Africa launched, but all administrative items, including the adoption of a manifesto, and the aims and character of the party, were endorsed. For all practical purposes, the Communist Party of South Africa was the local chapter of

Communist International, the global communist movement based in Moscow, Russia.

The 1921 conference also, as expected, elected leaders. One of those was English-born William Henry 'Bill' Andrews, who became secretary-general. Andrews had previously served as a member of parliament on the South African Labour Party ticket. The Labour Party was made up essentially of lower-middle-class white workers who, among other things, were concerned about the emerging threat of black African workers taking their jobs.

A year after the formation of the Communist Party of South Africa, the Rand Rebellion miners' strikes took place. It all started when mining companies, thanks to a lower gold price, decided to cut labour costs by replacing white employees with black ones, while paying darkies exactly the same salary as before. Basically, they would get the black employees to do the same job as their white counterparts, but for less. (I have a sense, and maybe it is just me, that this very practice still exists in South Africa today. Otherwise, how do you explain the obsession by private companies of preventing employees from sharing, and thus comparing, their salaries and perks?)

Although the strike was organised under the auspices of the South African Labour Party, the local Communist Party also supported it.

The racist tone of white workers towards their black counterparts was glaring. Among the posters and slogans used during the marches was, for example, 'Workers of the world, unite and fight for a white South Africa.'

Prime minister Jan Smuts's government sensed that this was more than just a labour issue; it was the start of a rebellion to undermine and eventually take over the state. Smuts therefore brought out the big guns. Literally. The Air Force was deployed, and before you knew it, it was raining bombs. By the time it was all over three months later, about 200 people, mostly workers and civilians, were dead.

This perceived heavy-handedness by Smuts cost him the 1924 general election. His South African Party lost to a coalition of the Afrikaner National Party and the South African Labour Party.

That same year, the Industrial Conciliation Act was passed, recognising white unions. And the Wage Act of the following year cemented, legally speaking, the wage gap between white and black workers.

Back to Bill Andrews, the first secretary-general of the local Communist Party. Throughout the 1920s the party focused on organising African workers around issues of trade-union rights and national liberation demands, and by 1925 it had a majority of black members. Andrews soon made it onto the central committee of Communist International, and spent time in Moscow being coached and mentored on the finer details of the imminent global revolution.

Within a decade of its formation, the Communist Party had its first black secretary-general, Albert Nzula. Nzula, a teacher by profession, soon made his way to Moscow for further ideological and military training because he was seen as a potential ultimate leader (read: chairperson) of the local chapter. After becoming despondent about communism and its variations (Stalinism, Leninism, Marxism, Trotskyism), he found solace and comfort in the bottle. He fell asleep while drunk in sub-zero temperatures, and died of pneumonia before his 30th birthday.

One of the first black people to join the Communist Party of South Africa was Josiah Tshangana 'JT' Gumede. Gumede was also a founder member of the ANC in 1912. Nothing illustrates the animosity between the ANC and the Communist Party like JT's case. After he'd been to Moscow, he was ousted from the ANC because of his Communist Party affiliations. (When he died in 1946, he was survived by, among others, his son Archibald Jacob Gumede. Archie, as he was fondly known, led the then Natal delegates to the 1955 adoption of the Freedom Charter in Kliptown. A lawyer by profession and a leader of the United Democratic

Front, he was elected as a member of parliament in 1994, and he died in office four years later, aged 84.)

Notwithstanding what happened to JT Gumede, seemingly the relationship between the two organisations stabilised and in time became very cosy. In fact, the relationship has been so cosy over the years that it has become the norm for an individual to hold senior positions in both organisations at the same time, to the extent that at one stage it felt like the ANC and the SACP, especially at leadership level, were two sides of the same coin.

Let us look at a few examples.

Two years after joining the Communist Party, aged 25, South African John Beaver 'JB' Marks was on his way, thanks to funding by the Russians, to study at the Communist University of the Toilers of the East, which operated under the umbrella of Communist International. Although he was at one stage suspended from the SACP, he came back with a bang: in 1962 he became chair. Six years later, while still holding that position, he also became the treasurer-general of the ANC.

Then there was the case of Moses Kotane, who was the secretary-general of the SACP for an astounding 43 years. (To put this into perspective, Blade Nzimande, who was first elected as secretary-general in 1998, would have had to serve until 2040 to break this record, but thank goodness Blade relinquished this position and was, in turn, elected chairperson in 2022.) While he was at it, Kotane also served for a number of years as ANC treasurer-general.

The two periods of Kotane's tenures as secretary-general (1933 to 1936, and 1938 to 1978) were separated by Edwin Thabo Mofutsanyana's tenure.

Let us detour for a second or two. Govan Mbeki, a prominent communist who was also a Rivonia Triallist, was so close to Thabo Mofutsanyana that when his (Mbeki's) first child was born, he decided to name the child after his friend and comrade. That boy grew up to be such a high-achieving man that two days short of his 57th birthday, on 16 June 1999, he was sworn in as the president of South Africa.

Seemingly, Moses Kotane took over from Thabo Mofutsanyana not just on Communist Party matters, but also on a personal level: years later, Mofutsanyana's wife had a child with Kotane. Of course, this is a private matter and none of us should be involved when comrades-in-arms end up in the arms of the same woman. It is comradely love. As one comrade once told me, 'Sihle, izinto ziyenzeka kuma-conferences' (Things happen during conferences).

Kotane was succeeded by Thomas Nkobi as the ANC's secretary-general. Many South Africans may remember Nkobi as the name of the company that was owned by Schabir Shaik, former president Jacob Zuma's financial advisor who was sentenced to fifteen years in jail for fraud and corruption. Shaik, by the way, worked as an assistant to Nkobi.

When Nkobi died in 1994, he was buried at South Park Cemetery, which years later was renamed Thomas Titus Nkobi Memorial Park. I must admit, before I came across this Nkobi cemetery issue, I had never thought about whether it is appropriate for cemeteries to be named after people. If yes, must it be limited to dead people? I think so. Imagine walking around and already you have a cemetery named after you. It would be enough to kill you. But then again, even if a cemetery is named after a dead person, how does that make the family members feel? Imagine driving past a cemetery named after your grandfather. Does it make you smile because your grandfather is buried in his own cemetery, or do you end up sad because it serves as a reminder that your grandfather is dead? (And buried in his own cemetery, which then brings a bit of a smile.)

Kotane suffered a stroke and died in Russia in 1978. He was succeeded as ANC secretary-general by Moses Mabhida.

Mabhida, like Kotane before him, held dual membership and

senior positions in both organisations. He'd joined the Communist Party of South Africa in 1942, when he was in his 30s; and in the mid-1950s, he was elected to the national executive committee of the ANC. He was always loved by the rank and file of both the ANC and the Communist Party. In 1969, at the Morogoro Conference in Tanzania, he was tasked with establishing the ANC's department of intelligence and security.

Mabhida died in 1986 of a heart attack in Maputo, after having suffered a stroke the previous year. This means two consecutive secretary-generals died of stroke-related complications. But not much must be read into it if you consider their ages, 73 and 63, at the time of their death. Therefore it would be a long shot to think that there were some shenanigans behind the deaths of such great communists.

I, however, just don't like it when senior leaders and other prominent people get very sick and, even worse, die all of a sudden, especially when on a business trip in foreign lands. Remember in 2012 when Radhakrishna Lutchmana 'Roy' Padayachie, then minister of public service and administration, died in his hotel room while on an official visit to Ethiopia? 'Natural causes', we were told. Personally, I struggle with coincidences but then, I am sure, it is just me.

Let us, for a minute or so, stick with the theme of prominent people suffering heart attacks. I have often wondered what would have happened if PW Botha had not had a mild stroke early in 1989. What if he had continued in good health?

Soon after his stroke, PW Botha resigned as leader of the National Party. Some say he was pushed out by other leaders within the party, and that his ill health was used as an excuse. For six months afterwards, there were two centres of power: PW held on as the president of the Republic, while FW de Klerk took over the leadership of the ruling party. But the writing was on the wall, and Botha eventually resigned when he felt he was not being consulted on critical issues. A key example was when, behind his back, De Klerk met Zambia's Kenneth Kaunda.

On the same day that Botha resigned, De Klerk was sworn in as the president of the country. The following year, on 2 February 1990, De Klerk announced plans for massive political reforms. These included the unbanning of political parties and the release of political prisoners.

So the question I have always asked myself is, what if PW Botha had not suffered that stroke? Do you, dear reader, understand the implications if Botha had continued as leader of both the party and the country? Would it have meant that political prisoners would not have been released? Would Nelson Mandela have died in jail?

Was that stroke a supernatural intervention?

Let's go back to the communists.

(PW Botha was not a communist. He was, however, a member of the Afrikaner Broederbond ... and he left it after he resigned as the president of the Republic ...)

Mabhida was succeeded as secretary-general of the SACP by Joe Slovo.

Born into a Jewish family in Lithuania, the young Slovo arrived in South Africa aged 8. As an adult, and by then a fully fledged communist, he was one of the founder members of Umkhonto we Sizwe, the Spear of the Nation, the ANC's armed wing.

While in exile between 1963 and 1990, and still MK commander, he was elected to the national executive committee of the ANC, thus making history as the first white person to make it onto the highest decision-making body of the party.

He was appointed by Mandela as minister of housing in 1994, and died the following year. He was buried in Heroes' Acre in Avalon Cemetery in Soweto, and is the only white person I know of buried there. (But then again, having grown up in KwaZulu-Natal, where an overwhelming majority of my family members, friends and ex-colleagues live, I do not know a lot of black people who are buried in Avalon.)

One of the best-known people to be a member of the Communist Party was none other than Nelson Rolihlahla Mandela. Although he consistently denied that he was a member, including during the Rivonia Trial, there were always rumours that not only was he a member of the SACP, but that he was part of its highest decision-making structure: the central committee. According to historian Stephen Ellis's 2011 article 'The genesis of the ANC's armed struggle in South Africa 1948–1961' in the *Journal of Southern African Studies*, as well as his 2016 article 'Nelson Mandela, the South African Communist Party and the origins of Umkhonto we Sizwe' in the journal *Cold War History*, this was not a rumour but fact.

It is now a matter of record that while he was on Robben Island, Mandela spent considerable time, effort and energy compiling a manuscript titled 'How to be a good communist'. During a raid of his cell, the handwritten script of about nine thousand words was discovered. In it he'd covered topics such as capitalism, feudal society, the political economy, materialism, dialectical method and dialectical materialism.

The first time, at least for me, when it was publicly and officially acknowledged that indeed Nelson Mandela had been member of the SACP was a few days after his death in 2013. Gwede Mantashe was given the monumental task of telling the country, and indeed the world, what Mandela had consistently denied. He delivered the news jokingly and in an informal manner in a clip that was shown on the TV news later that day. The reason Mandela was a communist, explained Mantashe, was because Walter Sisulu, Mandela's friend and comrade, was a communist. And that, according to Mantashe, was why Mandela decided he was going to be a communist too.

If that was indeed the case, it cannot be said that he was a communist because he believed in its ideology, theory, philosophy or principles. It cannot be said that he at a certain point in his life believed that it was what the world deserved. No, he joined the party because his friend was a member.

I am aware that there are scholars, historians, politicians, journalists and so on who are still debating whether Mandela was a communist or not. If it is not disputed that indeed Mandela wrote a manuscript titled 'How to be a good communist', that settles it. Why would a Christian, as an example, write a manuscript titled 'How to be a good Muslim'?

The reason why Mantashe was the ideal candidate to deliver this news to the nation is simple. It also fits in perfectly with this theme of the SACP and the ANC sometimes operate as two sides of the same coin. At the time of Mandela's death, Mantashe was not only the secretary-general of the ANC, a position he held from 2007 to 2017, but earlier that year he had stepped down as the chairperson of the SACP, his party role from 2007 to 2013. This means that for six years, while Mantashe was secretary-general of the ANC, he was also chair of the SACP.

Could it be that the Communist Party, at least within the South African context, has been the tail that has been wagging the dog? If in doubt, let's look at five ways in which the Communist Party shaped the political discourse in South Africa.

First and foremost: the Freedom Charter of 1955.

This is the statement of core principles of the South African Congress Alliance, which included the ANC and the South African Indian Congress. It opens, 'We, the people of South Africa, declare for all our country and the world to know: that South Africa belongs to all who live in it, black and white, and that no government can justly claim authority unless it is based on the will of all the people.' Reference is made in the charter to 'the country's wealth' being 'restored to the people': 'The mineral wealth beneath the soil, the banks and monopoly industry shall be transferred to the ownership of the people as a whole' and 'all other industry and trade shall be controlled to assist the wellbeing of the people'.

The Freedom Charter came together after a nationwide soliciting of 'freedom demands' by the people. But, actually, this is not true, at least according to Gerard Ludi, who wrote *The Communistisation of the* ANC (Galago, 2012). The travels around the country in order to collect these demands were just a public relations exercise, says Ludi. The charter, he maintains, was crafted mainly by a few white communists, including activist Lionel 'Rusty' Bernstein, later the only Rivonia Triallist who was found not guilty, and Ruth First, the wife of Joe Slovo who was assassinated in 1982 in Mozambique, where she was working in exile. (Notwithstanding this charge, it must be stated that one of the people who consolidated the document was ZK Matthews.)

Ludi, for the record, was recruited by the apartheid government's intelligence services while he was a student at Wits University in the 1960s. He infiltrated the Communist Party which, although banned, was operating underground. Senior communist leaders came to trust him so much that they sent him to Moscow for further training in – horror of horrors – intelligence work, under the capable hand of senior Soviet Union security agency operatives. His cover was only blown when he was instructed by his seniors to testify against Bram Fischer at his 1966 trial. Fischer, who at one stage was the acting chairman of the organisation, was found guilty of violating the Suppression of Communism Act and conspiring to commit sabotage, and got life in prison.

Only then did the penny drop that all that time Ludi had been working for the state as a spy. The account in his book, therefore, is that of an insider.

However, it is not one of someone who at one stage believed in communism, but then for whatever reason decided to drop it, and eventually decided to spite the organisation and spill the beans.

No, this was someone who from day one was there for one job and one job only: to spy.

So when someone like that writes a book, especially in his old age (Ludi was in his seventies when the book was published), you owe it to yourself to read it and get the lowdown on what was really happening in the communist organisation in South Africa and abroad.

Ludi, by the way, also wrote that Patrick Duncan, the white guy who not only joined but became a leader of the PAC, 'as the CIA's most important asset in Africa ... was tasked by the Americans with stopping a takeover of South Africa by the SACP/ANC Alliance'. The Central Intelligence Agency (CIA) focuses primarily on providing intelligence for the president and cabinet of the United States.

On an unrelated matter, Ludi wrote that Duncan was 'most likely' behind the split between the ANC and the PAC. Therefore, if we take this assertion to its logical conclusion, the ANC/PAC split had nothing to do with ideology but at a deeper level was all part of the West's divide-and-rule strategy. If, indeed, this is true, it makes me want to say what my kids often say to me when they discover something new: all this time my life has been a lie.

Do yourself a favour, read the book *The CIA's Greatest Hits* by Mark Zepezauer (Soft Skull, 2012). It covers 42 CIA covert operations worldwide, including not only the 1961 assassination of Patrice Lumumba, the first prime minister of the Democratic Republic of the Congo, but also how the CIA militarily propped up Angola's National Union for the Total Independence of Angola (Unita). South Africa soon got itself into this Angolan quagmire, funding Unita during the Angolan civil war of 1975 to 2002.

The PAC, fortunately (or unfortunately), does not feature in this astonishing work, but the book shows how intelligence services, especially the CIA, can and do manipulate events in other countries. It would be very naive to think that the CIA was, and is, not manipulating – or at least trying to manipulate – certain events in South Africa here and now.

Oh well, as recently as December 2021, the Independent news media group was interdicted, at the last moment, from publishing a story emanating from a classified report titled 'Top secret: US interest in ANC party dynamics'. The report reputedly deals with how certain senior members of the ruling party are being influenced and or controlled by foreign agencies – America, in this instance.

Still on the CIA, there had always been rumours and speculation that it was the CIA that tipped off the South African authorities about Mandela's whereabouts, leading to his arrest in Howick in 1962. Well, it turns out that there is no smoke without fire. A gentleman by the name of Donald Rickard, a CIA operative, who was officially employed as the US vice-consul in Durban, was the one who alerted the South African authorities, which led to Mandela's capture.

This story only made it into most mainstream global newspapers in 2016, when filmmaker John Irvin was in South Africa making the movie *Mandela's Gun*, about his experiences as a guerrilla fighter for the ANC. The story was first carried by the British *Sunday Times* under the screaming headline 'CIA admits: We sent Mandela to jail'. The following day the *Washington Post* published more or less the same story under the more subdued headline 'The CIA's mysterious role in the arrest of Nelson Mandela'.

Rickard explained to Irvin that Mandela, according to what the United States believed at the time, was 'completely under the control of the Soviet Union ... He could have incited a war in South Africa ... and things could have gone to hell ... We were teetering on the brink ... Mandela had to be stopped. And I put a stop to it.'

Two weeks after dropping this bombshell, Rickard died. Of

course, his confession and subsequent death were a mere coincidence. Nothing at all must be read into it. After all, he was 88 years old.

One of the hits carried out by the CIA, according to Zepezauer's book, was in Nicaragua. This Latin-American country had always been under the control of the USA, to the extent that Franklin D Roosevelt, US president from 1933 to 1945, is quoted as saying, 'Somoza may be a son of a bitch, but he's our son of a bitch.' Anastasio Somoza García was the leader of Nicaragua from 1937 until his assassination in 1956.

Coincidentally, in 1995, Gary Webb, an American investigative journalist, started publishing a series of explosive stories of how the CIA, in order to raise the huge amounts of cash needed to quell a challenge to the Somoza dynasty, hired a number of traffickers to buy, distribute and sell drugs in the USA. It was this very project, according to Webb, that led to the explosion of drug use in poor inner-city areas in the 1990s.

Webb persisted against all the odds to expose the truth. In 2004, he was found dead, with two bullets to the head. It was ruled a suicide. I promise, it was ruled – after an investigation that included a post-mortem report – a suicide.

Let's return to the Freedom Charter. This is the document that, to this day, most if not all ANC leaders and supporters consistently and constantly quote from, sometimes word for word. I find it strange that the Freedom Charter acts, for all practical purposes, as the founding document of the ANC and yet, in 1943, the African Claims document written by Dr AB Xuma, and including a bill of rights and a charter 'from the African's point of view', was adopted. And it was in this latter document that an overarching right – 'the granting of full citizenship rights such as are enjoyed by all Europeans in South Africa'– was demanded, including, first and foremost, 'abolition of political discrimination based on race'.

I wonder how many ANC supporters, as a percentage of the

total membership, have ever heard of the African Claims document. Why is it not regularly quoted by the rank and file? It is not abnormal, when discussing education-related issues (as was the case during the #FeesMustFall campaign), for the Freedom Charter to be quoted: 'The doors of learning (and of culture) shall be opened.' But have you ever heard anyone in this regard quote African Claims, which I think is more comprehensive: 'We demand ... the right of every child to free and compulsory education and of admission to technical schools, universities, and other institutions of higher education'?

Could it be that the SACP has always had a strategy, at least in South Africa, to play the backroom role? Or, if you insist, be the puppetmaster?

So important is the Freedom Charter that its opening phrase, 'We, the people of South Africa', made it into our constitution. I rest my case.

Let us look at the second way which the communists played a historic role in modern-day South Africa: Umkhonto we Sizwe.

Here is the context. On 16 December 1961, MK launched its first attack. A decision had been taken a few months earlier that the ANC needed this military wing. But Ben Turok (RIP) – a senior SACP member at the time – had always maintained that the decision was taken in 1960 where a handful key communists (Bram Fischer, Yusuf Dadoo, Ruth First, Moses Kotane etc.) were present.

Stephen Ellis (RIP) – a historian and professor at Vrije Universiteit in Amsterdam – after trawling through thousands of documents from the then East German secret police known as the Stasi, also made the startling revelation that the meeting at which the decision was taken to form the military wing was in 1960 and consisted of only 25 people, and Nelson Mandela was one of the very few black people present.

Mandela was then tasked, according to Ellis, to present the proposal to the ANC Working Committee the following year (1961).

What is known as a matter of fact is that the headquarters of MK were at Liliesleaf farm in Rivonia. It was on this very farm in July 1963 that ANC and MK leaders were arrested. And it was that arrest that led to the Rivonia Trial.

Ellis also laid bare the myths of an armed struggle against the apartheid government in his book *External Mission: The ANC in exile, 1960–1990* (Oxford University Press, 2013).

He goes even further, and says that MK's contribution to the downfall of the apartheid regime was nothing but theatrics.

Ellis was among the first to cover in book format the mutinies that happened in MK training camps at Quatro in Angola.

Another person, by the way, who published a book on torture and killings at the MK camps was journalist Paul Trewhela. What makes his book *Inside Quatro: Uncovering the exile history of the ANC and Swapo* (Jacana Media, 2009) even more compelling is that it contains first-hand accounts and testimony by former MK combatants who witnessed and experienced what exactly happened in 1984 at Quatro.

It gets worse.

Former spy Riaan Labuschagne's 2003 book *On South Africa's Secret Service* notes that for years, thanks to the generosity of Zambia's then president Kenneth Kaunda, the ANC had its headquarters in the capital city of Lusaka. But, according to Labuschagne, 'One of the best examples of ... a secret cooperation agreement was the one between National Intelligence and President Kenneth Kaunda of Zambia. He was recruited as an agent of influence and handled by Dr Daan Opperman. Kaunda also worked for the British MI6 [the UK's secret intelligence service]. At the same time he was giving ANC president, Oliver Tambo, a safe haven at State House in Lusaka and providing bases for MK.'

Therefore, if the book is to be believed, it would have been impossible to plan a real and comprehensive military revolution led by MK without the British knowing and, obviously, without them informing (no pun intended) their South African counterparts.

Given the ill-discipline, inadequate resources, mutiny and infiltration of MK, it is safe to conclude that the simple reason we never had a military revolution in South Africa, as happened in Cuba, for example, is because MK (or the PAC's military wing, Apla, for that matter) on its own was never going to fight day after day, week after week, and take one village after another, one town after another, all the way to Pretoria, where the president and his cabinet (if they had not skipped the country already) would be arrested and paraded in front of the TV cameras. It was always a fantasy for (some) people but it remained exactly that – a fantasy. A wildest dream.

The negotiated settlement, with hindsight, was always the one and only option on the table.

Again, just to be clear: the negotiated settlement, with hindsight, was always the one and only option on the table.

Kaunda, seemingly, was not the only leader who was recruited by MI6. *The Road to Zimbabwe, 1890–1980* (Jonathan Cape, 1987) by academic and historian Anthony Verrier spells out that a number of leaders, especially from southern and East Africa, were also recruited by the British. Those include, says Verrier, Nyerere, Banda and Nkomo. Julius Nyerere was Tanzania's first president; Hastings Banda became prime minister and, after independence, president of Malawi; and Joshua Nkomo became Zimbabwe's vice-president.

If Verrier's book is to be believed as far as recruitment of leaders is concerned, by the time these national leaders became presidents, they were already on the payroll of the intelligence service of the very country that, at least publicly, they were fighting. And, if we take this to its logical conclusion, the point here is very simple:

colonialism never died. It reminds me of that song by Whitney Houston: 'Same Script, Different Cast'.

But then again, I keep saying to myself, if indeed these leaders were, to use the modern term, captured, why did they, when they took over, look East and end up implementing socialism or communism in their countries? Or did they, when it was convenient, dump the West? Or, all along, were they part of the East and just stringing the West along until, once in power, they showed their true colours?

So, to round off the point, all the signs point to the communists as having led the conversation and made the decision about the launch of the ANC's armed wing.

The third way that the communists greatly influenced South Africa's political discourse was the Rivonia Trial.

In July 1963, the South African authorities made a surprise swoop on Liliesleaf farm in Rivonia outside of Johannesburg. (Admittedly, it is difficult to think that, back in the day, Rivonia was essentially farmland.) Leaders of the Communist Party of South Africa and the ANC were arrested.

At the time of the arrests, Liliesleaf was what you would call the headquarters and war room of the fight against apartheid. The money to buy the farm, and to sponsor all the operational requirements of the revolution, had come from the Communist Party. Without those funds, there would have been no Liliesleaf and there would have been no Rivonia Trial. The communists were right in the thick of things.

After the trial, all but one of the defendants – Denis Goldberg, Govan Mbeki, Ahmed Kathrada, Raymond Mhlaba, Andrew Mlangeni, Elias Motsoaledi, Walter Sisulu and Nelson Mandela – were convicted and sentenced to life imprisonment. It would take almost thirty years for some to finally be free.

*

The fourth way the communists played a key role in South Africa was the 'sunset clauses'. These clauses brought a broad smile to the faces of representatives of minorities during the pre-1994 elections.

Esterhuyse's 2012 book *Endgame* chronicles how unbendable the National Party government was on Joe Slovo, who was in the leadership of the Communist Party, not being a member of any negotiating party. But the ANC and the Communist Party put their foot down, saying they felt that the National Party must decide for itself who were going to be its representatives, and they would do the same. No party should decide the opponents' players. And in the end, Slovo was part of the negotiations.

The notion of 'winner takes all' was effectively squashed during the negotiations, and the person who presented such a conciliatory path, among others, was one of the top communists in the country – Joe Slovo. But it was also Slovo, strangely enough, who was asked to present the sunset clauses, chief among which was a power-sharing agreement in a so-called government of national unity.

I admit that this was not entirely the SACP's doing, but the communists yet again were right in the thick of things.

And number five, communist leaders have held key positions in the post-1994 era and thus have been, at the very least, high-level implementers of the new government's policies.

We've seen how some individuals occupied leadership positions in both the ANC and the Communist Party in the earlier years. Let us now look at the post-1994 scenario.

There are a number of individuals who are ministers, deputy ministers and premiers, thanks to the ANC winning elections, and yet (or because) they occupy senior Communist Party positions. Thulas Nxesi, as an example, has held different ministerial positions since 2011. He was elected as SACP deputy chair in 2017. You might not be sure when exactly he joined the party, but you do not join the party today and get elected deputy chair the following day, so we can assume he is an old communist. At the 2022 conference, Nxesi retained his deputy chair position.

At the same conference, deputy finance minister David Masondo was elected as the Communist Party's first deputy general-secretary.

In 2017, Senzeni Zokwana was elected chair, and at the time he was minister of agriculture, forestry and fisheries.

The deputy minister of higher education, science and technology is Buti Manamela – a former leader of the Young Communist League and a member of the South African Communist Party's central committee.

The current chairperson of the SACP Dr Bonginkosi Emmanuel 'Blade' Nzimande, who was the general-secretary of the same organisation for 24 years (1998 to 2022), has held different ministerial portfolios since 2009.

Godfrey Phumulo Masualle, premier of the Eastern Cape from 2014 to 2019, is a former ANC chair in the province and has held different Communist Party leadership positions. He is currently the deputy minister of public enterprises (until further notice). Phumulo, who was vying for the Secretary General (SG) position at the 2022 elective conference, was very vocal about Cyril not deserving a second term. He lost the SG position to Fikile Mbalula.

Jeffrey Thamsanqa 'Jeff' Radebe at one stage served on the SACP's central committee. He also holds the record as South Africa's longest continuously serving cabinet member. He started his 25-year tenure during Mandela's administration, way back in 1994, and finished off as the minister of energy in Ramaphosa's cabinet in 2019.

By the by, it was during the tenure of Radebe, a communist, that most state assets were privatised. While he was minister of public enterprises, from 1999 to 2004, he privatised or partly privatised state assets including Iscor and Telkom. And here I have always thought that communism strives for nationalisation of state assets. In Mzansi, seemingly, the communists are the biggest capitalists.

Soon after being appointed minister for higher education and training in 2009, Blade bought a BMW 750i. Other ministers were revealed to be similarly indulging themselves (albeit within the approved parameters of the ministerial handbook) and the ensuing scandal became known as 'Cargate'. The SACP, with Blade at its head, issued a very objective, unprejudiced statement noting that, as a matter of fact, he needed such a car in order 'to strengthen and increase his security'.

This behaviour of running with the hare and hunting with the hounds reminds me of the Turkish proverb about the shrinking forest in which the trees kept voting for the axe: the axe was clever and convinced the trees that because its handle was made of wood, it was one of them.

To be fair to the local communists, communist leaders abroad have also now and then been caught not practising what they preach. Take Cuba's Fidel Castro. His former bodyguard Juan Reinaldo Sanchez wrote *The Double Life of Fidel Castro: My 17 years as personal bodyguard to El Lider Maximo* (St Martin's Publishing Group, 2016), in which he mentions that Castro not only had a portfolio of twenty grand properties but also owned a 90-foot yacht. *Forbes* magazine estimated Castro's fortune to be US$900 million (about R14.5 billion).

And Nicolae Ceauşescu, the supreme leader of the Communist Party of Romania from 1965, owned fifteen palaces and a couple of yachts. As Romania's head of state for 22 years, he had plenty of time to accumulate this wealth (and possibly more), until the people revolted. He and his wife were executed by the army, live on national TV, on Christmas Day in 1989.

*

We have learnt that former president Mandela was at one stage a communist, before jumping ship; that former president Mbeki was at one stage a communist, before jumping ship; that former president Motlanthe was at one stage a communist, before jumping ship; and that former president Zuma was at one stage a communist, before jumping ship.

The points covered above highlight how for quite some time the SACP has played a key and central role in the country.

By the way, the local Communist Party newspaper was called the *New Age*. Its editor was Ruth First, a scholar and anti-apartheid activist in her own right. When the Gupta family started their media empire they, for whatever reason, also decided to call their newspaper *The New Age*. The Guptas were not communists. This, however, did not stop them from sharing their newfound wealth with, among others, Duduzane Zuma, the then president's son.

The SACP was not the first nor will it be the last political party to have a mouthpiece in the form of a media group. As we have seen, the very establishment of Naspers had everything to do with being a mouthpiece for the Afrikaner. Cecil John Rhodes, when he was prime minister of the Cape Colony, secretly owned a lion's share of the *Cape Argus* newspaper; and in the dusty streets of Kimberley he had a secret shareholding in the *Diamond Fields Advertiser*. HF Verwoerd, meanwhile, started out as the editor of a newspaper called *Die Transvaler*. The IFP at one time owned an influential Zulu newspaper, *Ilanga lase Natali*. During Zuma's administration, the SABC appointed Hlaudi Motsoeneng to the hot seat at the SABC. Notwithstanding not having a matric, Motsoeneng tried to implement an editorial policy that focused on 'sunshine news'.

Any way we look at it, communists have always been in the thick of things in South Africa's body politic. Now, with the rise of China, which is governed by the Communist Party, in the global arena, will we see the rise of the communists in South Africa – and the rest of the world – again?

A question must be asked, and James K McCollum made it the title of his book: *Is Communism Dead Forever?* (University Press of America, 1998).

Only time will tell.

Chapter 10
THE JEWS

Jews have been the victims of their own success for aeons. There are archives of documents and books containing accounts of how Jews were persecuted in different parts of the world.

Instead of some among us learning and observing how the Jewish community anywhere in the world manages to rise above their circumstances and make it work, we get jealous about other children's ingenuity, innovation and grit. Other people end up so resentful and envious that Jewish success is turned into anti-Semitic fodder. Great entrepreneurial spirit, hard work and commitment to the course in order to achieve big things – sometimes against enormous odds – make the Jewish community a group of people to marvel at and draw inspiration from.

What follows is an account of how members of the Jewish community, globally and locally, have consistently excelled in different fields and, as a result, the power they have.

For starters, according to the Jewish Virtual Library (which prides itself on being 'the most comprehensive online resource on Jewish history, politics and culture'), between 1901 and 2021, the Nobel Prize has been awarded to more than 900 individuals and organisations, at least 210 of which have been Jewish. Just to drive the point home, JInfo.org (whose objective is to 'provide an online resource that accurately describes the Jewish contribution to the cultural, scientific and technological evolution of civilization') tells us that since the year 2000, Jews have been awarded

24 per cent of all Nobel Prizes, and 26 per cent of those have been in the scientific research fields.

This is very impressive, especially if you consider that there are only about fifteen million Jews in the world's population of around eight billion (in 2022). Put simply, Jews make up 0.2 per cent of the global population.

In 2015, the South African Jewish Report, commenting on that year's *Sunday Times* 'Rich List', pointed out that no fewer than 47 of the wealthiest 225 South Africans, measured by the value of listed shares they held, were Jewish, a representation of at least 21 per cent of the list. 'This has to be seen in the context that South African Jewry represents just 0.014 per cent of the total South African population,' the report noted.

To put things into even sharper perspective, according to Statistics South Africa, the country's population was 54.96 million in 2015, and that means there were fewer than 8000 Jews. And yet they had managed to make up 21 per cent of Mzansi's economic crème de la crème.

Whatever the Jewish community is doing, it is working wonders and miracles. Combined.

Of all Jews who have had a massive impact on South Africa, Ernest Oppenheimer sits right at the very top. Born in Germany, he came to South Africa in 1902, aged 22, to take up a job as a diamond buyer. Ten years later, he was elected mayor of Kimberley, one of the most influential cities in the world at the time. (Ernest had his fair share of tragic events. At the age of 54, he lost his wife and the following year his son died in a swimming accident. Amid what would have been an emotional traumatic experience, he converted to Christianity.)

Following his three-year stint as Kimberley's mayor, Oppenheimer spent his efforts raising capital to start a company. In 1917, he founded that company: Anglo American. Half of the initial capital came from America, and the rest from Europe (and South Africa), hence the name. Africa, where it all began, especially from an operational perspective, is, oddly, not reflected in the name.

As an aside, the capital was organised through the JP Morgan Bank, founded by American financier John Pierpont Morgan in 1895. At the time of his death in 1943, aged 75, JP Morgan Jr had four children. One of them was Henry Sturgis Morgan who, together with other JP Morgan employees, most notably Harold Stanley, started Morgan Stanley, a multinational financial services group that is consistently ranked in the top fifth of the Fortune 500 list of the largest United States corporations.

In simple terms, one man (John Pierpont Morgan) started one bank, and his grandson (Henry Sturgis Morgan) started another. A question must therefore be asked: what did you and your grandfather start?

One of the wealthiest families in the world are the Rothschilds. They are Jewish. Conspiracy theorists insist that wealthy families like the Rothschilds are the 'power behind the throne' of democratically elected leaders. We can never know the real truth.

What I do find fascinating is the story of a 30-year-old investment banker who joined Rothschild Bank, which had been owned and controlled by the family for more than two hundred years. Four years later, in 2012, this young man left in order to pursue a career as a full-time politician. In 2017, aged 39, he became the youngest president in French history. His name is Emmanuel Jean-Michel Frédéric Macron.

Back to Ernest. Two years after launching Anglo, he started buying diamond mines in what was then South West Africa. In order to ensure that he had control of the supply and trade of the precious stones, he gained control of De Beers, which at the time was the world's biggest diamond mining company. Two years later, in 1929, he became chairman of De Beers.

Harry Oppenheimer (who was also a Freemason – see next chapter) succeeded his father. As an adult, he too converted to Christianity.

It just so happens that, by 1889, Cecil John Rhodes had been able to consolidate more than ninety per cent of the world's diamond production and supply, after offering the Barnato brothers, Henry and Barney, the deal of a lifetime – well over £5 million (about R16 billion in today's money) – to hand over their Kimberley Central Diamond Mining Company. That might sound like a lot of money – and it is – but just to put things into perspective, and to show how much money was made by the Joburg-based mining magnates who became known as the Randlords, let us have a look at one example.

In 1890, Sir Joseph Robinson (who was not Jewish) founded the Randfontein Estates Gold Mining Company, the largest individual undertaking on the Witwatersrand and one of the largest in the world. It made him an enormous fortune, and he retired to the family estate of Hawthornden House in Cape Town. When he died in 1929, he left a fortune for his family.

Hawthornden House, which still stands today in one of the southern suburbs of Cape Town, is a now a provincial heritage site. One of Robertson's grandsons, can you believe, donated this property to the government of the Western Cape. Who donates a house to the government? But then again, Sir Joseph left £12 million (about R20 billion today) for his children, which in time was inherited by his grandchildren.

The reason why Rhodes was able to offer such a ridiculous amount of money to the Barnatos was because he was sponsored by one of the (some even say *the*) wealthiest families in the world. Their wealth is almost impossible to quantify. They were the Rothschilds.

Alfred Beit, a Jewish guy who was Rhodes's business partner, was also instrumental in mining activity not only in Kimberley and Johannesburg but also in Zimbabwe. As mentioned previously, Beitbridge is named after him.

Based on this information, especially as it pertains to Ernest Oppenheimer and Barney Barnato (both Freemasons), we can easily conclude that at least two gentlemen who both happened to be

Jewish played a fundamental role in the development of the mining industry, which became the backbone of the country's economy for decades to come.

George Albu, another Jew, started what is known today as BHP Billiton, one of the world's largest mining companies. He arrived in Cape Town from Germany aged 19, and eventually moved to the diamond fields of Kimberley, where he started buying shares in diamond companies. He eventually sold out, at a huge profit, to De Beers, before moving north to what was then the Transvaal, where he bought an ailing mine and reconfigured it. Aged 38, in 1895, he co-founded (with his brother, Leopold) the General Mining and Finance Corporation, which was later bought by the Afrikaners and in time became Gencor, then Billiton, and eventually BHP.

The question that must be asked from the word go is, who is Jewish? The answer is simple. Well, sort of.

The term 'Jewish', first and foremost, describes an ethnicity. Therefore, you are born Jewish through ancestry, especially if you have a Jewish mother, and in that case you are regarded as a Jew irrespective of your religion. You can also become Jewish through conversion to the religion of Judaism. Therefore, technically speaking, a person can be Jewish by ethnicity but not necessarily believe in Judaism. This also means, just as anyone can be a Christian or a Muslim, anyone can be a Jew if that person chooses Judaism as their religion.

Before we dwell more on local Jews, and their immeasurable contribution to South Africa, let us deal with some members of the global Jewish community and see how they impact or have impacted your life on a day-to-day basis.

Back in September 1998, two Jewish boys, Larry Page and Sergey Brin, both aged 25 and PhD students at America's Stanford University, started something that would revolutionise research and information-finding. Google is by far the most visited website globally, and, through acquisitions of other businesses like You-Tube and Blogger, it has become one of the largest companies in the world, now called Alphabet Inc. I don't have to tell you that these two are billionaires, and they consistently feature on lists of the richest people in the US.

At the age of 20, in 2004, another Jewish boy decided to launch an online platform on campus on which students could chat. It soon expanded to other universities and, boom, by 2021 Facebook had 2.9 billion monthly active users. Mark Elliot Zuckerberg became a billionaire aged 23.

Facebook, now called Meta, later bought other social network services including Instagram and WhatsApp. Zuckerberg is now a media mogul, albeit not in the traditional sense. According to *Forbes*'s 'Real Time Billionaires', Zuckerberg's net worth is US$58 billion (approaching R1 trillion). (WhatsApp co-founder Yan Borisovich Kum, who was born in Ukraine, is, yep, also a Jewish dude.)

While Zuckerberg is playing in the new media space, another American businessman is an old-school media mogul. He was the mayor of New York City from 2002 to 2013, and for a very short period a Democratic Party candidate for the 2020 presidential elections. The majority owner and co-founder of Bloomberg LP, a financial, software, data and media company, he is Michael Rubens Bloomberg. In 2020, *Forbes* ranked him as the sixteenth-richest person in the world.

It seems that Jews have a knack for numbers.

It seems that Jews have a knack for *big* numbers.

A former French politician who was appointed in 2007 to lead the International Monetary Fund (whose aims include fostering global monetary cooperation, facilitating international trade and all those great things) is, ahem, Jewish. However, Dominique Strauss-Kahn left the fund under a cloud in 2011, amid allegations that he had sexually assaulted a hotel maid.

Alan Greenspan, an economist, who served for nineteen years

(1987 to 2006) as the chair of the Federal Reserve, the central bank of the United States, is also Jewish. The second-longest-serving chair, he filled the role under four presidents: Ronald Reagan, George Bush, Bill Clinton and George W Bush.

Greenspan was succeeded by another economist, who served two terms as chair of the Federal Reserve between 2006 and 2014; and Ben Shalom Bernanke is also Jewish. He, in turn, was succeeded by another economist of Jewish stock: Janet Louise Yellen, the first woman to hold this position, who served from 2014 to 2018.

Still on the knack for big numbers, Stephen Allen Schwarzman, co-founder of Blackstone, the world's largest private equity firm with, in 2020, assets under management totalling approximately US$619 billion (almost R10 trillion) is also of Jewish stock. The South African GDP in 2020, to put this in perspective, was hovering at about US$369 billion (almost R6 trillion). (GDP, or gross domestic product, is the total value of goods produced and services provided in the country during one year.) More proof, relatively speaking, of how small our economy is.

Most of us remember the attacks on the World Trade Center on 11 September 2001. But what most of us did not know at the time was that Silverstein Properties had, earlier that year, signed a 99-year lease on the so-called Twin Towers. After the attacks, Larry Silverstein had a protracted legal dispute with the insurers, because he saw the attacks on his buildings as two different attacks, and thus launched two different claims, whereas insurers saw it as one event. Eventually, a settlement of US$4.5 billion (about R72 billion) was reached in Silverstein's favour.

And on the afternoon of 11 September 2001, another building owned by Silverstein also collapsed. World Trade Center 7, which stood across the street from the Twin Towers, was not hit by an aeroplane but collapsed because of fires ignited by debris falling from the North Tower's collapse. According to the National Institute of Standards and Technology's final reports of the building and fire investigation of the World Trade Center disaster, this was the first time in the history of construction that a steel skyscraper (it had 47 floors) is known to have collapsed fundamentally and essentially due to uncontrolled fires.

Larry Silverstein is Jewish.

And, oh, how can I forget the premonition of the decade: the British Broadcasting Corporation (BBC) reported on live TV about twenty minutes before building 7 collapsed that it had collapsed, when those who knew its location could see it firmly standing in the background. Later a statement was issued to clarify this mishap: 'On 11 September 2001 Reuters incorrectly reported that one of the buildings at the New York World Trade Center, 7WTC, had collapsed before it actually did. The report was picked up from a local news story and was withdrawn as soon as it emerged that the building had not fallen.' Okay then!

The story of the 9/11 terror attacks reminds me of relativism. Nothing is 'big' or 'small'; it all depends on the perspective of one thing against another. On 10 September 2001, the day before the attacks, for example, then US defence secretary Donald Rumsfeld told a media conference that his department was unable to account for US$2.3 trillion (almost R37 trillion, and bear in mind – as mentioned before – that South Africa's GDP in 2020 was around R6 trillion) Yep, *trillions* of dollars were nowhere to be found.

The following day, America was attacked and almost three thousand people died – and, with this to occupy their minds, every-body, because of relativism, forgot about the unaccounted-for Defense Department fortune.

On foreign policy, it does not get bigger than the teenager who fled Nazi Germany with his Jewish family in the 1930s. He grew up to be an American national security advisor before, in 1973, taking on the role of US secretary of state – the president's chief foreign affairs advisor. His name is Dr Henry Alfred Kissinger.

Another heavy hitter who survived the Nazi occupation is

investor and philanthropist George Soros (born György Schwartz). Over time, he has donated US$32 billion (R512 billion), roughly two thirds, of his fortune. But according to some critics, he uses these donations to influence policy and regime change in different parts of the world. According to Bloomberg, in 2021 his net worth was US$8.6 billion (R138 billion).

On the legal side, the Jewish community was well represented by the late Ruth Bader Ginsburg, the first Jewish woman to be a justice of the US Supreme Court, and only the second woman to occupy that position. In 2002, Ginsburg was inducted into the National Women's Hall of Fame; and in 2009 *Forbes* magazine named her one of the hundred most powerful women in the world. In 2015, she was named one of *Time* magazine's hundred most influential people in the world. She died in 2019.

Still on *Time*, in December 1999 Albert Einstein was named the magazine's person of the century because he was a leading and paramount scientist in a century dominated by science. Of all Einstein's contributions, and there are many, most of us mere mortals will know the equation he came up with: e = mc². Effectively it means (and trust me, after all these years I still struggle to logically accept this) that energy is the product of mass multiplied by the speed of light squared. However, because the speed of light is fixed, it means – and this is confirmed by www.energy.gov – that 'mass and energy are related and can be changed from one to the other'. One thing that really messes me up, and I keep asking myself, is: what does the speed of light has to do with all of this?

In 1952, three years before his death and four years after the creation of the modern state of Israel, Einstein was offered the country's presidency (without him applying for it or standing for election). Ever so kind and polite, he turned down the offer, explaining, 'All my life I have dealt with objective matters, hence I lack both the natural aptitude and the experience to deal properly with people and to exercise official functions.'

The reason why, by the way, *Time* announced Einstein as the person of the century in December 1999 was because there was a general belief by almost everyone globally that the new decade and century would start on 1 January 2000. I could not believe how almost everyone could not see a very simple issue: there was no year zero, therefore, a new or second decade would start at 11, not 10. It is as simple as that. I was so touched by this issue, especially when I saw mainstream media celebrating 'the last decade' in December 1999, that in January 2000 I wrote a letter to one of the Sunday newspapers explaining this matter once and for all. My submission appeared titled 'What new decade?'

In the article, among other things, I quoted Frank Morgan, professor of mathematics at Williams College in Massachusetts in the USA, who had simplified this confusion by using the example of a vast army of soldiers with a thousand men in each row. 'In the first row are soldiers 1 to 1 000, in the second row 1 001 to 2 000, and in the third row 2 001 to 3 000,' he wrote. 'The third row starts with soldier 2 001 ...' Well, the byline of the newspaper article defeated me by stating, 'Count the soldiers and get back to me, writes Sihle Khumalo.' Eish!

I feel vindicated because now it is logically and scientifically accepted that the new decade, century and millennium – because there was no year zero – started on 1 January 2001, and not, I repeat, not, on 1 January 2000. Phew!

Isaac Carasso, who was born into a prominent Jewish family in Greece, grew up to achieve big things. After moving to Barcelona, he started a yoghurt company. In time it grew, thanks to the business acumen of Daniel, his son who inherited the business and turned it international. Daniel's nickname was Danone, and today the Danone Group, a Paris-listed multinational, sells its products throughout the world.

The year 1961 must have been an extremely busy one for

Lawrence Harvey Zeiger, the 28-year-old son of orthodox Jewish parents who had immigrated to the US in the 1930s. That was the year Lawrence married and divorced his second wife, and married his third wife. Two years later, he divorced his third wife and married his fourth. Four years later, in 1967, he got divorced and went back to his third wife, who then became – technically speaking – his fifth wife. Zeiger, a TV and radio host, ended up getting married eight times to seven different women. Most of us knew him as Larry King (RIP).

The literature scene is also well represented by, among others, a Jewish Canadian author and social activist. Naomi Klein, especially after the publication of her books *No Logo: No space, no choice, no jobs* (Knopf Canada/Picador, 1999) and *The Shock Doctrine* (Knopf Canada, 2007), is internationally recognised as an authoritative thinker on globalisation, politics and feminism. *The Shock Doctrine* claims that in certain countries, the government, whenever it wants to implement certain policy changes, starts by shocking its citizens through a disaster or upheaval, and once the citizens are distracted, voilà, the government can implement any policy it wants with almost no objections.

Consider yourself warned!

Another literary giant of Jewish stock is Avram Noam Chomsky, a social critic, philosopher, political activist and historian. He has written more than 150 books. So influential is Chomsky that he is sometimes referred to as the father of modern linguistics. Aged 42, in 1970, he was named by the London *Times* as one of the 'makers of the twentieth century'. In the past he has also been voted the world's leading public intellectual.

One of my favourite quotes by this professor emeritus is, 'The smart way to keep people passive and obedient is to strictly limit the spectrum of acceptable opinion, but allow very lively debate within that spectrum.' Next time you are debating and/or arguing with a fellow human being, remember what Chomsky had to say about thinking you are totally free while in fact you are being kept obedient and passive within a tolerable spectrum.

This reminds me of another marvellous quote by another writer, Elie Wiesel, Holocaust survivor and Nobel laureate. As he aptly put it, 'Always take sides. Neutrality helps the oppressor, never the victim. Silence encourages the tormentor, never the tormented.' Wiesel was of Jewish stock.

There is another fine gentleman, also in the arts, who represented the Jewish community on this planet and beyond. Stanley Kubrick was an American screenwriter, film producer and director. His 1968 movie *2001: A Space Odyssey*, which won an Oscar for best visual effects, is regarded by some critics as one of the greatest films ever made.

There have always been rumours among those who do not believe that human beings (actually, men) walked on the moon. These theorists state that NASA contracted the one and only Kubrick to produce a make-believe documentary of Neil Armstrong and his crew walking on the surface of the moon. It was all fake, conclude these naysayers. It is not a coincidence, this theory continues, that Kubrick's movie premiered worldwide in 1968, and the following year – yippee – men were walking on the moon.

Two things, mainly, have always bugged me (and I mean really bugged me) when it comes to the man-on-the-moon extravaganza. First, why did the missions to the moon come to an abrupt end? Given how advanced technology is today, compared to the 1960s, surely we should have permanent bases on the moon by now? Right? (Admittedly, technology was already cutting edge in the 1960s and that explains why President Nixon could make a phone call using a landline phone, live on national television, and – with only a two-second delay – speak to astronauts who were on a surface of the moon almost 400 000 kilometres away. Well executed, gentlemen!) Why didn't we, over a period of time, make the moon our home away from home? In fact, nowadays we even celebrate when ultra-high-net-worth (i.e., filthy-rich) individuals make it into lower orbit. Is that not regressing, or am I missing something?

My second issue concerns the second man to walk on the moon, astronaut Edwin 'Buzz' Aldrin. In 2002, Aldrin punched Bart Sibrel in the face after this documentary-maker demanded Aldrin swear on a Bible that the moon landing was neither staged nor fake. I must concede that Sibrel followed Aldrin through a hotel lobby, into the street and back into the hotel lobby. But the question must still be asked: why didn't Aldrin just tell the guy to buzz off? Why lash out, Buzz, if indeed you walked on the moon? Seriously, why didn't you just put your hand on the Bible and swear that you walked on the moon? How complicated can that be?

But then let's not get too excited and start questioning why Hollywood, a place synonymous with acting, honoured the three Apollo 11 astronauts (Aldrin, Armstrong and Michael Collins) who landed on the moon. It puzzles me nonetheless why plaques with the names of these three astronauts appear on what is generally accepted as the world's most famous pavement in Hollywood where the big-name actors are honoured. Could it be that these three gentlemen, as someone once quipped, were 'actornauts'?

This reminds me of a quote by scholar and cultural critic Henry Louis Mencken: 'The whole aim of practical politics is to keep the populace alarmed (and hence clamorous to be led to safety) by an endless series of hobgoblins, most of them imaginary.'

This Buzz Aldrin storyline nudges me to ask why President Rama-phosa fought tooth and nail – and even went to court – to hide who donated money to (or was it invested in?) his 2017 presidential election campaign, and where it was spent. For someone who took office promising a new dawn, new beginnings, clean governance, transparency and all those good things, what are you hiding, Mr President?

*

From a Jewish film producer who might or might not have been contracted by NASA, let's get closer to home.

A Jewish woman in South Africa who broke the glass ceiling was Gill Marcus, who in 2007 became the country's first woman to be a chairperson of a commercial bank when she headed the Absa board. She was also the first female deputy Reserve Bank governor and, if that was not enough, she was the first female deputy finance minister. In 2009 she reached her career zenith when she succeeded Tito Mboweni as governor of the South African Reserve Bank – the only woman to date to hold this position.

Magdalena Franciszka 'Magda' Wierzycka was born in Poland and moved with her poor family to South Africa in 1983, aged 13. By 2018, as a co-founder of financial-services company Sygnia, she was reportedly the wealthiest woman in South Africa. Two years later, *Forbes* magazine listed her among Africa's fifty most powerful women. Magda is also of Jewish stock.

And what about the Jewish boy who grew up to be the president of the Constitutional Court of South Africa from 1994 to 2001, and chief justice of South Africa from 2001 to 2005? Arthur Chaskalson was educated at Hilton College, studied law at the University of the Witwatersrand and, in 1963, was part of the defence team in the Rivonia Trial.

On the subject of the Rivonia Trial: five of the fifteen people (33 per cent) who were arrested were Jews. In fact, all the whites who were arrested at Liliesleaf farm were Jews (and communists). And nothing shows how Jews are central to the key and historic events of this country like the fact that both the prosecutor in the trial, Percy Yutar, and the defence's instructing attorney, Joel Joffe, were – yes, you have guessed it – Jewish. It was Percy who decided to prosecute the Rivonia trialists for sabotage instead of treason, which would have definitely meant, if found guilty, the death penalty. Therefore a question has to be asked: did Percy save Nelson?

Chaskalson was not the only Jew of the eleven justices of the

190

Constitutional Court of South Africa. Another who made it to the highest court in the land was Richard Joseph Goldstone. The national spotlight shone on Goldstone when in the early 1990s he chaired the commission investigating political violence in South Africa between 1991 and 1994. After the dawn of democracy, he was thrust into the international spotlight when he worked as chief prosecutor of the United Nations International Criminal Tribunal for five years, until 1999. The two massive cases that he had to prosecute in this regard were the former Yugoslavia and Rwanda genocides.

The third Jewish judge on the Constitutional Court was Albert Louis 'Albie' Sachs, who lost his arm in 1988 when the apartheid government planted a bomb in his car when he was based in Maputo.

A former Cape Town High Court judge who is now judge president of the Competition Appeal Court and honorary professor of law at the University of Cape Town is also of Jewish stock. Dennis Davis was the chair of the Davis tax committee from 2013 to 2018; its objective was to assess South Africa's tax policy framework and its role in supporting the objectives of inclusive growth, employment, development and fiscal sustainability.

Besides Gill Marcus, there is another Jewish woman who contributed immensely to the country we have today. At the age of 42, in 1959, she hosted a meeting of other disgruntled United Party members, and that led to the formation of the Progressive Party, which over time evolved into the Democratic Party. In 2000, the Democratic Party merged with the Independent Party to form the Democratic Alliance (DA), now South Africa's official opposition. She was born Helen Gavronsky and aged 19 married Dr Moses Suzman. Helen Suzman fought a lonesome liberal battle in parliament for 36 years.

Coincidentally, the first leader of the Democratic Party was a Jewish man. Born and bred in what was then Natal, he grew up to be the leader of the opposition and later in life was appointed South

Africa's ambassador to Argentina. His name is Anthony James 'Tony' Leon.

The irony for liberal organisations with Jewish roots that were the voice of reason during the apartheid years is the fact that Israel, a Jewish state, was one country that, for whatever reason, felt it necessary to support the National Party and its apartheid policies. Some might say, well, Israel is practising its own type of apartheid in Palestine.

Notwithstanding the Aliens Act of 1937, which aimed to minimise and restrict the number of Jews coming into South Africa, DF Malan, soon after being elected prime minister, went to Israel looking for international support. Israel did not hold back. In fact, you could even conclude that Israel propped up the apartheid regime.

The 1975 Israel–South Africa Agreement, as an example, was a secret defence cooperation agreement. The arms trade between South Africa and Israel goes back to the 1960s. It is in that context that the assault rifles that were standard issue for the then South African Defence Force and South African Police were variants of Israel's IMI Galil rifles.

And just a friendly reminder that bantustan leader Lucas Mangope's fiefdom of Bophuthatswana not only had a trade office in Israel but also – notwithstanding Israel not recognising Bophuthatswana as an independent country – was allowed to fly its flag at the mission office because, it was reasoned at the time, there was no law preventing flying any flag in a private office. In my home language, we have a saying, 'Ukucasha ngesithupha,' which literally means 'hiding behind a thumb' – and as I'm sure you can imagine, you can't hide much behind a thumb.

A major project in Bophuthatswana, the impractical Mmabatho Stadium, where some fans ended up facing up into the sky, was conceptualised, managed and constructed by an array of Israeli companies. By coincidence, Odi Stadium, almost 300 kilometres away in Garankuwa, north of Pretoria, looks almost identical to

Mmabatho Stadium. Garankuwa was also part of Bophuthatswana.

To show how messed up 'separate development' was, let's take a look at the history of Soshanguve. From the late 1950s, Mabopane had been, thanks to the Group Areas Act, a blacks-only residential area. By the 1970s it was a sprawling township, roughly divided into Mabopane West (the old section) and Mabopane East (the newish part). When Bophuthatswana was declared an independent state in 1977, it was decided that Mabopane West would be incorporated into Bophuthatswana because – wait for it – that was where mostly Tswana people lived. Mabopane East was more, shall we say, cosmopolitan. Hence, it got a new name: Soshanguve, for 'Sotho, Shangaan, Nguni and Venda'.

The result was that you had a township, effectively separated by a strip of land, with the western part being part of a fiefdom called Bophuthatswana, and the other part of what was then the Northern Transvaal administration.

Mangope, and all other bantustan leaders, as expected of the stooges of the apartheid government, vehemently defended separate development for years. In other words, homeland leaders not only sold out black people but also sold their souls in order to get the crumbs from the white people's table. Exactly the same thing happened a few decades later, when black people agreed to BEE deals (yet more about this later).

To be fair to Israel, it was not the only country that propped up the apartheid regime. According to the book *Apartheid, Guns and Money: A tale of profit* (Oxford University Press, 2018) by Hennie van Vuuren, notwithstanding economic sanctions, a number of countries traded with South Africa and thus supported the National Party and its apartheid project with all its shenanigans.

Van Vuuren, by the way, is part of Open Secrets, a non-profit organisation that exposes and builds accountability for private-sector economic crimes through investigative research, advocacy and the law. Van Vuuren trawled through thousands of documents for his book. It is shocking stuff and it is enough to make you realise once and for all that indeed truth is stranger than fiction.

Other countries, according to Open Secrets, that propped up the pre-1994 regime, and thus sustained apartheid, included Singapore and China. In fact, Singapore, given its strategic location on various sea routes, was instrumental in the importation of anything that South Africans desperately needed.

Singapore lost its trade partnership to – wait for it – China. While the ANC was being propped up by communist China, the same Chinese government, according to Open Secrets, was in bed with the Nats.

China was not the only country batting for both teams. Other countries were also paying lip service to the 'we are against the apartheid government' narrative while they were sleeping with the enemy. These countries, I guess, were hedging their bets.

Take Switzerland, for example. Through its banks, a mutual trust was set up as far back as 1948 to buy South African gold and thus ensure a steady supply of foreign currency for South Africa.

And French companies, especially those in the arms sector, consorted with apartheid South Africa, according to Open Secrets. The South African Air Force's Atlas Oryx helicopter, for instance, is a variant of the utility/transport Aerospatiale SA 330 Puma helicopter originally developed in France.

Al J Venter in his co-authored book *How South Africa Built Six Atom Bombs and Then Abandoned Its Nuclear Weapons Program* (Ashanti, 2008) not only writes about submarines bought from France, he even includes photos. These submarines, he says, were used during the 'Border War operations along the Angolan, Mocambique and Tanzanian coasts'.

Venter states that South Africa, with the help of Israel, developed medium-range intercontinental ballistic missiles that were eventually tested in the southern Indian Ocean. (Questions to self: What happened to all the nuclear parts and components that were used to build those nuclear bombs? Did they just disappear into thin air? Were they sold to other approved countries, and did all the money make its way into the correct account at Treasury?)

It has been speculated by different sources that the reason why Dulcie September, the activist and ANC representative who was assassinated in Paris in 1988, was killed was because she had stumbled on sensitive arms-deal information between France and South Africa. She had to be silenced. She had to be eliminated. She was shot five times, and no-one has ever been arrested for her murder.

In her book *Incorruptible: The story of the murders of Dulcie September, Anton Lubowski and Chris Hani* (Evelyn Groenink, 2018), Dutch journalist Evelyn Groenink writes in detail about the life and times of September. What came as a surprise to me is how the ANC ignored endless calls to headquarters in London when September was reporting threats to her life. Groenink mentions that after the assassination, September was succeeded in Paris by Solly Smith, 'an apartheid agent'.

Let us cut all the bullshit and state the obvious: one of the biggest trading partners with apartheid South Africa was Britain. In fact, British prime minister Margaret Thatcher at one point labelled Mandela a terrorist – notwithstanding that this was the same Britain that not only harboured ANC leaders for years but also rolled out the red carpet for the 'terrorist' after his 27 years of incarceration. The irony, of course, is that the ANC headquarters were at one stage in London, and yet Britain was the pillar without which apartheid would have crumbled and died a natural death decades earlier.

The bigger picture is that, at the time, apartheid South Africa had to be supported by the West at all costs. If not, the fear was, as had happened in other African countries that had gained independence, the communist East would take over ... and the mines and possibly the banks, among other strategic assets in the country, would be nationalised ...

The moral of the story is that the apartheid government was

propped up by many countries that would, in order to avoid being shamed in the eyes of the international community, do anything to hide the fact that they were lovers in arms with the oppressive National Party government and its apartheid policy.

It was not just the governments of different countries that supported and sustained apartheid, corporates did their part too. Many foreign companies continued trading with South Africa despite economic sanctions, and benefitted handsomely from, among other things, government-sponsored cheap labour practices.

This brings to mind the lawsuit filed in 2002 in the USA by a group of South African non-government organisations purporting to represent apartheid litigants. The accused included American technology companies, car manufacturers, banks and oil companies. In 2003, the government of South Africa made it clear that it did not support the lawsuit. Then minister of justice Penuell Maduna, in fact, filed a declaration with the US District Court in New York in which he quoted President Thabo Mbeki who a few months earlier had said in parliament, 'We wish to reiterate that the South African government is not and will not be a party to such litigation. In addition, we consider it completely unacceptable that matters that are central to the future of our country should be adjudicated in foreign courts.'

In the meantime, in a case argued in the USA Supreme Court, a group of Nigerians were of the view that Royal Dutch Shell had compelled Shell Nigeria, in conjunction with Nigeria's forces, to repress resistance to oil exploration in an area of the Niger River delta between 1992 and 1995. Ultimately, the court felt it could not preside in a matter that had happened in another sovereign state – in other words, an American company could not be sued in America if the alleged action took place in another country.

With that judgment, it was a foregone conclusion that the American companies in the South African case could not be sued in America for what they had done in South Africa. And that is how American companies, and possibly other companies from other countries, escaped (rightfully or wrongfully) facing the consequences of engaging in business with the South African regime.

Let's come back to these shores where, seemingly, backhanders have been happening for decades, if not centuries.

A man who happened to be Jewish was reported to have handsomely greased politicians' palms (in isiZulu, amantshontsho) during the apartheid years. Sol Kerzner, who died in 2020, built South Africa's first five-star hotel, the Beverly Hills in Durban, in the 1960s, but really proved his mettle when he established the Sun City holiday resort and casino in Bophuthatswana. That was one of the many hotels and casinos he opened in the 'independent states'.

In December 1986 Kerzner gave R2 million to then Transkei prime minister George Matanzima in order to get a licence for his Wild Coast casino. It was this bribe that led to Bantu Holomisa being fired by the ANC, after he spilt the beans at the Truth and Reconciliation Commission in 1996.

At the time of his death, Kerzner had an empire of hotels and casinos in Mauritius, Dubai, Mexico, the USA, the Maldives, the Bahamas and China. Could it be, as is often said, that he who pays the piper calls the tune?

A well-known property development, Sandton City, which incorporates Nelson Mandela Square, was not only the brainchild of but was also financed by a Jewish guy – Donny Gordon. Some might even say that it was Sandton City that started, and sustained, the rush to Sandton, which eventually became 'the richest square mile' not only in the country but on the African continent. And this was all thanks to the man who founded Liberty Life. (And as more and more companies and businesses left the central business district, it was only a matter of time before Jozi's city centre lost its glitz and glamour. But things are changing, or so politicians keep telling us.)

197

Raymond Ackerman needs no introduction. He bought three stores in Cape Town trading under the name Pick n Pay and turned his company into one of the largest supermarket groups in the country. Pick n Pay now has stores in South Africa, Botswana, Lesotho, Namibia, Swaziland, Zambia and Zimbabwe.

Ackerman's father, Gus, together with two other Jewish gentlemen, founded South Africa's first chain store. Gus sold these stores in 1940 but they still bear his name, albeit without the apostrophe: Ackermans. So, the next time you are shopping at Ackermans and Pick n Pay, just remember that it all boils down to the vision of a father and son.

Randlord Abe Bailey, thanks to his closeness to Cecil John Rhodes, was able to make serious amounts of cash. His son, Jim, who was born in England, was one of the co-founders of *Drum* magazine in the 1950s. Some of the well-known journalists, photojournalists and art critics of that era include Henry Nxumalo, Alf Khumalo, Can Themba, Es'kia Mphahlele, John Matshikiza, Peter Magubane and Nat Nakasa.

In 1984, *Drum* was sold to Naspers, a process that one of its editors, Sylvester Stein, referred to as selling 'a corpse to its executioners'.

Another Jewish gentleman who made a significant contribution to this country was Sammy Marks. Marks, on hearing the news that the Orange Free State government, because of the distance to Kimberley, was not interested in the coalfields along the Vaal River, sent geologist George William Stow to buy the farms on which the coal had been discovered – by Stow himself, in 1878. For the purposes of this business venture, Marks formed the Zuid-Afrikaansche en Oranje-Vrystaatsche Kolen en Mineralen Myn Vereeniging (South African and Orange Free State Coal and Mineral Association). This business venture proved to be such a success that in time a town developed that took its name from the tail-end of the company name: Vereeniging.

It was Sammy Marks, incidentally, who commissioned the statue of Paul Kruger, his friend, which still stands proudly in Church Square in Pretoria.

Talking of Paul Kruger's friends, one of those was the Jew Alois Hugo Nellmapius. Born Alois Neumann in Europe in 1847, it is not quite clear why he changed his last name to Nellmapius. What cannot be disputed was that as a trained engineer, he was drawn by the discovery of gold at Pilgrim's Rest in what was then the Eastern Transvaal in 1873, but subsequently made a living as a transport driver. He got his first transport concession to Delagoa Bay from Kruger's government.

Nellmapius established an estate in modern-day Centurion and named it after his daughter, Irene. Today Nellmapius Road runs through the Pretoria suburb of Irene.

It was Nellmapius, by the way, who commissioned and paid for Paul Kruger's official residence in Church Street in Pretoria. Kruger House, which is now a museum, was built using milk instead of water to mix the cement, because the cement available at the time was deemed to be of inferior quality. I can only imagine that modern-day entrepreneurs would be as willing to go that extra mile to keep the politicians happy who, in turn, will keep the fiscus's taps wide open.

Barney Barnato, another Jew, gifted Kruger on his birthday with the two stone lions that still lie on the veranda of the house. Barnato (born Barnett Isaacs) and his nephew Solomon 'Solly' Joel also made a fortune in the diamond and gold fields. Born in London to a Jewish family, Barnato came to South Africa in 1873 in his early 20s, and within ten years was a multimillionaire. Besides managing the family interests in the mining sector, he also had interests back in London in the railways, brewing and the arts. And he had great interest and investments in horse breeding and racing, both in South Africa and in England.

In 1897, Barnato died in mysterious circumstances when he went overboard on his way to Britain by sea. Some sources suggest that he committed suicide, while others claim it was murder. In any case, after his mortal remains were recovered, they were buried in London's Jewish Cemetery.

Gustav Imroth, a minor Randlord, worked with Ernest Oppenheimer (who was his cousin) and Solly Joel in the consolidation of the diamond industry through De Beers. Gustav was a co-founder of the Johannesburg Consolidated Investment Company Limited (JCI), which he managed for nine years before retiring in 1920 to his 'home town' of London (although he'd been born in Germany).

The pots that our parents used when cooking for some of us when we were much younger, Hart Cookware, was started by a Jewish man, John Hart. In fact, in almost all my homecooked meals, and in my memories, Hart is – bam – right in the middle. I love Hart with all my heart.

It does not end there. While enjoying food cooked in Hart pots, there is a possibility that some of the appliances in your house were bought at one of the country's biggest privately owned appliances shops, Hirsch's. It was founded by Allan Hirsch who is – yep – a Jewish guy.

If you are not in the mood for cooking, you could pop in to your local Spur. That fast-food chain was started in 1967 when a young Jewish man, Allen Ambor, opened the Golden Spur in Newlands, Cape Town. Now the Spur Corporation boasts more than 500 restaurants, and includes other brands like Rocomamas, John Dory's and Panarottis.

Of all the companies that were started and in time became conglomerates, it does not get bigger than Bidvest. Brian Joffe, Bidvest's founder, was a visionary. Bidvest has six divisions (freight, financial services, automotive, properties, branded products and commercial products) and operates on four continents.

As an aside, with the onset of BEE, Cyril Ramaphosa's first

major deal was through his company Millennium Consolidated Investments (later called Shanduka), when he became Alexander Forbes's BEE partner. Two years later, in 2004, he was part of Dinatla, a broad-based consortium that became Bidvest's empowerment partner.

The elephant – or should I say the buffalo – in the room (and this is a conversation we as South Africans still need to have one day) is, what social value was created by BEE beneficiaries in our communities, society and the nation at large? While BEE makes absolute sense, the way it was implemented in South Africa leaves a lot to be desired. Take the case of Bidvest inviting Cyril to be its BEE partner, and years later Cyril was the chairman of the board, while Bidvest CEO and founder Joffe was still the CEO. Do you honestly think Cyril, as the chair, had power – as corporate governance dictates – over the CEO? Dream on …

Let's go back to the real entrepreneurs.

Part of the capital that Joffe used to start Bidvest he got from Investec. Investec started out as a small finance company in the 1970s before getting a banking licence in 1980. Today it has a primary listing in London and maintains its listing on the JSE. It was Jewish men – Larry Nestadt, Errol Grolman, Stephen Koseff, Ian Kantor and Bernard Kantor – who started it all.

The founder of Sasfin Holdings, meanwhile, was Roland Sassoon, who has handed over the baton to his son, now the CEO, Michael Sassoon. David Shapiro is a deputy chairman at Sasfin Securities. Just think how these guys, all Jews, worked together to start these companies that changed the South African economic landscape forever.

As a South African, you will at one stage or the other come across Graham Beck's wines. Beck made his money in the mining industry before moving into winemaking and stud farming. And one of his key BEE partners was one Cyril Ramaphosa.

Ramaphosa also signed a BEE deal with Eric Samson's MacSteel.

Beck and Samson (both now deceased) were Jewish, and their legacies live on.

Two other Jews, Mick Davis and Ivan Glasenberg, who at one stage were lecturer and student, respectively, on the same University of Witwatersrand campus, went on to achieve great things: Davis became the CEO of mining company Xstrata in 2001, while Glasenberg was named to head up Glencore the following year. (Glencore merged with Xstrata in 2013, and Glasenberg became the CEO of an even bigger mining giant.) Glasenberg, who retired in 2021, has, according to *Forbes*, a net worth of US$9.1 billion (R145.6 billion).

Ramaphosa was, at one stage, the local BEE partner of Glencore.

Glencore was in the global news in May 2022 after agreeing to a settlement of US$1.1 billion (R17.6 billion) in an American court, pertaining to allegations of bribery and market manipulation. Of course, there was no admission of guilt in this regard. In November 2022 Glencore UK was fined £182.9 million (about R3.5 billion) for, in essence, bribing African politicians and or their representatives/ bagmen for favours, including licences. And subsequent to this, as far as I know, the South African authorities never investigated if Glencore South Africa was involved, either directly or indirectly, in any form of bribery and/or market manipulation.

Another massive company that was started by a Jewish man is Aspen, South Africa's largest pharmaceutical firm. Stephen Saad founded the company in 1997 in a house in Durban, and within seven years it had become a continental powerhouse. Aspen, by the way, is the pharmaceutical company that got the deal to manufacture the Johnson & Johnson Covid-19 vaccine at its world-class facility in Gqeberha.

Another pharmaceutical enterprise, the retail giant Dischem, was started in 1978 by pharmacists Ivan and Lynette Saltzman. Thirty-eight years later, in 2016, soon after opening their hundredth store, the group listed on the JSE. Mr and Mrs Saltzman are both Jews.

Let me stick with the health theme. It was Adrian Gore who

was a disruptor in that space, and who changed the medical-aid market forever. He realised that healthy and fit members (like me) were subsidising the sick, lazy and unfit. He therefore devised a scheme in which members would be rewarded for living a healthy lifestyle. The more you changed your lifestyle for the better, the more rewards you got through the Vitality programme.

Other medical-aid schemes have since done similar, but Discovery was already miles ahead. That explains why and how Discovery has been South Africa's biggest medical-aid scheme for years. The founder and group CEO of the country's largest medical aid is Jewish.

Meanwhile, siblings Bertie and Ronnie Lubner nurtured and moulded the PG Group – *the* name for glass in South Africa. In 1922, their father, Morrie, started the Johannesburg branch of Plate Glass, which was founded in Cape Town in 1897. He later took equity control of the company. His sons turned this small family business into the largest timber and glass conglomerate in southern Africa, then grew the PG Group into the world's leading vehicle glass repair and replacement business. Bertie, who died in 2016 aged 85, headed the timber side of the business; Ronnie died in 2018 at the age of 84. The Lubner brothers were Jews.

Another pair of Jewish siblings who played in the big league were Jonathan 'Jonni' Katz and his sister Karen. They spotted a gap in the market, a need for high-quality clothes for children, and that is how Earthchild, South Africa's leading kids' organic fashion brand, was born.

Another Jewish family that made a name for itself in the clothing industry is the Fabians. It all began with a Jewish woman who emigrated from Europe shortly before the Second World War and opened a small clothing store in Cape Town's District Six. Her son Jeff later founded his own fashion store. On a shopping trip to Italy in 1978, his hosts often mistakenly addressed him as Mr Fabiani, and that's how this famous brand came into being.

Jeff's son, Arie, who joined the family business, sold the brand to The Foschini Group (TFG) in 2011.

Sticking with TFG, the story goes that one Stanley Lewis acquired a controlling stake in Foschini in the 1980s. His father, Meyer Lewis, was the founder of furniture retail business Lewis. The current TFG chair is Michael Lewis, Meyer's grandson.

After Michael's first marriage ended in a divorce, he stepped it up a bit (don't all divorcees want to do better than their first spouse?) and married a British model thirty years his junior. His second wife, Kitty Spencer, is the daughter of none other than Charles Spencer, the younger brother of none other than the Princess of Wales, Diana (RIP). And, oh, the Lewis family is of Jewish stock.

Still in the retail space, in 1933, Philip Krawitz opened an army and navy shop in Cape Town, supplying visiting troops, whaling ships and fishermen with merchandise. This later became Cape Union Mart. The outlet's K-Way brand comes from the name of one of its factories, and is short for 'Mr Krawitz's way'. The group is now being run by the fourth generation of Krawitzes.

The guy who put the showerhead on former president Jacob Zuma, Zapiro, is without a doubt the country's best-known cartoonist. While some people regard his cartoons as controversial, others see them as entertaining and thought-provoking. What cannot be disputed, however, is that Jonathan Shapiro is Jewish.

On the sporting front, footballer Dean Furman, whose parents are South African, was born in Cape Town and moved to London when he was five years old. He made his debut for the South African national team in 2012. This one-time Bafana Bafana ace hopes to inspire other aspiring Jewish footballers. 'I would love to see more Jewish players,' he has said.

Let's move to the arts scene. A Jewish musician who put South Africa on the world map was the late Jonathan Paul 'Johnny' Clegg. Clegg crossed racial lines when it was dangerous and illegal to do so during the apartheid years. He co-founded Juluka, a group that specialised in mbaqanga and maskandi music. It is no wonder, given his musical talent (vocals and guitar), as well as his impressive traditional Zulu dancing (indlamu), that he was nicknamed 'the white Zulu'.

A writer who in 1974 became the first South African to win the Booker Prize was Nadine Gordimer. In 1991 she was awarded the Nobel Prize for literature. This daughter of a Lithuanian Jew died in 2014, aged 90.

On the academic front the Jewish community is well represented too. One example is the man who became the vice-chancellor of one of the highest-rated public universities not only in the country but throughout the continent and worldwide: Max Price at the University of Cape Town.

One of the most prominent and authoritative people in the history of humankind was a Jewish boy who was born in a stable, and today the biggest religion in the world follows his teachings. The irony of the whole thing is that Jews dispute the assertion that one of their own, Jesus, was a messiah. My question, therefore, is: who are we non-Jews to even get involved in this (Jewish) story?

It was only natural that while researching and reading about how Jews both locally and globally have contributed in different ways and forms to the world, I began thinking about my own people, the Zulus. All twelve million of us.

Given our numbers, our contribution could have been more meaningful and intense but, as the saying goes, we have been asleep at the wheel.

Let me say this: silitshelwe ukuneka amasende, which literally means 'we are busy drying out our balls', and it illustrates the worst form of laziness, where a person just sits and does absolutely nothing (while other children are changing the country and the world, as comprehensively illustrated above).

Indeed, iqiniso liyababa – 'the truth is bitter', the truth hurts. But as part of constructive criticism, we must be frank with one another and, in the process, speak, and write, the truth. Even if it hurts …

Chapter 11
THE FREEMASONS

Thirteen of the 39 men who signed the American Constitution belonged to an organisation called the Freemasons. Two of those were George Washington, the first president of the United States (1789–1797), and Benjamin Franklin, the statesman whose face has been on the US 100-dollar note since 1914.

Conspiracy theorists – who, I am told, prefer to be called public intelligence analysts – often state that Freemasonry is a secret club for the wealthy and powerful that decides on how to rule cities, countries and the world at large. There is much along these lines written about Freemasons, including that they are powerful individuals who want to turn the socioeconomic and political system into a new world order, with them seated right at the very top, while the billions below them are at best burdened with debt and at worst starving and living in poverty. Or both.

Admittedly, today there is a fair share of transparency for an organisation that is seen as secretive. Most lodges (which is the name for the buildings where Freemasons meet; they are also called halls or temples, and Freemasons are sometimes referred to as Masons) have their own websites and social media accounts. The South African grand lodge, for example, provides not only an online form for those who want to join, but also comprehensive answers to frequently asked questions. Many brick-and-mortar lodges are clearly labelled as such (for example, 'Masonic temple') and some even include the logo, which is a square and compass.

The conspiracy theorists still insist that the ones at the bottom do not really understand what the whole thing is all about, however. It is those at the very top, the argument continues, who know the strategy and the end goal.

The fact of the matter is that there are different levels, called degrees, within the Masonic hierarchy, and as you gain more degrees, the higher up you go in the system. It is just a coincidence, of course, that through the tertiary-education system you may also gain degrees that may influence whether you climb the (corporate) ladder. Or is it? Any way you look at it, there seems some type of coincidence between being a Mason and making it big in life. What are the odds that, for example, fourteen presidents (almost a third, to date) of the United States and 35 (out of a total of 116) US Supreme Court justices were all Freemasons?

So how did it all begin for the Masons here in South Africa? Well, back in 1772, Captain Abraham van der Weijden docked his ship in the Cape and decided to establish the South African chapter of the Netherlands grand lodge. The first meeting was attended by nine gentlemen, and it was decided to call the new branch the Lodge de Goede Hoop. One of those present, Abraham Chiron, a German-born banker, was elected as the grand master.

This means that Freemasonry celebrated 250 years in South Africa in 2022, and – according to the local Freemasonry website – this auspicious occasion was marked by visits from Masons from all over the world.

(Technically speaking, South Africa only got its first grand master in 1961, after the formation of the South African grand lodge. Before that, local leaders were considered to be part of European grand lodges. Also, a few months after he'd established the first local branch, Van der Weijden had a quarrel with another ship's captain and was stabbed to death. But his legacy lives on as the initiator and co-founder of Freemasonry in South Africa.)

Of the nine men who were at that first meeting, it was one

Christoffel Brand's family who went on to achieve great things. His grandson, also called Christoffel, grew up to be a lawyer and the first speaker of the legislative assembly of the Cape Colony. (We have, in fact, already met this Brand: it was he who named a town after his wife, Lady Brand.) He not only followed in his grandfather's Masonic footsteps, he became the grand master of Lodge de Goede Hoop in 1837 and remained in that position for 37 years. He died the following year, aged 77.

The son of Sir Christoffel Joseph Brand (yes, he was knighted), also a Freemason, whose name was Johannes Henricus 'Jan' Brand, followed in his father's footsteps by becoming a lawyer and politician. Although he did not become a grand master, he outdid his father by being named the president of the Orange Free State in 1864, a role he stayed in for 24 years, before dying in office. (And we have met this Brand before too: like his father, he named a town after his wife, Johanna Sibella Zastron.)

Before Jan Brand occupied the chair of president in the Orange Free State, it was the job of Marthinus Wessel Pretorius, Voortrekker leader Andries Pretorius's son. Pretorius Jnr was also a Freemason. At different times the president of the Zuid-Afrikaansche Republiek and the Orange Free State, at one stage he held both positions at the same time.

Coincidentally (I know it is a sheer coincidence and nothing further must be read into it), the man who preceded Pretorius as the president of the Zuid-Afrikaansche Republiek was yet another Freemason, Thomas François Burgers. And Brand was succeeded as Orange Free State president by Francis William Reitz Jr, who was – yes, you have guessed it – a Freemason.

Marthinus Wessel Pretorius, by the way, bought two farms where a new town quickly developed. The town was later named after his father, and that is how the capital city Pretoria got its name: by a Mason honouring his father.

Pretorius Jnr had one daughter, Christiana. The father, ever loving and powerful, named a town on the Vaal River after his little princess. But there was one thing that powerful father could never have granted to his beloved and only daughter, and that was membership of the Freemasons, because women weren't allowed.

There are a handful of accounts of how some women in the nineteenth century tried to join the Masons in Europe, with a few even resorting to disguising themselves as men. Some lodges were willing to be associated with women-only lodges, and more recently 'liberal Freemasonry' has no problem whatsoever with women members. In 2018 the United Grand Lodge of England issued new guidelines in order to clarify the matter of women membership, including the phrase 'A Freemason who after initiation ceases to be a man does not cease to be a Freemason'. Talk about muddying the waters! So if you are a woman and you want to be a Mason, it will mostly depend on which grand lodge you intend applying to.

The son of Reitz Jr, Deneys Reitz, was not a Freemason. At least, as far as I know Deneys Reitz was not a Freemason. He did, however, achieve great things, as a politician and a lawyer, and as a Boer fighter during the South African War and a colonel during the First World War. He wrote about these experiences in a series of autobiographical books. His biggest legacy, however, was the law firm Deneys Reitz, which he founded in 1922, aged 40. It became one of South Africa's major law companies. In 2011, more than 65 years after the death of its founder, Deneys Reitz Inc. joined the Norton Rose Group, a top global legal practice.

Deneysville is named after Reitz. However, Reitz, another town in the Free State, gets its name from Francis William Reitz Jr, Deneys's father. This means that two towns 130 kilometres from each other are named after a father and son.

In 1910, Francis William Reitz Jnr was chosen as the first president of the senate of the Union of South Africa, a position he held for eleven years, while – another coincidence – Louis Botha was prime minister. Louis Botha, a war hero for the Boers during the South African War, was – yep, you got it spot on – a Freemason.

Riaan Labuschagne's 2003 book *On South Africa's Secret Service* states clearly that, officially, those who worked for the country's intelligence services were not allowed to gather information of any sort on the illuminati and/or the Freemasons. Labuschagne does not explain why, so we will never know why the state made this policy not to interfere with the Masons. Could it be that – and I am thinking out loud here – some cabinet members and members of parliament were Masons?

'The illuminati' is a name given to several groups, both real and fictitious. The one founded in 1776 in what is today Germany is the secret society often referred to by conspiracy theorists. The logos and symbols associated with the illuminati include triangles, pentagrams, the all-seeing eye and the number 666. Conspiracy theorists spend their time looking for these signs and symbols in order to justify, first, that the illuminati do in fact exist; and, second, that, by using certain sectors of the economy, including the media and entertainment, they seek to create a new world order.

Another secret society, although perhaps not as famous as the illuminati, is the Knights Templar. Founded in 1118, with their headquarters at Temple Mount in Jerusalem, at their zenith the Templars were so rich that they owned not only Cyprus, the third-largest island in the Mediterranean Sea, but also a fleet of ships. Exempt from paying tax thanks to an order issued by Pope Innocent II, they loaned money to different monarchs, until – at least officially – the order was dissolved in 1312.

In 1832, at Yale University in the USA, a secret society was founded. It is called Skull and Bones. Reportedly, initiation into the society (which is also known as 'the brotherhood of death') includes swearing allegiance to fellow 'bonesmen' (as members are known), lying in a coffin, and revealing your entire sexual history in frank detail. In one report, it's all three of these at once: initiates must masturbate in a coffin while recounting their sexual exploits. In return, apparently, members are promised lifelong financial stability, which effectively buys their silence.

So, dear reader, do you want 'financial stability'? Then, if these reports are to be believed, go ahead and reveal your entire sexual history in detail and, while you are at it, masturbate in a coffin. If this is the only way to financial stability then, eish, I am going to be unstable for the rest of my days.

The Skull and Bones Society has included, among others, three presidents: William Howard Taft, George Bush and George W Bush. The last-named revealed in his political memoir *A Charge to Keep* (William Morrow, 1999), 'I joined Skull and Bones, a secret society; so secret, I can't say anything more.'

In 2004, two bonesmen ran against each other as presidential candidates: Bush (Republican, and then-incumbent president) and John Kerry (Democratic senator and future secretary of state). What are the odds?

Other bonesmen include Stephen Schwarzman, co-founder of Blackstone; Harold Stanley, co-founder of Morgan Stanley; Henry Luce, founder and publisher of influential magazines like *Time*, *Fortune* and *Sports Illustrated*; and Frederick Wallace Smith, founder of freight and logistics company FedEx. US Supreme Court justices Potter Stewart and Morrison R Waite, and national security advisor McGeorge Bundy, were bonesmen when they were at Yale.

Now, let's go back, way back, to the beginning.

Less than thirty years after the Freemasons were established on our shores in 1772, the coincidence of having Freemasons occupying powerful positions had already begun. Johannes Andreas Truter, who served a five-year term as the grand master of Lodge de Goede Hoop, from 1799 to 1804, was appointed chief justice of the Cape Colony; he was in office from 1812 to 1827.

Truter's stint as grand master was followed by that of Jacob Abraham Uitenhage de Mist (who we have already met in this book), who spent nine years in the position, from 1804 to 1813, before which he served about two years as the commissioner-general of the Cape Colony.

One of the longest-serving grand masters was Johannes Henoch Neethling, who filled the role for eighteen years. Armed with a PhD in law, within three years of serving as a judge he was appointed a Supreme Court justice. And after marrying a woman who, together with her brother, owned a wine farm, Neethling became a co-owner, and three years later bought the farm outright. Although it has since changed owners several times, it still carries the grand master's name: Neethlingshof.

The person who succeeded Neethling just so happens, like most grand masters, to have made it big in life. Besides being a prominent farmer, he was elected as the first mayor of Cape Town in 1840. It was Michiel van Breda, who was succeeded by Christoffel Brand (both of whom we have also previously met in this book).

More recent grand masters have also achieved senior positions, such as the late Armiston 'Watty' Watson, a DA councillor who was appointed the party's chief whip in the national assembly, a position he held for three years, from 2011 to 2014.

And talking of Freemasons and political parties, there has been some speculation – you may call it rumours – that some leaders of other political parties, including the ANC and the Economic Freedom Fighters (EFF), are Masons.

What cannot be denied is that the Freemasons – and this was not just in South Africa but globally – were, for quite some time, exclusively white men. It took not a hundred years or even two hundred, but 205 years for the lodges to be opened to people of all races. Someone in 1977 decided, for whatever reason, that black brothers could be invited in and, from that moment onwards, black folks officially became part of lodges countrywide.

In the United States, racial matters were just as complicated. Prince Hall – that was his official name – is regarded as the father of African-American Freemasonry. He had a keen interest in Masonry but was turned down for membership because of his race. Years later, in 1784, when eventually he, together with other African Americans, founded their own lodge, its functions and responsibilities were limited, for example, they could not confer Masonic degrees. This is like having a school that does not have the power or authority to say 'now you can go to the next grade'. (Black and white lodges are integrated today.)

Internationally, Masons who have achieved exceptionally great things include British royalty; politicians such as presidents (those already named, plus Bill Clinton) and heavyweights like Jesse Jackson and Mikhail Gorbachev (RIP); military leaders such as Napoleon, Simon Bolivar and the Duke of Wellington; entrepreneurs such as Henry Ford; and artists Wolfgang Mozart, William Shakespeare, Oscar Wilde, Duke Ellington, Ludwig van Beethoven and Nat King Cole.

What a list! It is a who's-who of global thinkers and shapers. Some of them might have had different beliefs (Republicans vs Democrats, capitalists vs communists) but when it came to Freemasonry, they sang from the same hymn sheet.

Two names that are also on this list stand out for me. Quite honestly, I just could not believe my eyes when I read them. These two are much closer to home: Nelson Mandela and Desmond Tutu.

Moving swiftly along ...

Okay, maybe not so fast.

Apparently, even the Archbishop of Canterbury was at one stage a Freemason. Rev. Dr Geoffrey Francis Fisher served as the Archbishop of Canterbury from 1945 until he retired in 1961. During this sixteen-year stretch, two events thrust him into the international limelight. The first was officiating, in 1947, the wedding of Princess Elizabeth and Prince Philip. Six years later, on 2 June 1953, he presided over the coronation of Queen Elizabeth II.

This is very elaborative ceremony includes taking an oath, anointing, investing and – eventually – crowning. And this was all done on that summer day in 1953 by the Freemason Dr Fisher.

Bear in mind that the Archbishop of Canterbury is the head of the Anglican Church, just like the Pope – the Bishop of Rome – is the head of the Roman Catholic Church. So, to round off the Desmond Mpilo Tutu Freemason issue, if the head honcho of the Anglican Church can be a Mason, why couldn't our very own archbishop be part and parcel of the craft? Rest in peace, Arch!

As for Nelson Mandela, he is apparently (according to some online sources) in the company of other prominent black civil-rights activists like WEB du Bois and Booker T Washington, plus former US sports star Shaquille O'Neal.

There is a Freemason who has indirectly touched almost all of us on our, er, private parts. It all started when two brothers, William (a Freemason) and James, as well as another business partner who was a chemist, tried out a new soap-making process to make bathing an even more pleasurable experience, and thus changed our bathroom habits forever. Their enterprise was so successful that, through organic growth and international acquisitions, it became one of the world's biggest companies. The brothers' surname was Lever.

In 1929, Lever Brothers merged with a Dutch company to form Unilever, which today has more than four hundred brands available in almost two hundred countries.

One of those brands is Lipton tea. Thomas Lipton, a Scottish Freemason, had a few grocery shops and was forever looking for products to stock them with. In the latter part of the nineteenth century, he ended up heading to Ceylon (modern-day Sri Lanka) where, in order to control the entire chain, he decided to plant his own tea. Through efficient processes and on-point marketing, Lipton's tea was soon selling in a number of countries.

Richard Byrd is best known for his Antarctic expeditions. The first two expeditions, in 1928 and 1934, were sponsored by private investors, including wealthy and influential individuals like Vincent Astor and John D Rockefeller Jr. That is why you will find Astor Island and Mount Astor, as well as Rockefeller Plateau and the Rockefeller Mountains, in Antarctica. And while on his naming spree, Byrd, a Freemason, established the first Masonic lodge on that southernmost continent.

Byrd's fourth expedition, a year after the end of the Second World War, was officially titled the United States Navy Antarctic Developments Program. Commonly known as Operation High Jump, it comprised at least 25 aircraft (some records mention over 30), 13 ships including an aircraft carrier, and almost 5 000 people. Why would so many people be needed for a scientific expedition/training exercise? Was there more to Operation High Jump than meets the eye, I keep asking myself.

This reminds me of Euripides, that most influential dramatist in classical Greek culture, who once said, 'Time will discover everything to posterity; it is a babbler, and speaks even when no question is put.'

One of Germany's most recognised literary figures, poet and playwright Johann Wolfgang von Goethe, was a Mason.

Another, this one Italian, whose name has lasted for more than two centuries, is Giacomo Girolamo. You don't recognise those first names? Well, he was a schemer and plotter of note, successfully wriggling himself into meetings with royalty in Spain, England and Prussia. In his 1882 memoir, *Histoire de Ma Vie* (Story of My Life), he is very candid about the loads and loads of women he'd slept with. To this day, anyone who is a womaniser is referred to by Giacomo's surname: Casanova.

Ernest Oppenheimer (who we've also already met in this book) was a Freemason – he was, in fact, the master of the Richard Giddy Lodge in Kimberley. His son Harry was a subscribing member of the lodge for fifty years and ultimately was made a master Mason.

Harry succeeded his father in running the family dynasty, and was chair of Anglo American and De Beers for almost three decades. He retired in the 1980s and died in 2000.

A Freemason who contributed immensely to the country we have today is the poet Cornelis Jacobus Langenhoven. One of his famous poems is 'Die Stem van Suid-Afrika' (The Voice of South Africa). He wrote it in 1918. Does that year cause any bells to ring? That was the year that, as part of the economic emancipation of the Afrikaner, Santam and Sanlam were formed. And CJ Langenhoven just happens to be one of the gentlemen who, four years previously, had decided to form a publishing company for the volk.

When the democratic government took over in 1994, it was deemed appropriate – because of nation-building and not forgetting that we were (are?) the rainbow nation, and because we had to sustain social cohesion – that 'Die Stem' should be the second half of the new national anthem.

Freemasons did not only dominate the political sphere; some of them dominated in other fields. Take Gerard Moerdyk (also spelt Moerdijk) as an example. An architect (and a Broederbonder), after studying in England and France he came back to South Africa with new ideas and was willing to experiment. Among his well-known buildings is the NG Kerk in Mkhondo (previously Piet Retief) in Mpumalanga. What put him on the map, however, was the Voortrekker Monument outside Pretoria, which was officially opened in 1949.

There is a fundamental link between Gerard Moerdyk and Piet Retief (besides the church in the town that was once named after the latter). Retief, the Voortrekker leader who was killed by the Zulus in February 1838, was also a Freemason. Ten months later, the Zulus and the Boers slugged it out on the banks of the eNcome River. Were it not for Piet Retief, there would not have been a Battle of eNcome; and we can safely conclude, therefore, that Moerdyk would not have been called on to design his masterpiece, so there would not have been a Voortrekker Monument. And 16 December would not be a public holiday.

Although the first Freemason lodge was formed in Cape Town in 1772, the first brick-and-mortar lodge was only built about thirty years later. The Freemasons bought some land on which to build their first temple, and the building was consecrated by Uitenhage De Mist in 1803.

In the 1840s, a banqueting hall was built next to the lodge, and this hall housed the Cape parliament from 1854 to 1884.

Over a hundred years later, in 2014, the grand master of the South African Freemasons, Geoff Edwards, accompanied the media around the premises, where he pointed out, 'People say we're on parliamentary grounds, but that's not true. Actually, parliament is on our grounds.'

Imagine a secret organisation (or should I say an organisation with secrets) that has the country's parliamentary precinct on its land! Talk about being a power broker.

Chapter 12
THE UNIONS

Of all unionists who have had a major impact on South Africa, no-one comes close to Cyril Matamela Ramaphosa.

Ramaphosa was supported in his earlier years by Clive Menell, the head of gold-mining conglomerate Anglovaal. In the 1970s, Menell helped the youngster complete his legal studies, which had been interrupted by his arrest for joining the anti-apartheid Black People's Convention and also following the 1976 Soweto uprising. Menell then recruited Ramaphosa into the Urban Foundation, which had recently been established by himself, Harry Oppenheimer and Anton Rupert to help finance and establish housing projects for 'urbanised blacks'. This taught Ramaphosa useful skills in dealing with powerful people and gave him a unique appreciation of business.

The Menell family, by the way, made its fortune through Anglovaal, which in the 1990s was separated into Anglovaal Industrial Holdings and Anglovaal Minerals (Avmin). And in 2003, Avmin was consolidated into African Rainbow Mining, a listed black-empowerment company that was founded and is majority-owned by the Motsepe family. Patrice Motsepe by then had been Cyril's brother-in-law since 1996, when Cyril had married Patrice's elder sister Tshepo. Of course, that did not play any role in the deal. It's just a small world out there.

And to further illustrate this point about the small world, what are the odds: Clive Menell's son Brian sold his Saxonwold property in 2005 to – drum roll – the Guptas. A decade later, we would learn how one president was being controlled by the Guptas, and how ministers and senior government officials would be summoned to what was later known as 'the Gupta compound'.

To take this point to its logical conclusion, this means that for the Gupta brothers to have been able to afford to buy property in one of Johannesburg's leafiest suburbs as early as 2005, they must already have made some sizeable money by then. I am sure you have figured this one out, but Zuma only became the president of the Republic in 2009, and before that other children had far more influence than him.

Moving swiftly along …

There is something, I must admit, that over a period of time I have struggled with but so far have completely failed to resolve. So Ramaphosa was not only helped financially by the Menell family, they were also instrumental in coaching and mentoring him, as well as introducing him to South Africa's business elite. But then, a few years later, Ramaphosa became a founder member of the National Union of Mineworkers (NUM) – which means that he would ultimately directly and indirectly challenge the Menells and other wealthy families who had made and were continuing to make millions – in fact, billions – in the mining sector. In short, Ramaphosa as a co-founder of NUM bit the very hand that had fed him when he had nothing. In his new position as NUM's secretary-general, he challenged his benefactors.

To this day I struggle to wrap my head around that one. Whenever I try to solve this conundrum, I find myself thinking about, of all people, Vladimir Ilyich Ulyanov, who not only led the 1917 Russian Revolution but who also served as the first and founding head of the government of Soviet Russia and the Soviet Union. Better known as Lenin, he once said, 'The best way to control the opposition is to lead it ourselves.'

And, indeed, in 1987, five years after the founding of NUM,

Ramaphosa led the biggest mining strike in the country at the time – which subsequently saw more than 40 000 miners lose their jobs. Remember, unlike now, when workers can embark on a protected strike, back then there was no legal way for workers to strike. Needless to say, mining companies fired thousands of workers for going on strike, and those employees who were not fired got absolutely nothing from the strike. Not even one extra cent was offered by the mining companies.

As part of an arrangement to end the strike, employers agreed to take back workers 'wherever possible'. As such, thousands of employees had to reapply for their positions. Some, in the process, were demoted. The troublemakers obviously never made the cut.

The general narrative about that 1987 mining strike has always been simply that it was 'the biggest mining strike', without asking a rather simple question: who, out of the employer and employees, benefitted from it?

A decade or so later, Ramaphosa was a mover and a shaker, thanks to BEE deals in various sectors of the economy, including mining. It was in that context that, as Lonmin's shareholder and non-executive director, he got entangled in a dispute at Marikana in which employees were demanding a measly R12 500 minimum wage. Within a few days, ten people, including two police officers, had been killed in the strike. Ramaphosa sent an email to the mine management calling the actions of the strikers 'plainly dastardly criminal'. 'In line with this characterisation there needs to be con-comitant action taken to address this situation,' he wrote.

The following day, 16 August 2012, police officers opened fire and 34 miners lost their lives.

Admittedly, Ramaphosa apologised five years later, stating, 'Yes, I may well have used unfortunate language in the messages I sent out ... I have apologised and I do apologise that I did not use appropriate language but I never had the intention to have 34 other mine workers killed.'

There you have it: an apology was issued – for use of inappropriate language.

The R1 billion civil claim, by the way, by family members of the Marikana victims and survivors of the massacre against Ramaphosa in his personal capacity, and their employer, still has to run its course in our courts.

Two other alumni the Urban Foundation can claim are Nkosinathi Nhleko, CEO and later chair of the MTN Group, and Peter Matlare, who headed up the SABC and Tiger Brands, and was deputy CEO of the Absa Group before passing away due to Covid-related complications in 2021.

Please, dear reader, indulge me as I pay tribute to Peter Matlare.

It was in 2016 when I received a call from Peter. I was expecting it. He was the leader of the ilobolo delegation that was going to come to my brother's home. Peter had been sent by his friend, Alex, who wanted to marry my niece, Ziyanda.

Over the next few years, Peter and I would bump into each other at family functions and gatherings. One thing that never ceased to amaze me was how humble he was. He was just a joyful guy next door, with a warm personality, charisma and an Anglicised African accent. I can imagine how pompous and stuck-up other people might have been had they occupied the positions that Peter occupied. Admittedly, I do not aspire to be the CEO of a multinational organisation but one day, when I am grown up and can finally achieve big things, I would love to be as humble as Peter Matlare – to basically let my works do the talking on my behalf. Peter was humility personified. Rest easy, humble soul. Rest in eternal peace, Peter Bhambatha Matlare.

Back to unionists … I know, I know – what an anticlimax!

Okay, maybe before we go back to the unionists, let's talk about another gentleman who at one stage was part of the Urban Foundation and also went on to achieve big things: the late Jabu

Mabuza, whose career path was stratospheric. He started out as a taxi driver before eventually buying his own taxi. He was a co-founder of the Foundation for African Business and Consumer Services (Fabcos). In the mid-1990s he got involved with the Urban Foundation, and soon thereafter became an advisor to the Union Bank of Switzerland. He then joined Tsogo Sun where in time he became group CEO. He held a number of board positions, including at Telkom and Eskom.

From being a taxi driver to being the most senior guy in board-rooms takes something special, very special. Whatever that thing might be, Jabu Mabuza had it.

Now, back to the unionists.

Ramaphosa, love him or hate him, is a high achiever. For starters, he is a billionaire. There are billions of people out there – no pun intended – who would love to be, yes, billionaires. Admittedly, most (if not all) the money he made was through BEE deals: white companies giving a minority share to black people, who were then locked in for some time in the hope that, through dividends that would pay off the debt and through share appreciation, they would become filthy rich. In simple terms – at least, in the way it was implemented – this meant white companies coopting politi-cally connected black individuals and keeping them happy, and so getting some BEE points. Improved BEE ratings ensured more business from government for the white companies, while the black masses were led to believe that working hard alone would make them wealthy ... until they died poor.

A 2014 study on BEE by global consulting firm Ernst and Young, which looked at deals made from the dawn of democracy, revealed that 72 per cent of the total deal value involved at least one of the top six BEE consortiums, namely African Rainbow Minerals (Patrice Motsepe), Mvelaphanda (Tokyo Sexwale), Safika (Saki Macozoma), Kagiso, Tiso – and Shanduka. This means that Ramaphosa, as founder of Shanduka, was in the thick of beautiful things from the beginning of the new South Africa.

Talking about being in the thick of beautiful things, Mark Wilcox co-founded Mvelaphanda in 1998 and six years later he had made himself a tidy sum of R300 million. Not bad for a white guy who turned 34 that particular year (2004). Wilcox died of a heart attack in 2022, age 52. Life well lived, if you ask me. If black people allowed, and still allow, white people to ride the BEE wave, surely that cannot be white people's problem. It is also not black people's problem. It is simply black people's short-sightedness and stupidity. It is our short-sightedness and stupidity.

Back to Cyril.

Besides being a billionaire, Ramaphosa is the president of the country. He is the president of a country that not only has the second-largest economy but also the most sophisticated economy on the continent. Some (I am tempted to say most) politicians in the national assembly, as well as those in the different provincial legislatures, would love – and some might be tempted to even kill – to be the president of South Africa.

So Ramaphosa has achieved both – being a billionaire and being a president. I can only imagine how many rivers you have to cross in order to be a billionaire. I can only imagine how many mountains you have to climb in order to be the president of a country. Now, what are the odds of being a billionaire *and* a president? Well, Ramaphosa achieved both … but so did Donald Trump.

Ramaphosa, by the way, is not the only former unionist who made it all the way to the executive arm of government. Others include Senzeni Zokwana, former president of the NUM, who was appointed by Zuma to serve as minister of agriculture, forestry and fisheries; Membathisi Mphumzi Sheperd Mdladlana, former president of the South African Democratic Teachers' Union (SADTU), who served a twelve-year stint as minister of labour before jetting off to be a high commissioner in Canada; and Thembelani Waltermade 'Thulas' Nxesi, the former SADTU general-secretary who is credited with growing the union's membership from about 30 000 to 250 000, who has served in different ministerial portfolios since 2011.

The same year that Ebrahim Patel ended his ten-year term (1999 to 2009) as the general-secretary of the Southern African Clothing and Textile Workers Union (SACTWU), he was appointed as a minister, and he is still at it. And the former national executive officer of the National Union of Metalworkers of South Africa (NUMSA), Alec Erwin, grew up to be a minister at different times overseeing various portfolios.

Of unionists who have had a major impact on South Africa, coming a close second to Ramaphosa is one Samson Gwede Mantashe. Mantashe is an achiever of note but, for whatever reason, some South Africans do not want to give him his due. He was, for example, the first trade unionist to be appointed to the board of a JSE-listed company, Samancor, in 1995. Three years later, he was elected general-secretary of the NUM. In 2007 he was elected secretary-general of the ANC, a position he held for ten years. And while he was in that position, he was also the chair of the South African Communist Party. In 2017, he was elected chair of the ANC. In 2019, aged 64, he was appointed minister of mineral resources and energy by President Cyril Ramaphosa.

Ramaphosa, incidentally, was succeeded by Kgalema Motlanthe as the NUM's general-secretary. Motlanthe, in turn, was succeeded by Mantashe. If you connect the dots, you can see that the first two general-secretaries of the NUM grew up to be presidents of the Republic. Why, then, I keep asking myself, doesn't Mantashe, also a former NUM general-secretary, have presidential ambitions? Or does he? In any case, Gwede, who is also affectionately known as Uncle Gweezy, was re-elected as the ANC's national chairperson at the 2017 conference. He beat Stanley Mathabatha by only 44 votes (2062–2018).

*

Soon after Jacob Zuma's resignation as the country's president, the term 'nine wasted years' gained traction in political and media circles. There was this narrative that portrayed Zuma as a man who'd acted all alone and had no support whatsoever from anyone. It was conveniently forgotten how ANC members of parliament, without fail, had protected Zuma whenever he was faced with a motion of no confidence, even after the Constitutional Court had found that he had failed to respect, uphold and defend the constitution.

The irony of this whole thing is that some of those members of parliament, now that Zuma is history, often portray themselves as men and women of integrity, high morals and exceptional righteousness who are beyond reproach. My. Black. Zulu. Arse. Whenever we talk of Zuma's 'nine wasted years', we must not conveniently forget that Ramaphosa and Mantashe, not to mention all those ANC members of parliament, were in the midst of it all.

Cyril Ramaphosa, for the record, is not the only unionist who grew up to be to filthy rich. Three other unionists who became rich – very rich – come to mind: Irene Charnley, John Anthony 'Johnny' Copelyn and Marcel Golding.

Three years after the 1993 Sanlam/NAIL BEE deal (discussed in Chapter 8), there was another huge BEE deal when Anglo American sold its majority stake in Johnnic to an entity called the National Empowerment Consortium, which was effectively a coalition of BEE companies, including – yep – NAIL.

Johnnic was a conglomerate in its own right. It had massive stakes in Times Media, Premier Foods, South African Breweries and, indirectly, MTN. This must be understood in the context of pre-1994 exchange controls: due to economic isolation, companies and individuals were not allowed to take money offshore. Therefore, big companies like Anglo could not make offshore acquisitions, and as a result they ended up buying other companies in South Africa, even if those other companies had no strategic fit for them.

M-CELL, a Johnnic Holdings company, was basically how the MTN Group started. Irene Charnley, as M-CELL chair, was in the right place at the right time. Her experience as an organiser for NUM must have come in very handy when, later, as MTN's vice-president for the Middle East and North and East Africa, she was instrumental in the growth of the group in countries like Iran, Côte d'Ivoire, the Republic of the Congo and Zambia. And for this, she was well rewarded, if *Forbes* is correct, by stock valued at over US$150 million (R2.4 billion).

After leaving MTN, Charnley started another telecommunications company called Smile. She retired as deputy chair at Smile Telecoms in 2021.

It is a pity that not a lot of black women have been well rewarded by BEE. The patriarchal system, I see, still reigns supreme.

On this gender note, one of the contentious issues regarding both BEE and affirmative action legislation is whether or not white women (and this point has nothing to do with Irene Charnley, because she is black) should be regarded as part of designated groups, meaning people who were once discriminated against, and, as such, need the legislative framework as a tool to uplift them. It is a highly emotional issue and also polarising because women, all women, were in one way or the other discriminated against, and yet white women – because of their race – directly and indirectly benefitted from racial discrimination. For example, their husbands could start businesses and/or get good jobs coupled with perks which they enjoyed with their families.

In her book *Sitting Pretty: White Afrikaans women in post-apartheid South Africa* (University of KwaZulu-Natal, 2018), Christi van der Westhuizen grapples with the fundamental question of how white Afrikaans-speaking women have responded to the liberating possibilities of constitutional democracy. It would be very interesting, I think, to get the views in book format from black women (the ones at the very bottom of the pile because of their race and gender) on this issue: should white women benefit from BEE and affirmative action?

Johnny Copelyn is, according to one media article, a 'walking contradiction': a white man who benefitted immensely from BEE. He started out as a unionist and ultimately became the general-secretary of SACTWU. After the historic 1994 elections, he became a member of parliament on the ANC ticket while at the same time he was CEO of the SACTWU Investment Group, because with the new dispensation came an opportunity for unions to form investment companies. Three years later, the SACTWU Investment Group, together with the NUM's investment company (headed by unionist Marcel Golding) became major shareholders in Hosken Consolidated Investments (HCI). HCI has investments in hotels and leisure (Tsogo Sun), media and broadcasting, Golden Arrow Buses, property, mining, and oil and gas. Copelyn has been HCI's CEO since 1997. (By the way, both Copelyn and Golding are of Jewish stock; these two gentlemen had a major public fallout in 2014.)

During the 1987 mining strike, Ramaphosa's deputy at the NUM was Marcel Golding.

An irony is that although seed funding for the union investment arms was taken from workers' savings, when those workers became employers, they did not become great employers, as you might expect from people who have been on the other side of the fence. A paper by academics Nicoli Nattrass and Jeremy Seekings titled 'Trade unions, the state and "casino capitalism" in South Africa's clothing industry' makes key observations about the focus of unions' investments on high-end property, media and hotels, and especially casinos, and notes that this shows that there was not much socialism in the form of capitalism they were engaging in.

Social capitalism is any capitalist system that is structured with the ideology of liberty, equality and justice. Whatever economic system you subscribe to, there is one general conclusion that I have made in this regard: almost everyone, given opportunity and space, has the potential to be a greedy, blood-sucking capitalist who screws workers 24 hours a day, seven days a week, in the name of creating 'shareholder value'.

In simple terms, just like any woman can potentially be a prostitute, any human being can potentially be an ass.

Chapter 13
TAXIS, RELIGION AND TRADITIONAL LEADERS

Nothing, absolutely nothing, proves that the taxi industry is a government in its own right like what happened in June 2020. During those few days, even some among us who had been living under a rock in this regard were exposed to the reality that taxi owners could be a law unto themselves.

In that month, the country, thanks to an unconstitutionally recognised body called the national coronavirus command council, had effectively insulated South Africa from the outside world, and our movements as citizens had been significantly curtailed. We were not even allowed to travel to other provinces. And taxis had been instructed to keep their passenger loads at seventy per cent of capacity.

The taxi industry, after feeling the economic pinch, decided, 'Fuck it. We will do it our way.' Well, the wording was not exactly that but the message was essentially 'screw this government'.

It is one thing for an organisation to have clandestine meetings and take secret decisions to break the law. It is something totally different when, after holding your meeting, you issue a statement not only telling the government that you will break the law but essentially declaring to all people of South Africa that you are not scared of the state. Effectively, the taxi industry was saying, 'Bring it on.'

I could not believe my eyes when, live on national television, as per the statement issued a few days prior, taxi owners and drivers made it clear that they could not care less about the Covid-19 regulations. Passengers had to be transported from one province to the other. Money had to be made. If it meant flouting the law, well, shit happens.

A spokesperson for the local taxi association highlighted that the restrictions had had a major economic impact on the taxi industry and, as such, they could not take it any more. Johannesburg-bound passengers boarding taxis at Durban station stated live on national TV how relieved they were that at last they were going to see their loved ones in Gauteng.

I remember thinking, *Maybe the soldiers will wait for these taxis along the N3 at the Tugela toll plaza, just before they cross into the Free State, and instruct them to go back.* Mind you, the soldiers had already been let loose on us, the citizens. And at that time, the soldiers had already allegedly assaulted a citizen to death. (Rest in peace, Mr Khosa.)

A few days later, when the minister of transport was questioned by the media regarding taxis flagrantly travelling between provinces, he jokingly said, 'Andizi,' which means, 'I am not going there.' In simple terms, the minister was saying he was not prepared to go toe-to-toe with the taxi industry.

A few weeks later, the regulations were amended to allow interprovincial travel. And we all forgot how the taxi industry had publicly defied the national government.

This is just one example of how powerful the taxi industry is in our country (or should I say cowntry).

It is common knowledge that the taxi industry is one of the most violent sectors of the economy, if not *the* most violent. The media often reports clashes between rival taxi associations. There is also rivalry between taxi bosses within the same association.

It is all about money and power. It is almost as if you cannot get yourself to the top without having, literally and figuratively, skeletons in your closet.

It is common knowledge that hitmen (in my home language, izinkabi) are contracted to eliminate the competition on an ongoing basis. Some of the taxi bosses, I am told, prefer not to contract izinkabi but to do the job themselves. The warfare in this industry, seemingly, will never end.

In recent times, a book series by Dudu Busani-Dube called *Hlomu the Wife* (HlomuPublishing, 2015) was adapted into the telenovella *The Wife*. It broke viewership records when it first hit the small screen, as viewers were glued to their TVs, shocked and dismayed by, among other things, the series' illustration of the brutality of the taxi industry.

The government looks incapable and/or unwilling to stop this carnage. Could it be that our government is weak? Or could it be, as some have suggested, that some politicians and government officials at different levels own fleets of taxis? If that were the case, then cleaning up the taxi industry could lead to skeletons coming out of currently tightly closed closets. (This brings to mind another theory that says the reason why the rail system is barely functioning has little to do with the state not being able to fix it, but everything to do with some influential politicians owning a fleet of trucks, and thus not wanting, for obvious reasons, an effective and efficient railway system.)

Don't get me wrong: I realise that the taxi industry plays a huge and extremely important role in the economy of this country. Various reports have claimed that about two-thirds of South Africans use taxis as their mode of transport; and that explains why it is estimated that there are a quarter of a million taxis on our roads (not all at the same time, although sometimes it feels like it). That translates into roughly R5 billion in annual revenue for the taxi industry. With that amount of money comes power, influence and greed. And some taxi bosses understand this all too well.

In recent years, some taxi operators have become bus owners. Piotrans, for example, entered into a twelve-year contract with Rea

Vaya, Johannesburg's bus rapid transit system, in 2011. Piotrans has three hundred shareholders in nine associations; these are three hundred taxi operators in nine taxi associations.

In Durban, the eThekwini metro had a multi-year contract with a company called Tansnat. When travelling in KwaZulu-Natal, especially around Durban, you are bound to spot taxis proudly emblazoned with 'Gcaba Brothers'. One of the Gcaba brothers co-owns Tansnat.

There is another grouping in South Africa that holds enormous power. You might be tempted to call it 'soft power' because the leaders in this grouping are forever literally preaching about peace, forgiveness and turning the other cheek.

I am talking about religious groupings, and considering that a vast majority (about 85 per cent) of South Africans identify as Christian, I will focus mainly on Christianity.

Nothing illustrates the power of Christian leaders such as bishops and pastors like how the leaders of all the big political parties now and then visit (and almost want to be publicly endorsed by) certain religious leaders.

I have, at times, thought, what if the founders of the big churches were to start a political party? What if the bishop of some church group told his congregants, followers and members, 'God says I must start a political party'? Can you imagine the potential threat that would present to the current political establishment? Could it be that there is almost an unwritten rule that political leaders and bishops must, as young people might say, stay in their respective lanes?

Imagine if the leader of the Nazareth Baptist Church, better known as Shembe or amaNazaretha, which has millions of members, were to start a political party. It would win KwaZulu-Natal easily and would possibly be a major force in Gauteng.

Even better – or worse – imagine if the leader of the Zion Christian Church were to start a political party. Bear in mind that, according to the late spokesperson Emmanuel Motolla, the church had ten million members in 2020. There would be no need for him to campaign. All he would need to do is tell his congregants, 'God says you must vote for me.' And that would be it: after the next election we would have a new president.

Now, can you imagine the power you would have as a person in that position, when politicians hope and pray that you never challenge them because they know, for sure, that if you did, they would lose?

There is another way in which religious groups, specifically the church, not only prop up the government but also encourage acceptance of the status quo, and thus less challenging of corrupt and bureaucratic systems. This is because of the narrative of 'accepting God's will' or 'not questioning God's plan' when, truth be told, the government is messing up and should be held accountable.

Were it not for Christians (or any religious group, for that matter), how much of this corruption and incompetence would we be tolerating? Does religion make us docile and gullible? Or are we docile and gullible, and politicians just take advantage of our stupidity?

You can never talk about religion and its impact on politics without talking about the church. As covered in the first part of this book, most towns grew around a church. That on its own shows the power of religion, where the building associated with it leads to the development of a town.

Within the South African context, the Nederduitse Gereformeerde Kerk (Dutch Reformed Church) has had the most important historical impact on the politics of the country. It not only defended, but endorsed and justified, by quoting scriptures from the Bible, the oppression of black people. That explains, for example, why and how Rev. Dr DF Malan ended up as the prime minister.

This oppression and subjugation were underpinned and justified by the word of God. Then again, there are verses in the Bible that justify slavery, rape and murder. But, dear reader, that is a conversation for another day.

Truth be told, the apartheid project was sustained by mainly two factors: moral/religious justification and international economic partnerships. Without these, apartheid would not have lasted as long as it did – almost half a century. Domestic brutality, harassment, and the torture and killing of freedom fighters and civilians (including women and children) were just add-ons.

Had the architects of the apartheid policy – and the general white superiority complex – not found a rationale for and a defence of their programme in the scriptures, the whole thing would not have gained much traction and it would have died a natural death. For the system to work, the church had to indoctrinate all and sundry that, to quote George Orwell, 'All animals are equal but some animals are more equal than others.'

Therefore, considering that almost everyone these days talks about 'state capture', the question must be asked, did politicians capture the church? If not, then why did the church allow itself to be used so much by politicians?

One day, as people of the world, we must have a forthright and unambiguous conversation about whether religion (and here I am not talking about any specific religion, but religion as a whole) has really benefitted us, and in what way.

This could be put another way: what if we, the people of the world, had never invented religion?

On a more personal note, I was born into a Christian family. Although officially a member of the Anglican Church, I mostly attended the Zion Church. This was because the Anglican preacher only came once a quarter to our village, whereas the Zion church was a stone's throw from home, and it was open every Sunday.

What I did not know when I was much younger, and now find very fascinating, is the fact that this Zion Church, like all of them in southern Africa, came to our shores as a result of a former Dutch Reformed preacher, who imported it from – wait for it – the town of Zion in Illinois in the USA.

The founder of this American-based church, John Alexander Dowie, was a British Australian who had relocated to the US and, through a catchy message and his gift of the gab, was able to muster a worldwide following. He made so much money that in the early 1900s he bought huge tracts of land, and this is where he built his church, named after Mount Zion in Israel.

While all this buying of land and building of the Lord's house was going on, it was discovered that more than US$2 million (about R32 million, but this was back in the 1900s) could not be accounted for.

It does not get better.

Some pastors, and by extension, some churches, are used for money-laundering purposes. Until I was told about this, I had never really thought how easy it would be for a church to be involved in such a criminal activity. In fact, the more I spoke to friends and family members, the more it seemed that this was almost one of those well-known secrets of which only I was unaware.

The modus operandi is very simple, and it uses the very nature of how the church operates. All churches take offerings; most take mainly cash. All the pastor has to do is to accept 'dirty' (ill-gotten) money from, for example, politicians or drug lords, and deposit it in the bank as part of the church's legitimate takings.

Our financial systems, through banks, are supposed to pick up suspicious transactions, especially those involving large amounts of cash. A church, however, has a genuine reason for dealing with loads and loads of cash. Therefore, if the founder of, say, the International Church of Jesus Who Arose on the Third Day deposits a big wodge of cash on a Monday morning, it would not cause as much alarm as if the cash came from someone who, say, owns a consulting company.

In order to get the 'clean' money back, I was told, you submit an invoice for any services that a church might typically require: construction, security, cleaning, sound, lighting, etc. As a successful entrepreneur, you can then go and splash out with your money any way your heart desires. And no-one, especially the authorities, will suspect a thing.

That is how, I was told, some churches clean dirty money.

And do you know what other industry deals in huge amounts of cash? That's right: the taxi industry.

When a taxi boss deposits loads of cash in the bank, it does not cause alarm because, well, taxis take cash. Period. Therefore, in theory, taxi bosses could also clean a lot of money for drug dealers, corrupt politicians, tenderpreneurs and crooked government officials. (Except that the tax man might one day come knocking at the door ...)

Churches, by law, pay no income tax. That got me thinking: if churches were to be taxed, would that mean the government was taking money that belongs to God?

Some churches, by the way, make a lot of money. Let me re-phrase that: some churches metaphorically print cash. For example, the Rhema Bible Church, the South African branch of which was founded in Johannesburg in the 1980s, raked in slightly over R100 million in 2008, about two-thirds of which was from tithes and offerings. If that was the case more than a decade ago, I can only imagine how much revenue is made today.

In recent years, a series of events in one of the biggest churches in South Africa, the International Pentecost Holiness Church, high-lighted, first, what might happen when a leader dies without a publicly endorsed heir; and, second, how much money may cir-culate within a church. In 2016, the church's leader, Glayton 'the Comforter' Modise, passed away. The following year, his second wife was accused of stealing more than R15 million, of which almost R3 million was in solid cash. Later in 2017, it was reported that the Hawks were investigating the church's executive committee for the disappearance of more than R300 million from the church's bank account.

Things turned violent three years later when armed men stormed the church's headquarters and opened fire, killing five people. The general sentiment was that this was part of in-fighting between three contenders: two sons of the late Comforter, and a third son (allegedly) born out of wedlock.

The top twenty richest pastors in the world in 2022, according to the website MoneyInc ('the one place for you to learn all about the culture of money'), include our very own Ray McCauley, founder of the South African Rhema Bible Church, with a fortune of US$29 million (R464 million). Shepherd Bushiri, who at the time of writing was fighting extradition to South Africa, is at number five, with US$150 million (R2.4 billion). (Bushiri and his wife Mary skipped bail in 2020 on several charges, including rape, theft and fraud, and fled to their home country of Malawi.) On top of the list is Brazilian televangelist, media mogul and founder of the Universal Church of the Kingdom of God, Edir Macedo, with a tidy sum of US$1.1 billion (R17.6 billion).

A good friend of mine, Nathi Nkwanyana, after listening to me addressing mourners at my mother's funeral in June 2022, jokingly remarked not once but twice, 'Kuzomele sivule isonto,' meaning we must start a church. His reason was simple: 'Uma ukhuluma abantu bayalalela' – people listen when I talk.

There is no doubt about it, and any way you look at it, opening a church is good business. No wonder that wherever you go, new churches are sprouting up.

In recent years, I have noted how churches operate as – to use the corporate term – franchises. That is the way pastors become wealthy: by diversifying their income, first by opening branches in different parts of the country, the continent and the world, and then by signing TV deals and through books, and CD and DVD sales. And how can I forget money that, in recent times, is made through people accessing content online?

The irony of the whole thing, where churches rake in millions, is that it is sometimes (or is it mostly?) the poorest of the poor who take their last cents to give to the church. I have since concluded that I must stop questioning how people spend their hard-earned money because I also hate it when someone questions me why I spend my money on wine, whisky, brandy, gin, rum, beer, liqueur, cognac ...

If we talk about religion and power, the pinnacle of that must be the Vatican. At least, that is the view of the late Italian writer and historian Avro Manhattan. The Catholic Church, as at the end of 2020, had about 1.4 billion members, which equates to about 17 per cent of the total world population. Manhattan's book *The Vatican Billions: Two thousand years of wealth accumulation from St Peter to the Space Age* (Paravision Books, 1982) tells how the Catholics inherited riches from the Roman Empire, and how today it owns prime real estate and shares of multinational corporations.

Another Manhattan book, *The Vatican in World Politics* (Gaer Associates, 1949), talks explicitly about how over time the church has dabbled in global politics. If, as a global citizen, you are keen on getting different perspectives in order to comprehensively understand the world you live in today, read Avro Manhattan's books.

In recent years, a number of articles have reported on how some pastors take worshipping to another level. One of those is Lesego Daniel, who ordered his congregation to eat grass in order to be closer to God. I wonder if the grassy means justified the godly end.

Some time later a 'prophet', Lethebo Rabalago, made headlines when it emerged that he would spray his congregants with Doom insect killer, insisting that it would heal them of their afflictions. He was subsequently found guilty of assault.

Soon thereafter, pastor Christ Penelope made headlines when a photo was leaked that showed him sitting on a person's face (none of the people in the photo were naked). This pastor claimed that his farts had healing powers.

And how can we forget Penuel Mnguni, a prophet who fed his

congregants snakes, claiming they would turn into chocolates? On another Sunday, he fed his followers dog meat as communion.

Seemingly not to be outdone, Light Monyeki fed his congregants rat poison, insisting that none would die because, he said, 'death has no power over us'. Well, as far as I know, no-one died. Maybe death indeed has no power over prophet Monyeki's congregants.

Stories like these, where people, for whatever reason, are willing to believe anything reminds me of a quote from the late American comedian George Carlin, who said, 'Think of how stupid the average person is, and realise half of them are stupider than that.'

(Another quote, by the way, by George Carlin that really – I mean really – hit me was 'Governments don't want an intelligent population because people who can think critically can't be ruled. They want a public just smart enough to pay taxes and dumb enough to keep voting and electing corrupt politicians.')

This phenomenon, where some pastors take advantage of gullible people, is not restricted to South Africa. There was a video, supposedly taken in Ghana, that went viral a few years ago in which a female pastor asked congregants to get holy milk from her breasts. The video shows a man eagerly waiting to get as much holy milk as possible as the pastor is loosening her bra. In front of the excited and jubilant congregation, the poor guy (who surely must have been sick and indeed required divine intervention) could not help himself. I can only imagine that he must have been thinking, *God works in mysterious ways.*

As someone who was born and grew up in rural areas, I have always been aware of the power held by traditional leaders. But somehow, because of living in the big city, we tend to almost forget this fact of life. Is it not strange how sometimes death makes us see things in perspective?

Remember how the passing (correct term 'ukukhothama kweNgonyama') of Zulu King Goodwill Zwelithini kaBhekuzulu brought to the fore not only how rich the Zulu culture is but also the power that such a person has? Due to the Covid-19 restrictions at the time, there were limits on the number of people who could gather for funerals but, regardless, thousands gathered at the palace during the memorial service, which was also attended by the president. But hey, who was counting people?

Seeing this, I thought, imagine if the King had passed on when there were no restrictions whatsoever? Then the true power of traditional leadership would have been showcased for the world to see.

Another incident, which is even more personal, highlighted for me the power of traditional leaders. On 31 May 2022, my cousin Inkosi Stevenson Khumbulani Sithole passed away after a really short illness. It was speculated that he had been poisoned. What amazed me, during his funeral, was the number of warriors who attended. It was, for lack of a better term, with all respect to my departed cousin, a spectacle to be cherished. I had never been in the company of so many warriors singing in harmony. As we say in Zulu, amabutho ayeviliyela! It was something to marvel at.

What struck me was the power of izinduna (headmen) who are leaders of these people from different villages.

The fact that at this funeral we never saw the coffin nor the grave being dug, because amakhosi (chiefs) get buried only at night, is a conversation for another day.

In Zulu we have a proverb that sometimes we conveniently forget: inkosi ayiphikiswa. Literally, it means you cannot argue with the chief. In other words, it means the chief (yes, the chief – we are not even talking about the king here) is always right. Imagine the power of a person who has a birthright to be always right.

Exactly a year before his passing, I visited my cousin in Qhudeni in KwaZulu-Natal. He spent less time with us and more time dealing with his subjects – community members who brought him their disputes and squabbles. This is something that city slickers are not aware of or tend to ignore: how amakhosi are forever dealing with issues between spouses, family members, villages, clans. It never ends.

Just as in towns and cities it is accepted that legal recourse is through the courts, where magistrates and judges can preside over matters, in rural areas some community members approach inkosi. Without such a traditional mechanism, some of these disputes would in time escalate and lead to violence.

Although, through our constitution, the traditional system is recognised and catered for, part of me still thinks that traditional leaders get the short end of the stick. As a country we still, I think, have to find an optimal way to ensure that, notwithstanding our form of government being a constitutional democracy, our traditional leaders get the respect, honour and dignity they deserve. Is it fair, really, that local ward councillors in rural areas sit there and twiddle their thumbs, because they are hardly recognised by these rural communities, and instead the chiefs and izinduna continue with what they have been doing for years, because the people subject themselves to the traditional system, as they have been doing for centuries? Could it be that some of the modern social ills are as a result, partly, of letting go of some of the well-established community/social structures – including traditional leadership – which ensured stability, bonding and coherence in the neighbourhoods amongst the people? Why are we warming up to an idea that land, even in rural areas, must be sold as a private commodity? Do we, black people, have to forsake everything in the name of the so-called progress and civilisation?

In 2017, the government tried to consolidate the power and recognition of traditional leaders through the Traditional Courts Bill but at the time of writing, notwithstanding approval by parliament, the president had not signed it into law. There were some indications that the minute it becomes law, it will be challenged all the way to the Constitutional Court. One of the key issues is that the Bill wants to take away the right of any person to choose whether they will be subject to a traditional court or not. It is felt that the Bill takes away the right of any individual to opt out of appearing at a traditional court; and traditionalists have countered that common-law courts do not have the opt-out clause. Once you are summoned by a magistrate's court or the High Court, you have no choice but to appear (everything being equal). But then, the counter-argument is that common-law courts have checks and balances, including legal representation and appeals, whereas traditional courts do not. As stated before, inkosi ayiphikiswa!

The question must be asked: what are the odds that one day this piece of land at the southern tip of Africa will be ruled, as it has been in the past, exclusively by kings and queens? One day, will democracy fail us to the extent that some among us will opt, instead of voting, for the traditional system, where an heir (a first-born child, sometimes a son, of the main wife/uNdlunkulu) becomes our leader?

Chapter 14
THE MASSES

There is nothing significant to report here.

I mean it.

If the masses had power – real power – and black people had not been indoctrinated into accepting the crumbs, the government would never have approved the R350 grant scheme (read: an insult to the very powerless masses) as part of the Covid-19 'social relief of distress' plan.

'The bewildered herd must be governed by a specialised class whose interests reach beyond the locality.' – Walter Lippmann (1889–1974), American author, journalist and political commentator.

PART III

Ama-Reflections: Let us pause and ponder

'Whenever you find yourself on the side of the majority,
it is time to pause and reflect.'
Mark Twain (1835–1910), American writer

PART III.

Final Reflections: Let us pause and ponder

Whenever you find yourself on the side of the majority,
it is time to pause and reflect.
Mark Twain (1835–1910), American writer

Chapter 15

WHEN DID THE FEEDING FRENZY ON STATE RESOURCES BEGIN?

When did the feasting start?

The first wildly publicised case was that of Willem Adriaan van der Stel, Simon van der Stel's son. In the 1700s he was accused by the independent farmers known as the free burghers – former Dutch East India Company employees – of using the company's resources to improve his wine estate, Vergelegen. The free burghers were so incensed by his behaviour that they officially complained to the head office in Amsterdam. Although initially cleared, Van der Stel was finally dismissed and had to leave the colony.

Back in the Netherlands, he was cold-shouldered by society despite being loaded with stacks of cash and writing a book, *Korte Deductie* (Short Explanation), which contained a refutation of the various charges as well as extracts from official records of every kind, designed to establish his innocence. He died an isolated man, aged 69.

Vergelegen was subsequently subdivided and, over the years, the farm changed hands a number of times. Since 1987 Anglo American has owned it, and as noted earlier in this book, Nelson Mandela, immediately after his release from prison in February 1990, visited the wine farm for a celebratory and ceremonious luncheon.

Simon van der Stel, Willem's father, was allocated an area in modern-day Constantia in Cape Town's southern suburbs in 1685, on which he developed the country's first wine farm. Are we to believe that Van der Stel Snr did all the work himself, and did not use the company's resources – especially employees on the lower rungs of the corporate ladder – to, as and when required, work the land? Were the tools and equipment used on this wine farm his personal property? And didn't he sell the produce of his farm back to the very company he was heading locally? For all we know, Willem learnt from his father that there is a grey area between company and family resources.

Over the centuries, besides just the obvious feasting, there has been exploitation of situations and circumstances by colonialists. These include the grabbing of millions of hectares of land, the use of cheap black labour, the taking of livestock (which, besides land, represent black families' wealth), and, of course, the picking of women as and when the body was craving something different or 'exotic'.

The Lie of 1652: A decolonised history of land (NB Publishers, 2020) by Patric Tariq Mellet is but one of several recently published books that question the narrative of Europeans having arrived in a Cape that was 'empty land'. The author asserts that the glorification of 1652 is wrong and factually incorrect, because locals had been dealing with seafarers for almost two hundred years before Jan van Riebeeck landed in South Africa on that autumn day.

The 'empty land' narrative, which was cemented officially by history books at schools and universities, is, in essence, what makes the descendants of the European settlers comfortable, sometimes even arrogant, on the question of land, because it means that their forefathers committed no crime. They conclude, wrongly, that land was not taken from anyone. Botlhale Tema's book title sums it up: *Land of my Ancestors* (Penguin Random House, 2019).

The land issue is one matter that we as a country, because it is difficult to resolve, have dismally failed to address. Tembeka Ngcukaitobi's book, *Land Matters: South Africa's failed land reforms and the road ahead* (Penguin Random House, 2021), besides also showing that black African people owned land, suggests practical solutions. Another legal eagle, Bulelwa Mabasa, recently penned her memoir, *My Land Obsession* (Picador Africa, 2022), in which she too gives pragmatic suggestions about what needs to be done. But nobody seems to be listening, as the time bomb keeps ticking …

Two weeks after the July 2021 insurrection, the *Washington Post* described our 'celebrated rainbow nation' as 'the global poster child of economic inequality, where deep poverty sits in the shadow of astronomical wealth. What happened in South Africa is what happens when the gross inequality that shapes a whole society boils over.' But nobody seems to be listening, as the time bomb keeps ticking …

Rogues' Gallery: An irreverent history of corruption in South Africa, from the VOC *to the* ANC by Matthew Blackman and Nick Dall (Penguin Random House, 2021) chronicles, albeit with a fair share of satire, some of the key rogue individuals who have occupied very senior political positions in our country. These are people who, through dubious activities, have milked the country dry.

I strongly recommend this book, especially because it challenges the mainstream narrative that goes out of its way to ignore shenanigans that happened before 1994 and thus create or maintain the mindset that says 'whites are incorruptible, while when it comes to corruption, blacks cannot be saved'. Reading it might lead you to admit that we have always been led by rogues.

As an example, on the issue of state capture, the authors' perspective is refreshing: 'The South African state was effectively captured during the peak of the Broederbond years. The Broeders shifted government contracts to their mates, packed the courts with their judges, changed the constitution to serve their needs, and ran bogus commission after commission, the findings of which were not worth the polyester safari suits of the men who wrote them.'

It is a highly appreciated joint effort by Blackman and Dall. The only gripe I have, and I am sure it is just me, is how do I trust a white man with the surname Blackman? (I wonder if he has a wife. If yes, she is Mrs Blackman. This reminds me of a woman I once met whose surname was Mycock …)

There are other individuals who were not regarded as rogues, and perhaps rightfully so, but in retrospect it is clear that there were glaring conflicts of interest. For example, take Sir Joseph Benjamin Robinson, whom we have already met in this book. Thirteen years after the discovery of diamonds, and after making a fortune in that commodity, he became the mayor of Kimberley, in 1880. Here was one of the richest individuals in the country, making his money from the biggest industry at the time, and yet he was citizen number one in the city where he was making his fortune.

The same could be said for Cecil John Rhodes when he became prime minister of the Cape Colony. Did or didn't Rhodes use his company to capture the state? Didn't Rhodes, as a shrewd businessman, ensure that he directed government business to his own company? Didn't the business mogul in the process become the state?

Paul Kruger, together with his private secretary, Frederik Christoffel Eloff, who also happened to be his son-in-law, did business with the government. He organised the government to, among other things, construct a road to his house.

In recent times, there were four instances in which, depending on who you talk to, feasting on state resources went into overdrive.

The first occurred in the mid-1980s and was kickstarted by the talks between the apartheid government and the leaders of the liberation movements. Although a vast majority of these talks, by their nature, were secretive, word soon got around. You may even call it rumours and gossip. The minute that happened, some (I am tempted to say most, if not all) white people in positions of power who could get their hands into the fiscus's cookie jar did exactly that.

The Dakar Conference, held in Senegal in July 1987, where ANC leaders met with mainly dissident Afrikaner leaders, and which was not a secret, made it clear that it was only a matter of time before black people would run South Africa, at least politically. The conference thus made some white people very uncomfortable. This must be understood in the context that nobody knew what the new South Africa with black people in power was going to bring – hence the need for white South African business people, politicians and government officials to feather their nests, not just for themselves, but for their children, grandchildren, great-grandchildren ...

The second period during which the feasting reached astronomical levels was after the unbanning of political parties and the release of political prisoners in 1990. It was clear from that moment that it was not a matter of if but when black people would govern the country. The stress levels for some were sky high, and so was the looting.

In Sampie Terreblanche's 2012 book *Lost in Transformation*, he states categorically that during FW de Klerk's tenure 'from 1989 until 1994, government deficit increased from R91.2 billion to R237 billion [2012 figures]. We can regard this outrageous increase in the public debt as part of reckless "plundering" in the final years of white supremacy and, therefore, as another example of Afrikaner/white corruption.'

Thinking out loud: If a judicial commission of inquiry into misappropriation of state funds had been set up in the post-1994 era to look into the administrations of PW Botha (1984 to 1989) and FW de Klerk (1989 to 1994), I wonder what type of smallanyana skeletons (if any) would have been found.

However, generally speaking, some among us pretend, conveniently, that there was no fraud, corruption, money laundering and racketeering before 1994. It is almost as if, mysteriously, such crimes are the preserve of and can only be committed by black people.

The two big feasting events in the new South Africa were the arms deal and Covid-19. Let me, however, first deal with two programmes that siphoned huge money from the state but somehow managed to, by and large, remain under the radar.

The first one was the taxi recapitalisation programme. I remember this one clearly because of the conversation I had with my late friend Sfiso 'Bru' Sibisi (RIP) at our favourite watering hole, Jack Rabbits, in Glenwood, Durban, around the mid-2000s. He asked me if any of my family members were in the taxi industry. The answer was no. A few weeks later, in passing, he asked again. And again I said no.

Later on that month, he asked for the third time. By then, I had to enquire why he was so interested if any of my family members were in the taxi industry. His response went something like this: 'Look, Sihle, there is a programme where government pays you off for your old taxi and, in the process, helps you buy a new taxi. Basically, government is helping the taxi industry modernise its fleet. But here is the thing: with the right connections, you only need one old taxi. You take it there, they scrap it, and you get your money. Except that you take the same taxi, which is supposed to be scrap, for it to be scrapped again. And again. And again. And again. By the time you are done, you could have four new taxis for the price of that one old one.'

After ordering another round of our favourite beverages, he continued. I was now, I must admit, eager to learn how things worked in the real world.

'There are a number of people involved. Some of the officials from the Department of Transport are obviously on the take, and so are the police, because scrapped vehicles get taken to the pound.'

It is such a pity Sfiso passed away before any of my family members moved into the taxi industry. I wonder if I should relay this information to the relevant family members now, just in case, in future, there is a taxi recapitalisation project reloaded.

The second instance that involved the milking of state resources but somehow did not get the angry attention it deserved was the 2010 FIFA World Cup stadiums price-fixing saga. Long after Spain had won the cup, information emerged that construction companies had colluded. It transpired that executives from the country's largest construction and engineering companies had decided, first, which firm was going to win which bid and, second, that a 17.5 per cent profit margin was what they should aim for. (To put things into perspective, the average profit margin in the construction sector in 2009 was five per cent, in 2011 it was 2.8 per cent, and in 2020 it was 2.2 per cent.)

Therefore, practically, there was no competition between them. It was all fixed.

Another way of looking at this is that the Nelson Mandela stadium in Gqeberha was built for R2 billion, and the Moses Mabhida stadium in Durban cost R3.4 billion. This translates into profits of about R350 million and R600 million, respectively. Cape Town Stadium cost R4.5 billion; that means a whopping R797 million profit.

The competition commission fined all fifteen firms involved a total of R1.5 billion – about R100 million per company. And we all moved on. No criminal charges were laid. There was no judicial commission of inquiry. There was no proclamation for the Special Investigative Unit to dig deeper into this fiasco.

If you consider that, first, this was the first time the FIFA World Cup was being hosted by an African country, South Africa was indeed hosting on behalf of all other African states. Failure to deliver, for whatever reason, would have embarrassed not just us South Africans but the whole continent.

Second, without the stadiums, there would have been no World Cup. It was as simple as that. Therefore, the executives of this handful of construction companies knew that they had the country – in fact, the entire continent – by the balls. We totally depended on them. That is why they wanted a blank cheque, and they got it. In other countries people who were to try such a stunt, and who were caught, would be charged with treason.

The reason these construction companies got away with it is, I think, because of BEE. This needs a bit of context. Big construction companies get a sizeable chunk of their revenue from government infrastructure plans. Construction companies, like all other companies that want to take part in the state procurement system, need – among other things – good BEE ratings. But, as mentioned, the way BEE was implemented in this country leaves a lot to be desired. That explains why a vast majority of signed BEE deals (i.e., those that gave away a smallanyana part of their shareholding) were with black politicians and/or politically connected individuals who were then termed 'empowerment partners'.

The billion-dollar question, therefore, is how could the government effectively deal with (for example, blacklist) construction companies when the ruling party's senior leaders were shareholders and beneficiaries of the price-fixing scandal?

And now to the Strategic Defence Package, or 'arms deal'. This was a multibillion-rand military acquisition, from Germany, the UK, Italy and Sweden, and the first major foray of the ANC into the world of multibillion-rand tenders.

Just to keep things in perspective, in 1987, the apartheid government spent about R54 billion, or 4.2 per cent of the country's budget, on defence. For the sake of comparison, according to Treasury, the defence budget for 2022/23 year was R49 billion, or 2.4 per cent of the total budget. The 1990s arms deal was worth US$4.8 billion (about R238 billion in today's money).

Now, take a moment to think about the state of the country in 1994. There had been decades – in fact, centuries – of underinvestment in black areas. The apartheid government had spent ten times more on white learners than on black African learners. Infrastructure in 'native' areas was, thanks to the bantustan system, inadequate at best. Health facilities left a lot to be desired for the majority of South Africans. But, even given all that, the ANC government, with Mandela at the helm, decided that the administration was going to spend billions buying arms.

Let us ignore for a second or three the allegations about kickbacks to some politically connected people. Let us rather talk about the actual decision to buy, of all things, arms. At the time, all our neighbours in the southern African region were happy that we were 'free at last'. The Cold War was over, the iron curtain had fallen, communism had been defeated and capitalism had won the day.

Could it be that the arms deal was actually not about arms per se? Could it be that it was, from the start, about kickbacks? Could it be that at the time it was the official way for some leaders to get a head start, to 'catch up' financially, after being in exile or in jail or both?

The justification was, I imagine, 'We will not be stealing taxpayers' money because the kickbacks will be from the arms contractors.'

I can picture a conversation in the 1990s between some senior leaders as they were sipping exclusive single-malt whisky. 'Comrades! Off the record, comrades! We need money. Loads of money. Look, we are ministers but we are broke. Some of us are already in our late fifties and we have just bought our first property. We don't have any investments. Only now have we started contributing to a pension fund. It is a mess. Comrades! Off the record, we need money. Loads of money. We also need money, by the way, to fund the movement, our movement – for the long term'

'Agreed, comrade, but how?'

'We must identify one massive thing that the government must spend millions – in fact, billions – on.'

'I see, comrade. How about nuclear?'

'Don't be stupid! We have so much power in this country already. How will we justify it to our people?'

'I see, comrade. How about a massive infrastructure programme?'

'Nah, it will be way too cumbersome, comrade. There will be too many players involved. Even the small schemers will want to get in on the action. No. We need something big, where we can deal with the big boys, internationally.'

'I see, comrade. How about an arms deal?'

'Now you are talking! But, eish, how will we justify buying arms when it is clear, thanks to black power, that we are now friends with all our neighbours?'

'Don't worry, comrade. We can sell the arms deal to our people by talking about offsets. Trust me, comrade. The word "offsets" will confuse the living daylights out of them. It will be a spin, hot air. They will fall for it. In any case, come to think about it, they are still happy that they voted for the first time, thanks to us leading the struggle. They are still happy that the Springboks won the World Cup, and they are over the moon that Bafana Bafana won the Africa Cup of Nations. Now, on top of all of that, let's give them offsets.'

'Remember, comrades, all of this is off the record. Let us all stand as we toast the imminent arms deal!'

The government did not need a spin doctor to sell the benefits of the arms-deal ruse because – and you can quote me on this – some, I am tempted to say most, South Africans are gullible and highly susceptible to bullshit.

In his brutally blunt and uncompromisingly frank book, *Eye on the Diamonds* (Penguin Random House, 2012), retired banker Terry Crawford-Browne writes, 'Foreign politicians – but especially British politicians and even Queen Elizabeth – flocked to South Africa after 1994 to pay tribute to Nelson Mandela and our new democracy with one hand, and to peddle weapons with the other. The royal yacht *Britannia*, when docked in Cape Town harbour for the Queen's visit in March 1995, also doubled as a floating British armaments industry exhibition ... The urgent needs of South Africans for poverty eradication were deemed secondary ... Huge bribes were paid with deliberate British government connivance to unleash a culture of corruption to subvert a young and immature democracy.'

It must not be forgotten that the government, ever so reluctantly, eventually approved the investigation of the arms deal through a judicial commission. There was a general sense, after the report was released, that the entire investigation had been a whitewash. As renowned (Jewish) author Ayn Rand put it in her book *Atlas Shrugged* (Random House, 1957), 'When you see that men get richer by graft and by pull than by work, and your laws don't protect you against them, but protect them against you – when you see corruption being rewarded and honesty becoming a self-sacrifice – you may know that your society is doomed.'

Except that if I were to paraphrase this quote, it would be, 'If the judges protect the guilty, your country is fucked.'

The arms deal was not the first time, however, that comrades, at best, turned a blind eye to fraud and corruption. Remember earlier in this book, when we learnt how Bantu Holomisa had told the Truth and Reconciliation Commission in 1996 about how a senior ANC leader had taken money from a businessman who wanted a licence to develop his casino and hotel on the Wild Coast in the then Transkei? Remember how, soon thereafter, then President Mandela fired Holomisa as the deputy minister of environment and tourism? Remember how, two months later, the ANC fired Holomisa for bringing the party into disrepute?

Imagine if the ANC had investigated and swiftly dealt with allegations of fraud and corruption among its senior leader(s) there and then.

It is convenient for some amongst us to talk about the alleged Jacob Zuma corruption but things are much more complicated than some of us want to admit.

Still on complicated matters, it came out during the Shabir Shaik corruption trial that Nelson Mandela had given Zuma R2 million. A cool two million! The South African media never asked a very pertinent question then: where did Mandela get the money from?

*

257

Most recently, Covid-19 became an avenue for the state to be milked for the umpteenth time. And what hurts the most about the Covid-19 corruption is that many of us lost loved ones due to the pandemic.

While we were concerned about our future, while our movements were restricted during lockdown, some among us were scheming how to lay their hands on the loot.

There is a delusion that says fraud, corruption, money laundering, racketeering and so on only happen in the public sector. Nothing could be further from the truth. As mentioned – and this is public knowledge – the construction companies that built the FIFA World Cup stadiums colluded in order to maximise their profits. Not to be outdone, the private pathology laboratories creamed it for about twenty months at the height of the pandemic.

In December 2021, the competition commission reached an out-of-court settlement with the country's two largest private pathology laboratories, Ampath and Lancet, in which it was agreed that prices would be decreased immediately by more than forty per cent, from R850 to R500 per test. The third-largest company, Pathcare, a few days later also agreed to lower its price to R500. (Thinking out loud: is it not still price fixing if the top three biggest private laboratories charge exactly the same amount for their service?)

Any way you look at it, these private pathology laboratories got away with it. There was no criminal investigation, no media frenzy about how whenever we went for Covid testing, we ended up being screwed.

We all simply and quietly stood in another queue, to be tested for another variant.

As I was finalising this book, the competition commission raided the offices of the country's biggest eight insurers for allegedly colluding on premiums to charge consumers. And while we are at it, the banks look like a logical next chapter, I say. And, dear competition commissioners, please do not forget to look into telecommunication firms and have another look at medical-aid companies and airlines and ...

On the public-sector side, the fiscus was cleaned out thanks to Covid-19. There has been so much focus on corruption almost exclusively in personal protective equipment that you would think contracts for other services and products procured in the name of the disease were squeaky clean.

But think of the millions spent unnecessarily on 'deep cleaning' and 'sanitisation' of schools, even after the Department of Health had made it clear that this was not required. How about field hospitals that were half built and then dismantled but service providers still claimed all the money? What about the stealing of food parcels or money earmarked for food parcels as part of the Covid relief fund? And how about fraud at the Unemployment Insurance Fund where, it was reported in the media, government employees, minors, the deceased and the imprisoned successfully lodged claims?

Why hasn't the state, if it is serious about fighting corruption, instituted a judicial commission of inquiry into all the shenanigans pertaining to the Covid-19 pandemic? Could it be that, as noted, if sweeping things under the carpet was a sport, South Africa would get a gold medal every four years? Is the ruling party hiding the fact that some, if not most, comrades plundered state coffers during the pandemic, thus turning that global period of fear and misery into a plandemic?

Or is it because, with the 2024 elections looming, the ruling party cannot afford to have (yet another) judicial commission of inquiry, and thus risk having some its leaders exposed as fraudsters and crooks day after day, week after week, live on national television?

This episode reminds me of a quote from George Orwell's

1949 dystopian novel *1984*: 'The party told you to reject the evidence of your eyes and ears. It was their most essential final command.'

Is the current leadership following in the footsteps of Willem Adriaan van der Stel?

Chapter 16

PONDERING THE ANC ELECTIVE CONFERENCES OF 2007, 2012 AND 2017

At the ANC's 1991 conference – its first after being banned for thirty years – Walter Sisulu was elected deputy president to Nelson Mandela. At the time, it was clear that whoever deputised for Mandela would in all probability eventually succeed the old man (who was 73 at the time) as the president of both the ANC and the Republic.

Rumours have always done the rounds that both Thabo Mbeki and Chris Hani, who was also the secretary-general of the South African Communist Party (SACP), were gunning for the deputy presidency: both had been nominated and both had accepted their nomination.

The ANC, especially the elders, were concerned about leaders slugging it out for positions. It was felt, this narrative continues, that while no-one was against internal democracy, the party, which was going through the rebuilding process after its unbanning, could not afford to have factions. But no agreement could be reached with regard to who, Mbeki or Hani, should stand down. It was in that context, the tale concludes, that both were asked to stand down, and that Sisulu (who was then 79, and who apparently had made it clear that he did not want to stand for any position) was asked to stand unopposed for the position.

Two years later, in April 1993, Hani was assassinated. Right-wingers were arrested, convicted and sentenced for the crime.

A year later, in May 1994, Mbeki was sworn in as the deputy president of the Republic of South Africa.

It has been documented by various authors that Mandela, aware that a perception might be created that the ANC preferred Xhosas for senior leadership positions, named Cyril Ramaphosa as his deputy, but that some other influential elders wanted Mbeki, who had been mentored for years by OR Tambo, who had passed away the previous year.

What also worked in Mbeki's favour, because he'd lived in London and Lusaka, was that he was well known internationally and, let's not forget, he had a master's degree in economics. By contrast, Ramaphosa, a lawyer and trade unionist, had been in South Africa the whole time. He stood no chance. The international community is, make no mistake, always a key stakeholder in different countries' big decisions, including succession races.

In any case, Ramaphosa was still relatively young in 1994. He was just 42. Imagine if, as per his original plan, he had suc-ceeded Mandela; it would have meant he would have been deputy president from 1994 to 1999, then president from 1999 to 2009, after which – as the constitution only allows for two five-year terms – he would have had to retire, aged 57. Talk about not knowing what to do with the rest of your life! (Of course, he could have gone on to do other stuff but, let's face it, it's all an anticlimax, I imagine, when you have experienced being citizen number one.)

Ramaphosa's age, at the time, could explain why he acted so childishly. After failing to be in line to succeed Madiba, he was angry. He was so pissed off, in fact, that he did not even attend Mandela's historic inauguration. He also turned down an offer to be the minister of foreign affairs (now international relations and cooperation).

Such behaviour, irrespective of age, can never be justified. He was behaving like a spoilt brat who throws his toys out of the pram when things are not going his way.

There is, by the by, a narrative that says Ramaphosa was mandated by the ANC to make money so that he could donate a certain portion to the movement. The biggest risk, it was reasoned, was that the party would always be begging for funding from white-owned big business, which in turn would use the fact of these donations to try to influence policy. Therefore, this narrative concludes, the story that Ramaphosa was angry and turned down an offer to join the executive arm of government was a smokescreen. His venture into business was all part of a long-term plan, and that explains why, after fulfilling his obligation of making money and donating religiously to the party, he was duly rewarded with the organisation's deputy presidency in 2012.

Let's go back to 1994, which must have been a great year for Thabo Mbeki. He was sworn in as the deputy president of the country, and he was elected unopposed as the deputy president of the ANC. Remember that: unopposed.

Three years later, in 1997, Mbeki was elected president of the ANC, also unopposed. Remember that too: unopposed.

It was at this 1997 conference that it was resolved, among other things, that conferences should be held every five years. So, five years later, in 2002, in Stellenbosch, Thabo Mbeki, who had by that stage also been the president of the Republic for three years, was re-elected president of the ANC, unopposed. Remember that as well: unopposed.

In 2005 Mbeki fired Zuma as the deputy president of the country after Zuma was linked to alleged wrongdoing in the arms deal.

Fast-forward another couple of years, and you end up at the 2007 Polokwane conference, and the first time Mbeki had to slug it out against another candidate. And it was not just any other contender, it was Jacob Gedleyihlekisa Mhlanganyelwa Zuma.

In 1994, Zuma had won convincingly (with 77.6 per cent) when he was vying for the chairmanship of the party against Pallo Jordan (who got 11.8 per cent) and Jeff Radebe (10.5 per cent). And Zuma had been elected, unopposed, as deputy president at both the 1997 and 2002 conferences.

We all know what happened in Polokwane in 2007. Mbeki's faction lost all top six of the contested positions. (The ANC's national executive committee is headed by the president of the party, with the other top six leaders being the deputy president, the chairperson, the secretary-general, the deputy secretary-general and the treasurer-general.) What also helped Zuma's cause was the fact that he was endorsed by the SACP and the Congress of South African Trade Unions (Cosatu).

Nine months later, Mbeki was 'recalled' by the ANC as president of the country, but for the fiasco to work in terms of our constitution, he had to officially resign from this position.

It was a messy business that would haunt the ANC for a very long time.

Rev. Frank Chikane, who was the director-general in the presidency and secretary to the cabinet during Mbeki's era, subsequently wrote a book, *Eight Days in September: The removal of Thabo Mbeki* (Picador Africa, 2012). It gives a blow-by-blow account of what happened during those handful of days that ended with Mbeki submitting his resignation. The Reverend stops whimsically short of calling the whole fiasco a coup d'état.

Well, what goes around, comes around. Zuma, within two months of completing his second term as ANC president in December 2017, resigned as the president of the Republic the day before he was to face his umpteenth vote of no confidence in parliament. He knew he was going to lose this one, and he decided to quit in order to secure his benefits, including a salary and paid-for security for life.

It is safe to assume that it is difficult, to say the least, for an ANC president to serve two full terms as the president of the country. We wait to see if Ramaphosa will make it all the way to 2029.

Interestingly, Ace Magashule, who was elected ANC secretary-general at the Nasrec conference in 2017, penned a scathing open letter, out of the blue, in 2021, to Mbeki in which he wrote, 'The confusing mess of Cope [the Congress of the People] that ended up in four years of court drama is directly linked to the fact that you never came to occupy your reserved seat, leaving the surrogate mothers to fight forever. Comrade, you failed to condemn the breakaway because you could not since it had you as its raison d'etre.'

A political party, Cope had been formed by some of Mbeki's former colleagues, comrades and possibly friends after his recall in 2008. Patrick Mosiuoa 'Terror' Lekota was at the forefront of ten ministers who resigned en masse in that year, in protest at the ANC's actions.

It sounds straightforward but Magashule was right about one thing: it was chaotic. If you want to fully understand the confusion, backstabbing and gatekeeping that was prevalent during the formation of Cope, do yourself a favour and read *Misadventures of a Cope Volunteer: My crash course in politics* (Tafelberg, 2011) by Michiel le Roux. It gives a behind-the-scenes look into the confusion and disorder that ensued in Cope while some South Africans genuinely believed that the new political party was the future. No wonder Cope only managed less than eight per cent of the national vote (which got them thirty out of four hundred seats) in 2009. And it has been one way from there: in the 2014 and 2019 general elections, Cope got three and two seats, respectively.

I have often wondered if Cope was infiltrated. Otherwise, how do you explain that seemingly there was no coordinated effort on some of the basic things? The whole thing was so messy that the 2009 election campaign posters had Lekota's mugshot, as did the ballot paper, yet – horror of horrors – the presidential candidate was Bishop Mvume Dandala. You cannot make this stuff up. It was indeed a stuff-up of major proportions.

And soon thereafter there was a legal wrangle for the party presidency between Mosiuoa Lekota and Mbazima Shilowa. It took more than three years for the matter to be finalised by court judgment, and Lekota won; but the voters had long left. And they never returned.

In 2022, Lekota was suspended for 'lack of energy' and allegedly sowing division. He, in turn, suspended the faction of the leaders that had suspended him. A few days later, when he attempted to address members of the media, a scuffle broke out. I will be extremely surprised if Cope gets even a single seat in the 2024 general elections.

Another party, incidentally, that could have been infiltrated was the National Democratic Convention (Nadeco), which was formed in August 2005 by, among others, Ziba Jiyane, a former IFP chairperson. The following year, Jiyane was suspended by the party for misconduct. After a long legal dispute with another founding member, Rev. Hawu Mbatha, Jiyane left the party in 2007. The following year he formed the South African Democratic Congress (Sadeco). Everything, in time, fizzled out. When was the last time you thought or heard of Nadeco? My point exactly.

Another case where there might have been infiltration was that of the National Freedom Party. It was formed in 2011 by, among others, another former chair of the IFP, the late Zanele KaMagwaza-Msibi (RIP). In the 2014 general elections, it won six seats. Then, in 2016 – and this is where the possible infiltration comes in – its then treasurer completely forgot to pay the Independent Electoral Commission the required deposit and, as a result, the party was unable to contest the municipal elections. In the 2019 general elections, with 0.35 per cent of the vote, it could only garner two seats. As was the case with Nadeco, the National Freedom Party may in time fizzle out.

A question has to be asked: why did Thabo Mbeki stand for re-election as ANC president in 2007? He had, by then, been deputy president of the ANC for three years, from 1994 to 1997, and president for ten.

There are a number of possibilities. Let's look at two of them.

Could it be that Mbeki was going to be one of Africa's 'big men' who amend the constitution of the country in order to stay in power forever? Bear in mind that in the 2004 elections, the ANC had achieved more than 66 per cent of the vote, which is the threshold required to amend the constitution. Could it be, if Mbeki had won at Polokwane in 2007, that ANC members of parliament could have democratically amended the constitution to enable Mbeki to run for a third term as president of the Republic?

It sounds far-fetched but some of those presidents who eventually amended the constitution of their country started out as democrats, until they realised that serving a limited number of terms is, er, limiting. Isaias Afwerki, president of Eritrea, for example, started in 1993 as a democrat, and 29 years later, in 2022, is still at it. Exactly the same thing happened with Yoweri Museveni of Uganda: when he became president in 1986, he was seen as a democrat; in 2022, 36 years later, he is still running his fiefdom. Robert Gabriel Mugabe was Zimbabwe's president for 30 years (1987 to 2017) until he was ousted in a military coup.

There could be a number of reasons why some people are so power hungry. One of them, besides just greediness, is that with a loss of power comes possible investigations that could lead to prosecutions and eventually jail time. Another reason, psychologists tell us, is that people who hold on to power genuinely believe they are so great at what they are doing that no-one could possibly do a better job than them. They genuinely believe they are intellectually superior to everyone, so much so that no-one is worth being their successor. Hence the logical thing to do, they strongly believe, is to stay put. Forever.

Besides the possible amendment of the constitution in order to enable a third term as president of the country, could the reason why Mbeki stood for re-election as head of the ANC at Polokwane in 2007 be that, had he won, he would then have continued running the country from Luthuli House, the ANC headquarters? In all probability, whoever was the deputy president in the Mbeki faction, if we take this option to its logical conclusion, would have then ended up at face value succeeding Mbeki as president of the country. But Mbeki, the theory concludes, would, for all practical purposes, have continued running the country.

If this train of thought (Mbeki running the country from Luthuli House) has any merit to it, it means Nkosazana Dlamini Zuma would have, in all probability, been elected the president of the country in 2009. How so, you may ask. Nkosazana was the deputy-president candidate in the Mbeki faction at the 2007 Polokwane conference. Therefore, had Mbeki remained the president of the party post 2007, but been barred by the country's constitution for running for a third term as the president of the Republic post 2009, the second most senior person in the party would have been, logically speaking, deployed as the president of the Republic.

This boggles my mind: if Mbeki had had no intention of running the country from Luthuli House, then why did he contest the party elections in December 2007, knowing full well that in sixteen months' time (April 2009), as the constitution of the Republic dictates, he would have to yield to someone else as the president of the country?

This issue of why Mbeki stood for election in 2007 refuses to die down. As recent as 2022, retired newspaper editor Peter Bruce, writing in the *Sunday Times*, summed it up as 'Jacob Zuma might never have won the ANC leadership in 2007 had Mbeki stood aside and allowed in another candidate'.

One thing I have constantly asked myself is, why didn't Trevor

Manuel get a shot at any of the top six positions? In fact, the key question is, if Trevor Manuel had been born in, say, Gugulethu (read: if he had been of a particular race), would he have stood a better chance of being president of, first, the ANC, and eventually the Republic? Is it one of the unwritten rules, especially in recent times, that one race and one race only holds the monopoly on certain positions within the top six (now top seven) of the ANC?

Imagine if Mbeki had not stood for re-election at Polokwane. The Jacob Zuma and Nkosazana Dlamini Zuma factions may have then fought it out. Maybe the ANC would have had a female president in time for its centenary celebrations in 2012. Maybe we as a country would have had our first female president in 2009. If so, then Dlamini Zuma would have been Africa's second elected woman president, after Liberia's Ellen Johnson Sirleaf, who took the reins in her country in 2006.

Sirleaf's tenure, by the way, had its fair share of nepotism. One of her sons became chair of the National Oil Company of Liberia, while another acted for some time as interim executive governor of Liberia's central bank; and her stepson became the head of the national security agency. Talk about keeping it in the family ...

Another dilemma – and maybe this is just me obsessing about practical stuff – is, what if Phumzile Mlambo-Ngcuka, who was vying for the treasurer-general position in the Mbeki faction, had won? Bearing in mind that she had been appointed deputy president of the Republic in 2005, you would have thought she was a step closer to eventually occupying the highest office in the land. The problem there was that being treasurer-general is a full-time job. Therefore, if she had won, she would have had to be happy with a 'demotion' from being the second citizen of the country to the treasurer of a party. Talk about being a disciplined cadre of the movement!

I really hope that one day former president Mbeki will explain, perhaps in an autobiography, so that all the gossip, theories, what-ifs, assumptions and questions can be answered once and for all. In the meantime, let me gently sip on a single-malt whisky as I, and surely other people of the world, await the publication of what will no doubt be a poetically written book, in which the former president finally states, among other things, what he was thinking when he stood for re-election at the ANC's 2007 Polokwane conference.

And oh, while His Excellency is at it, it would be appreciated if he would include a chapter on Zimbabwe and another on HIV/Aids. With the benefit of hindsight, does Mbeki still think the 'quiet diplomacy' strategy that South Africa adopted towards Zimbabwe was the best option to deal with what other people saw as a mounting political and economic crisis in that country? And much has been written about Mbeki's inexplicable stance on the HIV/Aids issue, which included his refusal to listen to scientists, and a delayed antiretroviral rollout, leading to 300 000 deaths, and ultimately a court judgment that effectively forced the government to release a drug that prevented HIV-positive pregnant women from infecting their unborn babies.

Mbeki, officially opening the 13th International Aids Conference in Durban in 2000, noted that 'as Africans, we are confronted by a health crisis of enormous proportions'. 'It seemed to me that we could not blame everything on a single virus,' he went on. 'The world's biggest killer and the greatest cause of ill health and suffering across the globe, including South Africa, is extreme poverty.'

On that note, I might as well ask: given that tuberculosis (TB), that 'disease of the poor', killed about 58 000 people in the country in 2019 (according to Statistics South Africa), why don't we, as was the case with Covid-19, which killed 52 648 people in the same period, have daily rolling media coverage of TB infections and deaths? Why don't we talk about TB, which in 2018 accounted for 44 per cent of all deaths, or about 200 000 people? Why, I ask, is the biggest killer in our land not a daily topical issue?

Put differently: are poverty-related deaths not newsworthy?

And now, on to the 2012 conference.

Let us recap. In 1997 Kgalema Motlanthe was elected as secretary-general of the ANC, succeeding Cyril Ramaphosa, who was still pissed off at the time, and who, to that end, left the political stage in a huff after not having got the nod as Mandela's deputy for the country three years earlier. It was at that 1997 conference that Thabo Mbeki was elected president.

Motlanthe, like Mbeki, was re-elected in 2002 in Stellenbosch. Five years later, in 2007 at Polokwane, Motlanthe was elected deputy president of the ANC.

After Mbeki was recalled as the president of the country the following year, Motlanthe found himself warming the seat for Zuma.

However, there was this smallanyana thing that Zuma still had to deal with. Let's call it a hurdle. Just a smallanyana hurdle. He had been charged with fraud and corruption stemming from the arms deal, and still had those charges hanging over him. It was impossible for the ANC to go to elections with a presidential candidate who was facing criminal charges.

Just before the 2009 national elections, the acting national director of public prosecutions, advocate Mokotedi Mpshe, dropped all fraud and corruption charges against Zuma. Part of his reasoning for dropping the charges was, he said, that 'it is not so much the prosecution itself but the legal process that is tainted'. He was referring to a recorded phone call between Bulelani Ngcuka, national director of public prosecutions, and Leonard McCarthy, then head of the Scorpions, the nickname given to the independent agency that investigated organised crime and corruption, in which they discussed when exactly Zuma should be charged.

A few weeks later the ANC won the elections, albeit a few per centage points down from the previous election, and Zuma was inaugurated as the president of the Republic of South Africa.

As an aside, the national director of public prosecutions, advocate Vusi Pikoli, had been suspended by President Mbeki in 2007, but a subsequent inquiry found that the government had 'failed to prove' its allegations and had not demonstrated that Pikoli was no longer fit and proper to hold office. Motlanthe, by then the president of the republic, fired Pikoli anyway, and Pikoli was succeeded by advocate Mokotedi Mpshe, in an acting capacity. Pikoli challenged the termination of his employment contract, and a R7.5 million out-of-court settlement was reached literally on the stairs of the High Court.

(Another thing that happened during Motlanthe's presidency was, in accordance with a resolution taken at the 2007 Polokwane conference, the disbandment of the Scorpions. That independent multidisciplinary agency was clearly proving to be too independent for those in power.)

Now, imagine if Motlanthe had not fired Pikoli. We possibly would never have known advocate Mpshe, and there is a possibility that, in that case, Zuma's fraud and corruption charges would have stood. The big implication is that Zuma might have not ended up as president of the country, because although everyone is assumed innocent until proven guilty, really now, we could not have had a sitting president attending a court case. Zuma's ascension to power totally relied on all those charges being dropped, and that's what happened. Years later, the charges were eventually reinstated but by then Zuma had already been president for nine years.

After the 2009 general elections, Motlanthe, as the deputy president of the ANC, became the deputy president of the country. Do you remember the confusion after those elections about how much Motlanthe should be paid? The rule is clear: former presidents get their salaries until they die. Other people just love to make drama when there is none. FW de Klerk had gone through exactly the same thing: he was the last president of apartheid South Africa and, after the historic 1994 elections, he became deputy president to Nelson Mandela.

Leading up to the 2012 Mangaung conference, Julius Malema, who was the president of the ANC Youth League, had been over-stepping the line, and Jacob Zuma had to clip his wings. Malema at one stage had said he was willing to kill for Zuma, and months later Zuma had reciprocated by saying Malema had the potential to be the future president of the country. It all went to Malema's head, and he and Zuma had a public fallout. Malema was disciplined. The best of friends became the worst of enemies. Malema was fired by the ANC. He appealed.

The 2012 Mangaung conference took place against this back-ground: Malema on appeal, and hoping that whoever challenged Zuma would win so that he could be readmitted to the movement. After all, Malema is on record stating that his blood is black, green and gold.

At that 2012 conference, Motlanthe decided to challenge Zuma. Why?

It was at that point, four months after the Marikana massacre, that Cyril Ramaphosa found himself being handpicked to deputise for Zuma. It could have been almost anyone, and that individual would have won as deputy to Zuma. That is how powerful JZ was in 2012.

Zuma's faction, as had happened in Polokwane five years ear-lier, won 6–0.

Now, imagine if Motlanthe had defeated Zuma in 2012. Would Malema have been readmitted to the movement? And would that have meant that after the 2014 general elections, he would have been appointed a minister?

The biggest possible implication, if Zuma had been defeated at the 2012 conference and Malema reinstated in the ANC, is that there would be no EFF today. There would be no red overalls in parliament. Most of us would never have known a 'people's bae', Mbuyiseni Ndlozi. Our political lingo would not include 'pay back the money'. And parliament would still be a boring place with very bad TV ratings.

Imagine, again, if Motlanthe had not stood against Zuma in 2012 but had instead agreed to deputise for him, as he had done five years earlier at Polokwane. That would have meant that Motlanthe would have been the secretary-general of the ANC for ten years, from 1997 to 2007, and the deputy president of the ANC for the following decade, up to 2017. Had that been the case, there is no individual who would have stood a chance against Motlanthe at Nasrec in 2017. It would have been a foregone conclusion that he would have had to succeed Zuma.

Did the following two issues cloud Motlanthe's judgement? First, was his age a factor in his deciding not to wait any longer? He was born in 1949, so that meant he would have been president (again) in 2019 at the age of 70. That in itself was not so bad, if you consider that Mandela became president aged 76. (Zuma, for the record, was inaugurated in 2009 aged 67.)

Although age may have been a factor, could there have been another reason that made Motlanthe impatient? Could it have been the fact that he had tasted power? Could it be that the eight months he had spent as head of state had made him feel the sense of importance that, I can only imagine, comes with being in control of such levers of power? Is that how his judgement was clouded? Is that what made a seven-year wait (until 2019) feel like a lifetime?

There is another theory that says Motlanthe challenged Zuma (instead of being Zuma's deputy, as he had done five years earlier at Polokwane) in order to ensure that another person (Ramaphosa, in this instance) could deputise for Zuma and, in time, that person could take over as head of the ANC. Motlanthe, the narrative continues, knew he stood no chance of winning against Zuma in Mangaung, but it was just a strategic move. This explains why, this theory concludes, when the results were announced that Zuma had won convincingly, Motlanthe raised a victory sign, something that was captured by a press photographer and made it into a number of newspapers.

For this theory to be credible, Zuma's faction must have been infiltrated by people who were going to suggest their own guy – Ramaphosa – as the deputy president. Otherwise, with Motlanthe out of the way, Zuma could have just as easily co-opted another person as his deputy. And then the entire cookie, of making space for a specific individual who would in time challenge Zuma, would have crumbled.

So why did Motlanthe challenge Zuma in 2012?

Could it be that the two factors, of his relatively advanced age and that taste he'd had of real power, clouded his judgement? Or was it indeed to make way for Ramaphosa? Bear in mind that in 1991 Motlanthe had succeeded Ramaphosa as NUM secretary-general, and six years later, in 1997, Motlanthe had again succeeded Ramaphosa, this time as ANC secretary-general. So, in 2012, could it be that Motlanthe was paving the way for Ramaphosa to stand a better chance to be in line, in time to become the president of both the party and the country?

I hope that one day Mkhuluwa (the Elder One, the Wise One) will take us into his confidence and tell us why he challenged Zuma in 2012.

And now to the 2017 Nasrec conference.

What did Jacob Gedleyihlekisa Zuma think would happen when he eventually left the presidential stage? Could it be that JZ messed it all up, as far as his exit plan was concerned, at the 2012 Mangaung conference?

Let us look at the facts.

In 2012, Zuma was a very powerful person; politically speaking, he was the most powerful person in the country. He had been the president of the Republic for three years, since 2009, and was about to finish his first term as president of the ANC, a position he'd held since 2007.

What we did not know at the time – but do now, thanks to the Zondo Commission – was that he had access to information compiled by a parallel intelligence-gathering/spy structure. He was untouchable.

Also, bear in mind that he had been written off a number of times before, but had come back even stronger. In 2005 and 2006, some (I am tempted to say most, if not all) media groups ran editorials stating as a matter of fact that Zuma was a goner, that he would never be the president of the Republic. Besides editors and journalists, some (again, I am tempted to say most) political analysts stated publicly that it was all over for JZ. But, against the odds, Zuma survived it all.

The year 2005 must have been a very difficult one for him. His relationship with Shabir Shaik was found by a court of law to have been 'generally corrupt'. Shaik was sentenced to fifteen years in prison, and Zuma, who had not been charged, was fired by President Mbeki as the deputy president of the Republic. At the tail end of the same year, he was charged with rape. He was acquitted of those charges the following year.

In isiZulu we have a saying, 'Ukuhlehla kwenqama akusho ukuthi iyabaleka, isuke ilanda amandla': when someone is retreating, he is just taking a break in order to come back with more strength.

Zuma came back with a lot of amandla. Eighteen months after being fired by Mbeki, he ousted his nemesis at the ANC's watershed Polokwane conference, and less than eighteen months later, he was sworn in as the president of the Republic.

What a comeback!

(The biggest comeback, in recent times, that comes to mind is that of Benni McCarthy. He was fired as the coach of Amazulu FC, which had won only two major trophies in the past forty years – the last one in 1992 – and a few months later he was unveiled as part of the technical team of Manchester United in England.)

Back to JZ ... Could it be that after getting over so many hurdles, it was only natural that Zuma, as the president of the ruling party and of the country, felt that he could survive anything and everything? Did he feel untouchable? Did he feel invincible? And maybe, just maybe, people around him were telling him that, as such, his reign would last for a very long time.

Did Zuma pick a deputy whom he thought would never be able to challenge him for the top spot five years later?

As mentioned above, Motlanthe, who had been Zuma's deputy since Polokwane in 2007, was vying for the presidency, and this move must have made Zuma even more convinced of the importance of having a weak deputy who did not have a lot of support on the ground through the branches.

Enter Cyril Matamela Ramaphosa. He had been out of day-to-day politics for a while. ANC secretary-general until 1997, he had then spent the next fifteen years making billions of rands, thanks to BEE deals, in the private sector. It must be noted, however, that Ramaphosa had remained a member of the ANC's national executive committee even after 1997.

If Zuma had indeed been thinking about the ANC presidency without him post 2017, why didn't he ensure that his anointed successor became his deputy in 2012 in Mangaung? In other words, did Zuma undermine Ramaphosa? Didn't Zuma and his advisors undermine Ramaphosa by thinking that he had been out of the day-to-day running of politics for such a long time that he would have no base to challenge JZ in five years' time? In simple terms, was Zuma looking for a very weak deputy?

There could be some logical reason why Zuma was, while powerful, also paranoid. After all, three of the people who five years earlier had stood by his side at Polokwane were now in the faction that was challenging him. Motlanthe was taking Zuma head-on for the presidency. Mathews Phosa, who had been a member of the ANC's national executive committee since 1999, and had been elected treasurer-general at Polokwane, was now eyeing the deputy presidency. And Thandi Modise, who had become deputy secretary-general at Polokwane, had her eye on the chairship. That must have made Zuma realise – once again – that there are no permanent friends in politics.

There were others in Zuma's top six who could have been his deputy. The Zuma faction had Zweli Mkhize down as the treasurer-general. Mkhize had been the ANC chair in KwaZulu-Natal for more than a decade by then. Gwede Mantashe, meanwhile, had been secretary-general (read CEO) of the organisation since Polokwane. And Baleka Mbete had been elected chairperson at Polokwane and, more importantly, had in 2008 become deputy president to Motlanthe.

But these three, to a lesser or greater degree, had support of some sort on the ground that they could have used as a springboard to challenge Zuma in 2017, and in the position of his deputy Zuma wanted someone he thought weak. Could this have been the context in which Zuma and his advisors approved Ramaphosa – whom they thought of as an outsider – as the deputy president of the ANC in 2012?

From about 2014, things started changing.

The first massive scandal to hit the Zuma presidency was the revelation that millions of rands of taxpayers' money had been spent on renovating and upscaling JZ's private residence in Nkandla. A subsequent public protector's report on the matter found that he had not been entitled to the work, and she recommended that he pay back a portion of the funds used for the upgrades. The report was, however, set aside by the national assembly after Zuma made submissions on why he should not pay back the funds, after which the DA and the EFF (among others) took the matter to the Constitutional Court. A 2016 Constitutional Court ruling found that Zuma had 'failed to uphold, defend and respect the constitution', and should pay back the money.

From that moment on, the end was nigh.

By 2015, Zuma could feel the ground moving beneath his feet. Late that year, after firing finance minister Nhlanhla Nene and replacing him with a little-known backbencher called Des van Rooyen, he was literally instructed by business leaders to fire Van Rooyen, and then either reinstate Nene or appoint another, competent finance minister. Pravin Gordhan ended up getting the nod, while Van Rooyen has since been known as the 'Weekend Special', for the position he essentially occupied for a single weekend.

As an aside, not much attention was paid – especially by the mainstream media, #WeSeeYou – to the legality of a handful of business leaders telling, in fact instructing, the president who to appoint and who not to appoint. Our constitution is very clear in this regard: the president, and the president alone, hires and fires ministers. The reason for this intervention by business leaders, the mainstream media told us, was the economic implosion the country faced if nothing was done: upwards of R100 billion would have been lost by the South African economy if Van Rooyen had been allowed to stay.

What we did not know at the time, it must be added, was that Zuma was also getting shall we say 'recommendations' about who to hire and fire from the Gupta brothers at their Saxonwold compound.

Prior to the 2016 local government elections, Zuma was seen (rightfully so, because as president of the ANC and part of the collective leadership he had to concur with the decision) as behind the nomination of Thoko Didiza as the mayoral candidate for the Tshwane metropolitan council in Gauteng. There was an upheaval. Some people did not want anything to do with Didiza. There were strikes, marches and mayhem in the streets. Even tribalism came into the picture.

There was a narrative that said Zuma, a Zulu man originally from KwaZulu-Natal, was imposing Didiza, a Zulu woman originally from KwaZulu-Natal, on a city in which Pedis and Sothos (correctly, Bapedi and Basotho) made up almost 35 per cent of the population, compared to Zulus with less than nine per cent.

In those elections, the ANC lost a whopping 8.04 per cent of the general (nationwide) support. Even more importantly, the ANC lost three metropolitan councils – Tshwane, Johannesburg and Nelson Mandela Bay – to a coalition of opposition parties. (In the 2021 local government elections, the ANC lost 7.87 per cent of the vote nationally; Ramaphosa is also treading on thin ice. (Notwithstanding these results, the ANC re-elected Cyril for his second term as the president in its 55th conference in December 2022. The country, and the world, await the results of the 2024 general elections ...)

The tide was fast turning against Zuma. He was in crisis mode. The noose was tightening around his neck. He was a man under siege. He was panicking.

Surely, at the same time, some senior ANC members had already started talking to Ramaphosa about taking JZ head-on in 2017? And Ramaphosa did not need much convincing. He had unfinished business: he had always harboured presidential ambitions. His life plan was coming together nicely. The stars were aligned for Matamela to rise to the occasion. As young people say when a plan works perfectly, the combos were communicating for him.

For Zuma, notwithstanding his charm, song and dance, things were just not working out. There was no way he could stand for a third term as ANC president: his advisors surely told him so and, it is apparent, he listened. He had to find his anointed ANC presidential candidate, and fast – someone he would be very comfortable with. Only Zuma knows why he did not (again) trust any of the people in his top six, including Zweli Mkhize and Gwede Mantashe. He had to bring in someone from the outside.

To that extent, he felt he had some power left. Did he think that since he'd been able to organise a deputy presidency for Ramaphosa in 2012, he could do even better for Nkosazana Dlamini Zuma, and make her the president in 2017?

In 2012, Dlamini Zuma had been elected chair of the African Union Commission – the first woman to fill the role. The commission, which is based in Addis Ababa, Ethiopia, is the secretariat of the African Union, and undertakes the day-to-day activities of the union. There is a theory that says the reason why Dlamini Zuma was elected to the position had less to do with woman empowerment and more with ensuring she was very far from South Africa during the critical 2012 Mangaung conference. Considering that she had a solid fifteen-year tenure (1994 to 2009) as a minister in different portfolios, she was seen as a potential future president, and certain people saw that very track record as a threat. And the fact that she had agreed to be on the Mbeki slate (as his deputy; she had lost to Motlanthe in 2007) made some in Zuma's camp not trust her at all.

If this theory is true, it means the very person JZ had worked so hard to neutralise five years earlier was now, in 2017, the one on whom he was pinning his entire hope and future. As a colleague in the publishing industry put it, 'As a man, when your first option in life is your ex-wife, you must know you fucked up.'

This reminds me of the funeral I attended in KwaZulu-Natal, just outside Tongaat, in the second half of 2017. A good friend of mine, Nathi Nkwanyana, had lost his son, Ntuthuko, as a result of a tragic case of mistaken identity.

Greg Ardé's book *War Party: How the ANC's political killings are breaking South Africa* (Tafelberg, 2020) chronicles this story, among others. Nathi, a revenue protection manager at the electricity department of the eThekwini metropolitan council, refused to sign and approve certain invoices and was asking too many questions. First he was suspended but his employer struggled to come up with an exact charge, and therefore he had to be killed. Hitmen who had been following him buzzed at the gate soon after he got home. Thinking it was his son's friends, he asked Ntuthuko to go and check who was there.

Gunned down, the young man died on the spot, in the arms of his father. Ntuthuko had been due to write his final exam the following week and complete his electrical engineering degree at the University of KwaZulu-Natal.

At the time there were rumours that the invoices Nathi had refused to sign were linked to the then upcoming Nasrec ANC conference. It is now public knowledge that money plays a huge role in ANC conferences, especially at provincial and national levels. (More about this later.)

So, I ask again, what was Zuma's exit plan – the one that should have been cemented at the Mangaung conference in 2012? Did he and Ramaphosa have a gentleman's agreement that went spectacularly wrong? Did Zuma undermine Ramaphosa? Did Zuma think he would just stand for re-election in 2017? Did he think he could pull off what Mbeki had failed to achieve – winning a third term as ANC president?

If not, Msholozi, Nxamalala, Mafahleni (Zuma's clan names), what was your exit plan? (Time will tell if Paul Mashatile's election as the deputy president of the party at the 2022 conference – instead of Cyril's staunch supporter Oscar Mabuyane – will, in the medium to long term, haunt Ramaphosa.)

Chapter 17

WHAT WERE THE CONSTITUTIONAL COURT JUDGES THINKING?

Although the Constitutional Court is the court of last resort, which means matters must first be dealt with by other courts, there are instances in which you can approach the apex court directly. The overarching issue – the litmus test, if you like – for direct access to be granted is very broad: it must be 'in the interests of justice'.

In the recent past there have been three instances that perplexed and mystified me as to how the Constitutional Court judges reached their decision to grant, or not to grant, direct access.

The first instance involved the family of Collins Khosa (RIP). Khosa, from Alexandra, died after allegedly having been assaulted by soldiers and Metro police officers during the Level 5 lockdown in April 2020. His family approached the court for an effective and swift intervention.

First, obviously, they applied for direct access. Second, they asked for a series of court orders to explicitly deal with the conduct of soldiers during the lockdown. And third, they requested orders dealing with reporting and investigating the misconduct of soldiers, including a tribunal to be chaired by a retired judge.

The Constitutional Court, in its wisdom, did not grant them direct access.

This means, as things stand, that if there were to be another disaster and soldiers were once again let loose on us, we would be on our own. If those soldiers were to kill a loved one, what would be the recourse? Or would you expect the soldiers to investigate themselves?

And, for the record, at last count, eleven other people were killed by the police and/or soldiers during the lockdowns. The families of those people were left in, for lack of a better term, no-man's land. They just had to bury their loved ones, and move on as if nothing had happened.

The second instance was when the DA approached the court questioning the constitutionality of the Disaster Management Act, which enables the president and the executive to declare a national state of disaster and, so long as the disaster persists, to bypass some of the legal constraints ordinarily placed on the exercise of government powers. The main argument by the DA was that the Act, under which the state of disaster was declared in response to the Covid-19 pandemic, was unconstitutional because it effectively sidelined any type of oversight by the legislature. To top it all, the so-called national coronavirus command council, a body that does not feature anywhere in our constitution, was taking all the big decisions, including what the different levels of lockdown should be.

While announcing that the country was effectively going to be closed, President Ramaphosa told us that the council had 'decided to enforce a nationwide lockdown for 21 days with effect from midnight on Thursday 26 March'. A few weeks later, the president was at it again: 'After careful consideration of the available evidence, the national coronavirus command council has decided to extend the nationwide lockdown by a further two weeks beyond the initial 21 days,' he told the country on 9 April 2020.

The Constitutional Court, in its wisdom, did not grant the DA direct access either.

The matter ended up at the North Gauteng High Court in Pretoria, where two of the three judges in March 2021 felt that the Disaster Management Act was constitutional. Interestingly, at least for me, was the minority judgment (or dissenting opinion) of the third judge: that that section of the Act was indeed unconstitutional.

I have struggled to wrap my head around this issue ever since I became aware that this is standard practice in law. So, people who underwent the same legal studies (even if at different universities) and went on to practise the same law, and who in time became judges, could differ in their judgments when presented with the same arguments and counter-arguments. To my mind, the Act is either constitutional or it is not. That is why, surely, parties approach a court of law to deliberate on the matter and hand down judgment. I struggle when the judges, the very people whom we mere mortals depend on to clarify matters, differ. And it comes down to good old democracy: the majority wins.

Surely there has to be a better way to judge matters?

I once posed this question to a friend who is a lawyer. His response was philosophical: 'Sihle, why do people sometimes seek a second medical opinion? Exactly: because nothing in life is absolute.'

I might as well, while I am at it, as a slight detour, deal with two things that, besides the one mentioned above (judgments based on majority rule), bug me about the justice system, not only in South Africa but globally. The first is, why must the judge who finds you guilty be the same judge who decides whether to grant leave to appeal or not? In other words, the very person who has publicly pronounced that you are guilty and even sentenced you is the same person who has to approve the application where his own decision will be scrutinised and put to the test? Isn't that a classic case of conflict of interest?

The second thing is, why must the judge or magistrate against whom you are lodging a recusal application be the same person who decides whether to recuse himself (or herself) or not? Doesn't logic, and logic alone, dictate that the judge ends up being a player and a referee?

Moving expeditiously along ...

Let us recap. A man was allegedly killed by soldiers during a lockdown, yet the Constitutional Court saw no 'interests of justice' in the direct-access application. And the decision to decide whether the Disaster Management Act is constitutional or not boiled down to a simple two-to-one majority win at a High Court after the Constitutional Court had refused to grant direct access.

And yet, down the road from the Constitutional Court, a man walked out of the State Capture Commission without permission from the chair. It was, rightly, a big issue. It was what breaking news is made of.

When former president Zuma walked out of the commission, he was showing a middle finger to both the commission and the entire country, which had been waiting for months – in fact, years – for him to respond to some serious allegations made by numerous witnesses.

The chair of the commission, live on national TV, stated that a criminal complaint would be laid against Mr Zuma for leaving without his permission.

Isn't the criminal complaint avenue a standardised way, in law, of dealing with people who do not want to live within and abide by accepted societal norms? So what made the Zondo Commission all of a sudden (or, as we say in isiZulu, gwijiji or jiki jiki) apply for direct access? Could it be that there was, sooner than later, a realisation that there was a problem, in fact two, with this criminal complaint avenue?

It takes 18 to 24 months for a court case to be finalised in this country. And that excludes appeals. It is common cause that by the time a court case is finalised, the commission would long have finished its work.

Could it be that the second problem with this route, it soon became apparent, was that the contravention of the Commissions Act, in the bigger scheme of things, was not such a big deal? The culprit could walk away with, believe it or not, a fine totalling £50 pounds (about R1 000). The reason the fine is in pounds is because the Commissions Act was passed before 1961, when we started using the mighty, but sometimes staggering, rand.

It is general knowledge that the commission, which was chaired by the then deputy chief justice, approached the Constitutional Court for direct access. In essence, and this is the part some among us do not want to delve into, the deputy chief justice was asking his colleagues – in fact, mostly his juniors – to grant his commission direct access to the highest court in the land.

One very simple learning from this fiasco is that the deputy chief justice should never have been, and must never again be, the chair of any commission. We have so many retired and full-time judges who could do justice (pun intended) to any commission.

Imagine, as part of the review process of the findings and/or recommendations of the Zondo Commission, if the matter ends up in the Constitutional Court? Of course, Raymond Zondo, who is now chief justice, could recuse himself and let other judges – his subordinates – deal with the matter. But it is something that, with the benefit of hindsight, should have been avoided from the beginning.

Another learning, which leads to action that must be taken, is to repeal the Commissions Act of 1947. It is old and outdated. Someone has been asleep at the wheel for a very long time.

You don't need a crystal ball or to be isangoma to know that it is only a matter of time before there is another serious commission of inquiry which will be investigating this or that. Therefore, having such an old Act where you can simply ignore being summoned by the commission and then, after a lengthy trial, take the option of a light fine, is ridiculous, to say the least.

So what happened to the criminal complaint? Did it die its natural death after the direct access application was granted, or was it before; or is it still in the pipeline?

Back to the direct access application ...

The Constitutional Court, in its wisdom and – it must be stressed – without any prejudice and preconception, granted direct access to the commission, which was chaired by the then deputy chief justice, who is now the chief justice.

Now, we know as a fact that if, first, soldiers are let loose on civilians again and in the process a family member of yours gets killed, oh well, shit happens; and if our rights are curtailed again because there is some disaster, oh well, suck it up, suckers. But when you walk out of a commission without the permission of the chairperson, you are constitutionally fucked.

This reminds me of what was once said by Nigerian political scientist and academic Chuba Williams Okadigbo: 'If you are emotionally attached to your tribe, religion or political leaning to the point that truth and justice become secondary considerations, your education and exposure is useless. If you cannot reason beyond petty sentiments, you are a liability to mankind.'

Interestingly, Ziyad Motala, a professor of law at the Howard University School of Law in Washington DC in the USA, wrote in the *Sunday Times* in August 2021, a month after the 2021 July insurrection, that some decisions of the highest court in the land 'smack of personal predilections and politicking', and noted that 'making stuff up from thin air based on the personal predilections of the judges, like the Constitutional Court, is haemorrhaging into lower court decisions'.

And, oh, when Zuma decided not to appear at the Zondo Commission after having been ordered to do so, the same court – horror of horrors – wrote him a letter (a love letter, if you insist) asking him what an appropriate sentence would be. You cannot make this stuff up: the highest court in the land asking someone what an appropriate sentence would be!

What are the odds of you, or anyone for that matter, receiving a communiqué from the highest court in the land (or even from a magistrate's court) asking you what an appropriate sentence would

288

be? Bear in mind, here we are not talking about an acceptable legal practice, such as mitigation of sentence where the accused in a criminal matter has already been convicted and found guilty, and all he is doing is asking the court for mercy. Here, the highest court in the land is requesting someone who was in contempt of that very court to suggest his own sentence.

Hence, at the time, and even now, I still ask myself: what were the Constitutional Court judges thinking?

Chapter 18

IS SOUTH AFRICA A FAILED STATE?

A few things in the recent past have made me look at my country differently. This handful of incidents has left me very uneasy about not only my future in this country but, worse, the future of my children. Some of the decisions in the recent past have left me very uncomfortable about the state of the state.

The reason why I take this failed-state matter to heart is because in my travels I have been through a number of such states. Therefore a failed state is, for me, a lived experience.

First things first, let us define a failed state. According to the Cambridge Dictionary, a failed state is 'a country whose government is considered to have failed at some of its basic responsibilities, for example keeping the legal system working correctly, and providing public services (= electricity, water, education, hospitals, etc.)'

Here, just to be clear, I am not even going to touch on Eishkom, which has been keeping us in the dark intermittently for more than a decade of loadshedding. I am also not going to dwell on the fact that – in a rich country like ours – we still have learners attending classes in mud schools or under a tree, where there is a real risk of falling into a pit latrine and drowning in human excrement. Have you ever asked yourself why middle and upper classes send their children to International Examination Board (IEB, commonly known as private) schools instead of the public ones? In this chapter I will also not even touch on how the middle and upper classes have access to better health care (by paying exorbitant monthly medical aid premiums) whilst the rest of South Africans have to queue, sometimes for hours, just to see the general practitioner. I will also, in this chapter, avoid potholes.

One of those questions I had to ponder in the recent past is, why didn't the Zondo Commission summon Arthur Fraser to tell his side of the story?

Let us recap.

Arthur Fraser, a former boss of the country's state security agency, was implicated by about ten witnesses at the Zondo Commission. Although he was appointed to the director-general position in 2016, while a deputy director-general, he had long been running (according to a statement read at the commission) a unit called the principal agent network, in which (the allegation continued) fraud and corruption in the region of R600 million was committed. In fact, one of the statements read to substantiate how bad things were during Fraser's tenure sounded like a fictional story, the figures quite unbelievable: R19 million here, R5 million there, R1.9 million, R2.5 million, R2 million, R2.4 million, R1 million, R1.3 million ...

All this money was drawn by various agents in cash, and therefore it would be extremely difficult to even start tracing who benefitted from these transactions. What cannot be denied, however, is that the dates this cash changed hands, December 2017, coincided with the ANC's 54th conference at Nasrec.

The same submission stated that in the 2017/18 financial year, about R9 billion-worth of fixed assets were nowhere to be found, and R125 million was not accounted for. I must admit, I had never imagined that a spy agency would have fixed assets amounting to so many billions of rands. And the R9 billion-worth would, I assume, be only a portion of the total fixed assets which, by the way, can include land, buildings, vehicles, furniture, computer equipment and machinery.

My question, therefore, is how is it possible that a person

who was so implicated not be summoned by the commission? Wasn't the commission established to investigate this very type of issue; and also, equally importantly, to invite implicated people to state their side of the story? Could it be that the statement that was issued by Fraser, and read into the record by his legal representative in July 2020, made the commission think twice about taking Fraser on?

What was read into the record was that Fraser, as part of clearing his name, would need to divulge state secrets, and that those secrets might implicate 'the president, or the presidents of this country, past and present ... judges ... [and] parliamentarians'.

If we take away all the frivolities, could it be that what Fraser was really saying to the commission was, 'I have dirt on a number of high-profile people'?

If we cut to the chase, was Fraser saying to the commission – to quote tough guys in the movies – 'Back the fuck off'?

And the commission duly backed off.

Why?

Could it be that the information that Fraser had (and possibly still has) had the potential to collapse not only the commission but all three arms of government? If he had divulged state secrets on the present president, then there goes the executive; on parliamentarians, eish, there goes the legislature; and on judges, oopsie, there goes the judiciary.

Then we would have been left with the fourth estate – the media, and possibly the South African National Editors' Forum – holding the fort as the government of the day. Until further notice ... Or were we going to see for the very first time in South Africa an army intervening by forming a military transition council for a few months, which inadvertently ends up, as has happened in other countries, being a couple of years or, heaven forbid, a few decades?

The state of decay and corruption in our country is so bad that in all honesty it is no longer surprising when a politician is exposed as corrupt. There is almost an understanding that our political leaders are corrupt and that 'these things happen'.

However, what shocked me to my core was the fact that the word 'judges' came up in Fraser's statement. Judges! What is this information that implicates judges? Are they cheating on their partners? While that is not a good thing, surely that can never, in essence, be a state secret? Except, of course, if in the process of cheating, judges end up enjoying themselves so much that they are willing to amend judgments for the sake of another exxxciting, scintillating round of rompfulness.

Judges' sex lives, while not ideal to read about in newspapers, are just tabloid fodder. A case in point: remember a few years ago when a tabloid reported how two ministers were sharing the same woman? No, sucker, it was not a threesome. The lady was, at different times, juggling very important balls. We soon forgot about it.

But before we get sidetracked from important judicial issues ... Could it be that one day the people of this country, in their numbers, will ask a pertinent question: 'Can the South African judiciary be trusted?' And that, as part of answering that question, there will be a need for a commission of inquiry into the judiciary? But then the problem will be, among others, who will chair such a commission, when some judges will be facing a barrage of judiciary-related questions, live on national TV? Or will we need to import the services of the evergreen Judge Judy?

While, thanks to the Zondo Commission, we now know things that we never would have known otherwise, what exactly are these state secrets that made the commission – which was, as per legislation, chaired by a judge – back off?

A question must be asked: did the commission, in its failure to summon Arthur Fraser, protect certain presidents, certain parliamentarians and certain judges?

Another bigger-picture issue that has been bugging me for some time, and something about which most South Africans – for whatever reason – were, and are, not outraged, has to do with a specific incident that occurred during the July 2021 insurrection.

Remember how a container that had left the Port of Durban illegally was broken into at a private container depot in Mobeni? Apparently the container contained about a million (some reports say 1.5 million) rounds of ammunition. Other reports, months later, highlighted how not one but two containers filled with 'AK47-type' rifles went missing during the insurrection.

I am not a military analyst (and I have never been either a police officer or a soldier) but common sense, and common sense alone, tells me that a group of individuals with rifles that filled two containers plus more than a million rounds of illegal ammunition are a threat to national security.

But instead of focusing on this very important incident, the government launched Operation Khiphi'risidi (Operation Show Us The Receipt). The state, to save face, distracted us – helped by mainstream media – by launching an illegal Khiphi'risidi mumbo-jumbo. And, live on national television, the police and soldiers were asking for receipts. Looted goods (and in some cases non-looted goods) were confiscated and loaded into trucks.

No-one was arrested for being in possession of alleged stolen goods. The trucks disappeared with looted goods to some warehouse. We all saw that no-one was taking stock of what was being loaded onto trucks; and surely no-one was counting when the trucks eventually reached the warehouse, in order to confirm that everything that was loaded onto the trucks actually made it to the warehouse. And I can bet my last Zim dollar that no-one was taking stock (no pun intended) of what was in the warehouse.

Is there a possibility (in fact, a huge possibility) that police officers and/or soldiers ended up helping themselves to the looted, non-looted and 'recovered' goods?

Why didn't the state pour resources into finding out who stole those million bullets? Why did the executive promise us, the nation, that the instigators were known and would face the full might of the law, and yet when it came to arrests, dololo? Could it be that the government, after some preliminary investigations, discovered that hunting and arresting the real instigators, and trying to get the bullets back, would lead to more bloodshed? So the state, ever weak and not functioning coherently, decided to back off. To back the fuck off ...

What if I were to put it to you, dear reader, that the state of the state is, at best, shaky and, at worst, shady?

Could this mean that one day, when the government finally grows some balls, we will have a well-balanced fight, with millions of civilians caught in the middle, between government forces on one side, and the people who consistently steal firearms from police stations and now have ammunition stolen during the insurrection on the other side? And even this worst-case scenario assumes all government forces will work with a single objective in mind, i.e., to protect lives and property ...

Those few days of insurrection led to the deaths of at least 340 people, and the destruction of property totalling billions of rands. And yet the government has been reluctant to get to the bottom of what caused it. With respect to the South African Human Rights Commission, which investigated what the president called a 'failed insurrection', why didn't we have a judicial commission of inquiry, with witnesses beamed out live on national television, investigating who the true masterminds of the insurrection were?

We will never know what the findings of such a judicial commission would have been, because the government (and, by extension, the ANC) is seemingly not willing to risk it. Could it be that, a few days into the work of such a commission, it would become clear that some members of the executive and some leaders in the governing party were the brains and sponsors of the failed insurrection? Could it be that, within weeks of the commission, there would a split within 'the movement'?

The good news is that the insurrection could have been worse but – thank goodness – the taxi industry came to our rescue. You know you are in the doldrums when, as communities, you start relying on one of the most violent sectors in your economy to protect malls and shopping centres. Even white people, who have never been the biggest cheerleaders of the taxi industry, were all in awe at how the taxi bosses took a stand. You know what they say about desperate times …

It gets worse …

In the same month as the insurrection, a police station sixty kilometres outside Kuruman in the Northern Cape was robbed of two shotguns, three R5 rifles and ten pistols, as well as ammunition. Four months later, the Malamulele police station in Limpopo was robbed; unknown people took R5 rifles, 9mm pistols, shotguns and an undisclosed quantity of ammunition. Almost a year later, it was the turn of Grootvlei police station in Mpumalanga, where a number of firearms and ammunition were taken. And in spring of 2022, October to be exact – just #ForControl – thugs struck again. Devon police station in Ekurhuleni was robbed of ten firearms, including three rifles.

It is one thing for thugs to rob a citizen in his home but something totally different when criminals brazenly rob police stations. Don't such things only happen in a banana republic?

And just when we thought the insurrection was over, towards the end of July 2021, boom, Transnet's IT system suffered a cyber-attack, security intrusion and sabotage incident. In simple terms, it was hacked.

Was that a coincidence or was it another arm of the insurrection?

Transnet, for the record, is a state-owned enterprise, and is the country's largest logistics company. The hacking of their system has a direct impact on imports and exports. And that has a direct impact on the country's economy.

Was this a sophisticated way of bringing the economy to its knees? And with a collapsed economy leading to, among other things, barely anything on supermarket shelves and extremely unhappy citizens, starting an even bigger and even more violent insurrection would be as easy as 'On your marks! Get set …' And all hell would break loose.

And, oh, did Transnet and/or the government pay the hackers a ransom, as is the case sometimes with hackings?

More than a year after the insurrection, some people who were allegedly involved were arrested. I keep thinking to myself, *When will they arrest the kingpins?*

Then, in September 2021, the Department of Justice was – click-click – hacked. Why would anyone hack the Department of Justice? In order to erase all files with incriminating evidence that has painstakingly been put together by prosecution teams? In order to, as a convicted criminal, change the criminal record against your name (or your clients' names)?

The department was very reluctant at first to even acknowledge that it had been breached and never comprehensively stated to what extent it had been hacked.

A few weeks later, in October 2021, two ministers and a deputy minister were held hostage at a conference centre in Irene, Pretoria, by 'military veterans' who later faced abduction charges. The government officials managed to escape after the intervention of the country's elite police unit, the Special Task Force.

As if that were not enough, the parliament building in Cape Town (a national keypoint, nogal) was set alight by a lone man in January 2022.

A few days later another lone man smashed the windows of the Constitutional Court building in Braamfontein. And then it was revealed that 158 guns had been stolen from Norwood police station in Johannesburg. It would be funny if it weren't so sad.

In one weekend in July 2022, in two separate incidents (subsequently called 'tavern massacres'), twenty people in Soweto and Pietermaritzburg were gunned down by unknown assailants. The following weekend, a further ten people were shot and killed in three different incidents. These incidents highlighted, once again, the dangers of having so many unlicensed and illegal firearms on our streets and in our neighbourhoods.

On this issue, political scientist Masixole Booi hit the nail on the head when he pointed out in the *Daily Maverick* in July 2022 that the violent nature of taverns in townships must be located 'within their historical context of colonial-apartheid violence that is still deeply embedded and normalised in townships'. Trying to investigate the motive behind these mass shootings without clearly understanding the structurally violent nature of townships is shortsighted, he said. 'South African taverns have a history of keeping black people in a permanent state of drunkenness to demobilise them and mesmerise young black people in particular ...'

In his book *Blame Me on Apartheid* (House of Masefako, 2020), Thamsanqa D Malinga eloquently and lyrically delves into – amongst other things – his view that instead of glorifying townships and township life, we should see townships for what they are: places that keep 'black people in mental slavery'; later on he says townships 'continue to be a psyschological tool of oppression to this day.' I agree wholeheartedly.

Maybe it's just me, but sometimes I get a sense that the centre is not holding. Sometimes I get the feeling that we are a cowntry on autopilot. Matamela is a strategic guy, we are told by his fans. He is in it for the long term, we are told by his cheerleaders. In my home language we have a saying, 'Uhleli ngesinqe esisodwa', which means he is sitting with only one cheek of his bum on the chair. It is used figuratively when a leader is not sitting comfortably on the throne and thus is not leading properly, because there are (powerful) forces who are challenging them every step of the way. From where I am seated, uCyril uhleli ngesinqe esisodwa. As we await to see how he will fare in his second term as the president of the Party (and the country?).

So, fellow South African, believe in the 'new dawn' all you want, but Cyril at times strikes me as a guy who is overwhelmed with the responsibilities and seemingly insurmountable challenges at hand. Have you ever asked yourself, fellow South African, where was Cyril during the insurrection of July 2021?

And then, boom, we discovered that in February 2020, thugs had broken into the president's farm in Limpopo and stolen what was initially reported as US\$4 million (about R60 million) but was later 'corrected' to R9 million in cash stored in a cupboard/mattress/under the bed; who knows. And we only got to know about it two years later, when it was reported to the police. As this book went to print, Ramaphosa, as cunning as ever, was trying by all means necessary to ride the wave, including a constitutional inquiry dealing with the removal of a president. After a preliminary investigation by the independent panel (which included a former chief justice) concluded that Cyril may have a case to answer, the ruling party publicly instructed its members in parliament to, literally, protect him by voting against the adoption of the panel's report. And that is how Cyril got away without fully disclosing publicly what happened at his farm. So much for the 'new dawn'. (Question to self: how can a president who says he is fighting corruption ask his party members to protect him from accounting to parliament?)

In any case, a few days after winning in parliament Cyril was re-elected as ANC president. (At the time of going to print, other investigations by the public protector, the police etc. were ongoing). (See Appendix I, Phala Phala, the poem.)

*

These are just some of the incidents, fellow South African, that have left me extremely uncomfortable about where we are as a nation. I keep asking myself: is South Africa already a failed state?

Maybe the fact that I am even asking myself something that to other people is as clear as daylight means I am in denial. Maybe it means, because I do not want my country to fail, even when the signs are staring me in the face, I find myself hopeful, against any practical proof, that one day we will turn the corner and, in the nick of time, avoid falling off the cliff.

The only question left, as someone (in another country) once asked, is, does this banana republic produce any good bananas?

And the answer – and I hope this consoles you, fellow South African – is, yes, our banana republic not only produces good bananas but is also home to award-winning wines.

Bottoms up, and chin up, everyone ...

Chapter 19

WHEN EXACTLY WAS THE STATE CAPTURED?

The term 'state capture' has been used frequently in recent times, thanks to the Zondo Commission.

Did the Gupta brothers capture former president Jacob Zuma? If not, how did the Guptas leave the country with, at last count, about R50 billion?

The question that must also be asked is, was this the first time ever that the state had been captured? If we as patriots are genuinely interested in knowing about the people and companies that, while we are blindfolded by the word 'democracy', run the country from the shadows, then why don't we have another commission of inquiry looking into the shenanigans of the other administrations, and not just Zuma's, with exactly the same kind of scrutiny, coupled with exactly the same kind of rolling media coverage?

In the early 1990s, when the leaders of then recently unbanned organisations came back from exile or were released from jail, who paid their rent? Who paid their kids' school fees? Who gave them money to make settling in back home stress-free? Pieter du Toit's latest book *The ANC Billionaires: Big Capital's Gambit and the Rise of the Few* (Jonathan Ball, 2022) gives a blow-by-blow account of how corporate South Africa laid red carpet for some ANC leaders, even going as far as making private jets available for them to make travelling throughout the country stressless.

And when, years later, these political leaders occupied strategic positions in government, didn't they bend over backwards to ensure that their former benefactors got a lucrative deal, or five, from the government?

Sampie Terreblanche's 2012 book, *Lost in Transformation*, comprehensively yet in simple terms tells the riveting story of the secret deals that were signed away from the cameras, the media and the general public. These secret deals, as explained earlier in this book, were of an economic nature.

Now, what if an even more sinister deal – you can call it a gentlemen's agreement, if you like – was signed just before the watershed elections of 1994? Have you ever asked yourself why, given that in 1998 the Truth and Reconciliation Commission referred more than three hundred cases to the country's national prosecuting authority, the governing party was so reluctant to prosecute apartheid killers? Why has the ANC (as a party and, even more importantly, as the ruling party) not pushed for justice in this regard? Why are those criminals enjoying their sunset years while there are still thousands of families patiently waiting for justice for the disappearance, torture and/or deaths of their loved ones?

What is holding the ANC government back? Surely this could never be simply and naively attributed to incompetence, laziness and dysfunctionality within the prosecuting authority?

Former national director of public prosecutions Vusi Pikoli is on record, as per an affidavit he submitted in 2015, after he left office, as part of the Nokuthula Simelane case. Simelane was an MK courier who disappeared in 1983, and her family in 2015 was asking the court to prosecute her alleged killers. Pikoli stated as a matter of fact that there was political interference that 'effectively barred or delayed the investigation and possible prosecutions of the cases recommended for prosecution' by the Truth and Reconciliation Commission. Simelane's sister, Thembisile Nkadimeng, also filed an affidavit in this regard, stating that the government had 'put in place measures to manipulate, control or obstruct prosecutorial decisions dealing with political cases of the past'.

So why has the ANC government at best been reluctant to pursue these cases, and at worst interfered with the justice system when it comes to the prosecution of apartheid killers? Could it be that some National Party head honchos, especially those within the security structures of the apartheid regime, have some dirty secrets on senior leaders within the liberation movement? Could it be that all we have are leaders who from day one have been blackmailed over and over again? Could it be that the minute apartheid killers were charged, they would spill the beans, including on who was a spy, and that this would destroy the liberation movement, because some of its very senior leaders might be on that spy list?

This reminds me of ex-MK member Barry Gilder's novel *The List* (Jacana Media, 2018), which tells the story of a list of the names of spies who had infiltrated the ANC all the way to the top that is handed to the newly elected president. The president secretly appoints a task team to investigate it. The story is told by a fictional ANC intelligence officer, Jerry Whitehead. The fact that Gilder is himself a former ANC intelligence officer is, of course, entirely coincidental.

Therefore, first, if the list actually exists, and, second, if it indeed has the names of former spies on it, and, finally, if the apartheid securocrats used it, and continue to use it, as leverage for their freedom, would that not mean that the new South Africa has always been captured?

Can we honestly say that the Guptas were the first people to capture the state?

How do you explain, for example, that Eric Taylor, one of the police officers who was involved in the June 1985 killing of the Cradock Four (Matthew Goniwe, Fort Calata, Sparrow Mkhonto and Sicelo Mhlauli), confessed to the murders at the Truth and Reconciliation Commission; but that there was also a revelation, during the commission hearings, that a request had been sent in 1984 to the state security council, which was then the highest decision-making body on national security, to 'remove permanently from society as a matter of urgency' the Cradock Four? Future president FW de Klerk and other ministers, including PW Botha, Pik Botha and Barend du Plessis, sat in on state security council meetings. None of the ministers who attended those meetings applied for amnesty. Only Du Plessis is (at the time of writing) still alive.

The commission felt that Eric Taylor (and his ilk) had not divulged everything and, as such, he was not granted amnesty. But Taylor died in 2016 a free man. Forget being convicted, he was neither charged nor prosecuted. And here, once again, I am talking about someone who had publicly confessed to committing the act of murder.

In the second half of 2021, the minister of justice and correctional services announced that the national prosecuting authority would accelerate prosecutions of Truth and Reconciliation Commission cases. Quite frankly, I am not holding my breath. And neither should you. Because this same Department of Justice (I am tempted to call it the Department of Injustice), in 2004, denied filmmaker David Forbes access to the commission's amnesty committee's recordings and inquest records about the deaths of the Cradock Four which, by law, are public documents. It took Forbes two years, following the legal route, to finally gain access to the records.

Interestingly, the independent South African History Archive states that, while working with David Forbes in trying to get the tapes, it was surprised by the 'obstructive stance' taken by the Department of Justice – a stance that went so far as to see the department approaching the widows directly and forcing them to sign affidavits refusing the release of the records.

Eugene de Kock, as mentioned earlier, was given a house and a salary by the state after he was paroled. At the time of his parole, the then minister of justice, Michael Masutha, said De Kock had been paroled 'in the interests of nation-building'. This is the same De Kock who, given the atrocities he had committed, including murder, attempted murder, conspiracy to murder, kidnapping and assault, was dubbed 'Prime Evil' by the media and the nation. He was sentenced to two life sentences plus 212 years in 1996 and got parole in 2015.

To be fair to the NPA, in 2019 it did reopen the inquest into death of Dr Neil Aggett, the trade unionist, labour activist and medical doctor who died while being held in detention. According to the official report at the time of his death, in 1982 Aggett had committed suicide whilst in police custody. Police officer Stephan Whitehead had interrogated Aggett, including electric shock and beatings, for a marathon 62 hours shortly before his death. NPA announced the reopening of the docket on 3 May 2019 and Whitehead had died of cancer on 23 April – exactly ten days earlier. When in shock, some people say 'oh my gosh' or 'oh my word'; I prefer the isiZulu expression 'Hawu!' or even more impressive 'Hhawu!'.

In this book, I have covered at length how the Afrikaner Broederbond captured the state for more than forty years, from 1948 to 1994. Who is to say that the Broederbond volk are not still calling the shots behind the scenes? It would be naive to think that people who had wielded so much power and held so many resources simply disappeared, just like that, just because everybody voted in 1994. The real world does not work that way.

What happened to all those networks? What happened to that comaraderie, secrecy, the will and desire to dominate and to be perpetually in power? Isn't power addictive? Did all that just dissipate because of a historic event on 27 April 1994? Did the real power of the Afrikaners – and the English – simply go up in smoke? Or is the Broederbond, albeit in a different form or manner, still running the show? Are the political leaders we watch on the news just puppets of the wealthy and the powerful? Do we have mighty puppetmasters lurking in the shadows?

This brings to mind Ebbe Dommisse's book *Fortunes: The rise and rise of Afrikaner tycoons* (Jonathan Ball Publishers, 2021), which looks at the past thirty years during which we have seen 'a remarkable rise of Afrikaners in business'. In light of the government's comprehensive BEE programme, this has been one of the 'unexpected features' of the South African economy, Dommisse writes. The book examines in detail leading business Afrikaners such as Whitey Basson, Christo Wiese, Johann Rupert, Douw Steyn and Jannie Mouton, looking at how they have made and continue making serious money, not only in South Africa but internationally.

Imagine the amount of power, economic and otherwise, wielded by these few individuals, some of whom are dollar billionaires? Could such economic power, especially in the hands of a few, be used to, for example, strong-arm the state on certain economic policy decisions? Could it be, to borrow from Pieter du Toit's book *The Stellenbosch Mafia: Inside the billionaires' club* (Jonathan Ball Publishers, 2019), that the 'Stellenbosch mafia' runs the entire country from their picturesque wine farms dotted around that university town?

But the capture of the South African state, seemingly, started with neither the Guptas nor the Afrikaner Broederbond.

How, for example, did South African industry manage to get away with the cheap black labour system? Of course, it is quite clear that the beneficiaries of that cruel and inhumane system, in which black people were paid just enough for them not to die of hunger, were the owners of capital. The mining sector, by virtue of being the biggest employer at the time, benefitted handsomely from that injustice, which lasted for decades. How did the owners of capital and captains of industry manage to convince the government not just to look the other way when citizens were being exploited but to actually come up with a legislative framework that made sure that indeed black employees – the vast majority of the work-force – were legally exploited?

There is only one way that that cheap black labour policy could have been instituted in this country. Capital had to capture the state, and from that moment onwards, politicians were dancing to the tune of business.

Just in case some among us have conveniently not been able to connect the dots between cheap black labour and dysfunctional black African families, here it is: the Natives (Urban Areas) Act of 1923 legally classified all urban areas as 'white', and all black African men in cities and towns were required to carry around permits called 'passes' at all times. Black people were permitted in 'white' and urban areas only to work. If a black man was found by authorities without a 'pass', he was in deep shit: he would immediately be arrested, then shipped back to the 'native reserves' in the rural areas (years later called bantustans). And in the 1940s and 1950s there was further legislation prescribing the permitted living places and curtailing the movement of black people in the land of their birth.

Linked to this 'migrant labour' system were single-sex hostels, housing compounds exclusively developed for black migrant workers. These workers, bear in mind, 'belonged' to the native reserves and as such had to be accommodated and controlled in urban areas until they returned to their homelands.

The social impact of fathers leaving their wives and children in the native reserves, and only seeing them twice a year (during the Easter and Christmas breaks), has not, I think, been fully appreciated. The migrant-labour system led to black African children growing up without fathers. Now, generations later, it has been normalised that, as per a 2021 Statistics South Africa report, less than 32 per cent of black African children live with their biological fathers, as compared to the same situation for 51.3 per cent of coloured children, 80.2 per cent of white children and 86.1 per

307

cent of Indian/Asian children. And, as we all know, the family is the most basic unit of any community, society and nation.

The destruction of black African families and communities, the results of which we see today, was a direct consequence of the cheap black labour system – a direct product of the apartheid system. And yet the Truth and Reconciliation Commission officially recognised only about 22 000 victims of human-rights violations. For context, there were 10.9 million black Africans in 1960; ten years later, that figure had grown to 15.3 million; and in 1980 there were 16.9 million of us. And yet only 22 000 officially suffered human-rights violations.

In any case, it was recommended that these victims be given reparations of R126 000 a year for six years. The ANC government decided to drop this to a once-off R30 000 payment. And about 16 000 of the 22 000 received far less than R30 000. (Interestingly, Brett Herron, a Member of National Parliament, asked a very pertinent question in an online article published in November 2022: 'What's happened to the R2 billion in the reparations fund?')

We as a nation have not even scratched the surface on the social ills caused by the cheap black labour system, as well as by broader apartheid policy. In this regard, I am reminded of nineteenth-century African American author and social reformer Frederick Douglass, who said, 'It is easier to build strong children than to repair broken men.'

So – fellow South Afican – when will we, as a country, have a real conversation, as part of genuine and practical nation-building, about redress which will lead to authentic and bona fide reparations?

The state was so captured by business that it bent over backwards to ensure that business got away with whatever it wanted, and expeditiously so. As an example, soon after the end of the second Anglo-Boer War (oops, the South African War), it became clear that a vast majority of black South Africans (basically, Zulus) were not willing to work on the British-owned farms and plantations of Natal; they preferred to go and work in the gold mines of the Witwatersrand.

And some of those men preferred to stay at home with their loved ones and live contentedly off the land.

That is where, yet again, capital owners dictated to the state how the issue could be circumvented. In 1906 the government decided to introduce, over and above an already existing 'hut tax', a one-pound 'poll tax' on every adult. Naturally, those men who had opted to live at home had to find a way to raise this money, and so had to go to work.

That is exactly what Chief Bhambatha (often written as Bambatha) KaMancinza Zondi was totally against, and it led to the 1906 rebellion that caused the deaths of 3 000 to 4 000 Zulus. It was a fight against an unjust policy. It was a fight, to use a modern term, against state capture.

At about the same time that the new tax was introduced in Natal, black workers were fighting wage cuts in the mining sector. Again, as if on cue, the government intervened on the side of business, and brought 60 000 Chinese labourers into the country. Problem solved! Within three years, gold production had almost doubled.

Indian indentured labourers were also brought into the country as cheap labour for the sugar-cane estates in Natal at the end of the 1800s. Unlike the Chinese labourers, who, when their contracts ended around 1910, returned to their homeland, most Indians stayed. That is how the country's demographics changed forever. That is how South Africa ended up with Indians/Asians making up almost three per cent of the population. That is how Durban became the city outside of India with the most Indians.

Let's go way back ...

The South African Native Affairs Commission was instituted in 1903 in order to deal with 'the native question'. Essentially, if we cut all frivolities, the question was, what must the government do with all these natives?

Based on the recommendations of the commission – again, if

we take out all the frivolities – it was decided that the natives must be slaves in their own country. However, before the recommendations could be implemented, a key legislative framework had to be sorted out.

In 1909, the British parliament finally gave permission for the formation of the Union of South Africa, which was proclaimed in 1910. The following year, the Mines and Works Act reserved certain skilled positions for whites, obviously with better pay. Also in 1911, the Native Labour Regulation Act was promulgated to regulate the recruitment and employment of 'natives'; for example, it made it legal for black employees injured in industrial accidents to receive less compensation than their white counterparts.

Both these pieces of legislation dealt exclusively with labour-relations matters. How was business able to pull off these miracles if it had not first captured the state?

Within three years of the formation of the Union of South Africa, the Native Land Act of 1913 became law. As Sol Plaatje so evocatively put it in his 1916 book *Native Life in South Africa*, 'Awaking on Friday morning, June 20, 1913, the South African native found himself, not actually a slave, but a pariah in the land of his birth.'

Plaatje nailed it. His book should be prescribed for learners in our schools. This is the type of history, if the government was sincere and genuine about nation-building and social cohesion, learners should be exposed to and tested on. But alas. And what can we expect, when some comrades in senior positions in the party and/or the government have never even heard of, never mind read, Plaatje's book. That is how bad the situation is in this country.

Some people need to, and here comes a swear word, read (yep, read) George Orwell's *1984*, in which, as he eloquently put it, 'Who controls the past, controls the future. Who controls the present, controls the past.'

The 1913 Land Act, which gave black people only seven per

cent of the country's land, meant that with a stroke of a pen African farmers who had been sharecropping on the property of white farm owners were chucked off those farms and had to move to the native reserves. And those native reserves meant – and this was a major prerequisite for the gold sector to be massively profitable – the mining sector could have unlimited access to cheap unskilled black labour, as and when required.

It did not end there ...

Exactly ten years later, as mentioned, the Native (Urban Areas) Act of 1923 created 'influx control', by calling urban black people 'temporary sojourners' whose main objective for being in urban areas was to attend to the wants of the white population; those duties discharged, they had to leave the area. Then, three decades later, with the promulgation of the Natives (Abolition of Passes and Coordination of Documents) Act of 1952, black South Africans were forced to carry a number of documents including a photograph, employment and tax payments records, proof of place of birth, and criminal records.

This 'dompas' law, along with a plethora of other oppressive laws, was introduced in parliament by none other than Hendrik Verwoerd, then minister of native affairs. These laws enabled the government to further restrict black South Africans' movement in the country of their ancestors. Restriction of the number of black people (read savages) living in or even near urban areas where white people lived and/or ran businesses was deemed important for the sake of the safety, order and peace of mind of the white population. Therefore the state, on behalf of business, had to intervene. The state, on behalf of business owners, had to keep the natives where they belonged: in the native reserves.

Doesn't all of the above point to one thing and one thing only: a state captured by business?

Now let's go even further back, to that autumn day when Commander Jan van Riebeeck docked at Table Bay. Van Riebeeck was employed by a private firm, the Dutch East India Company, to effectively be the head of state/government/cabinet, king of kings and leader of parliament all wrapped up in one. And all subsequent Dutch governors were appointed by the Dutch East India Company.

Given all these facts, dear reader, what if I were to put it to you that the state was captured a long, long time ago?

Given what we know now, as a matter of fact: money plays a big part in who gets elected during ANC conferences. For example, Cyril Ramaphosa told the Zondo Commission that his campaign for president at Nasrec in 2017 raised 'about R300 million'. Another prime example was when ANC member Aaron Motsoaledi, who was overseeing the Eastern Cape provincial conference in 2022, stated that he was 'not going to stand here and lie to you and say there are no ANC members who offer other money'. Just after the national elective conference, Gwede Mantashe (the national chairperson) admitted on national television that 'This time around you have people at branch level and regional level phoning you: "I have this number of delegates, please give me so much money",' before getting specific: 'It depends. One person phoned me and said, "I have 140 delegates, give me R100 000".'

Although superficially it might look as if the so-called leaders buy their way to the top, it is actually the exact opposite. The 'leaders' *sell* their way to the top. By the time you reach the top, my brother, the people who invested in your campaign have you by the balls. By the time you reach your political zenith, my sister, the people who backed you financially have you by the tits. In general terms, it is called 'you scratch my back, I scratch yours'. In politics and business, there is no free lunch. The fact is, investors want a return on their investment.

Given all the facts above, dear reader, what if I were to put it to you that the state was captured from day one?

What if, as you are reading this passage, the state is still captured?

It is just a question.

Think. Rethink.

Do not subcontract your thinking about your country, our country, to the self-appointed (or is it self-anointed?) thinkers.

Pause.

And think.

PHALA PHALA, THE POEM

Phala Phala was on the news.
Phala Phala farm was on Phalaphala FM.

What really happened?
Who would have thought?
Where did the money come from?
Why, oh, why?
How can he really explain this?

Phala Phala was on the news.
Phala Phala was the news.
It was shocking news.
It was good news.
It was great news, for some.
It was awful news, for others.
It was awesome news, for some.

The money was under the mattress.
The money was in the mattress.
The money was on the mattress.
The money was in the cupboard.
The mattress was in the money.

The money was in the mattress in the cupboard.
The money was in the cupboard under the mattress.
The money was in the mattress on a cupboard.
The money was on the cupboard under the mattress.
The money was on the mattress on the cupboard.

Oh, his audacity ...
The audacity of the people
who strategised to protect him,
The audacity of the people
who protected him in parliament,
The audacity of South Africans
who keep voting for the same protection scheme.

Kuthi angiPHALAze ...
I feel like throwing up ...

Dedicated to the late Chris van Wyk, who wrote 'In Detention'.

GREAT CONVERSATION STARTERS

Here are questions that ideally should be directed at a stranger in order to break the ice at your local pub, shebeen or shisanyama. I prefer to call them #GreatConversationStarters.

- Why, out of the blue in 2017, a few months before the ANC's national elective conference, did South African rapper Cassper Nyovest release a single titled 'Tito Mboweni'? Did Tito have presidential ambitions? If not, then why, when he was governor of the Reserve Bank, and before then President Mbeki's intervention, did he authorise the printing of notes on which were written 'President Governor'?

- Why, of all the things they could have called false memory – in which facts and events are collectively misremembered by thousands of people – did they choose 'the Mandela effect'? Fiona Broome, a paranormal researcher, coined the term in 2010 to describe collective false memory when she discovered that a significant number of people at a conference she was attending shared her memory that Nelson Mandela had died in prison during the 1980s. Does Fiona know something most of us do not?

- Did the auditor-general's office audit the various bantustans and homelands? How much of their spending was irregular, fruitless and/or unauthorised? And what was Pretoria's intervention? Or was it a matter of bantustan leaders not being exposed as corrupt? Was Pretoria willing to look the other way in the name of proving to the international community that 'separate development' (#apartheid) was a workable and practical solution for the Republic of South Africa?

- Why didn't Tendai 'Beast' Mtawarira at one stage or another become the captain of the Springboks? Could it be that although we South Africans loved him to bits and would all scream 'B.E.A.S.T' whenever he ran with the ball, when it came to the captaincy role, we would suddenly remember that he was born in Zimbabwe, and that a 'Zimbabwean' could not under any circumstances captain the South African team?
- Was it a coincidence that rugby player Mahlatse Chiliboy Ralepelle, a former captain of the under-21s, was found guilty and was subsequently suspended for using a banned substance a few months before the Rugby World Cup in England in 2015? Was it also a coincidence that, four years later, exactly the same thing happened again – he was found guilty and suspended for using a banned substance a few months before the 2019 Rugby World Cup, this time in Japan?
- Was it a coincidence that Aphiwe Odwa Dyantyi, the 2018 Break-through Player of the Year and the first South African (not the first *black* South African, just the first South African) to get that accolade, was found guilty and subsequently suspended for using a banned substance exactly a month before the start of the 2019 Rugby World Cup?
- When and how will South Africa's senior cricket team, the Proteas, win the Cricket World Cup?
- When, if ever, and how will the Democratic Alliance achieve 33.3% in the general elections?
- Now that Morocco has broken the record by becoming the first African country to reach the semi-finals of the FIFA World Cup since its inception in 1930, a question must be asked: when and how will any African country win the FIFA World Cup?
- When and how will a black African from anywhere on the continent win the 100m/200m butterfly or breaststroke at the Olympics?

- Why, even during the height of apartheid, did the state not prevent the gathering of thousands of black people for soccer matches? Could it be that sport in general, and soccer in particular, was being used as a distraction and thus gave the oppressed a false sense of freedom and liberty?

- Why has the ANC government been treating (alleged) racists – from a legislative perspective – with kid gloves? Remember how the government passed the Promotion of Equality and Prevention of Unfair Discrimination (Pepuda) Act No. 4 of 2000 which, amongst other things, created the Equality Court where the magistrate or judge becomes a 'Presiding Officer'? Why, given our past as a country, can't alleged racists be charged and be processed in a normal court where – if found guilty – they face, say, a prescribed minimum sentence?

- Why hasn't the ANC government officially probed the death of its leader Inkosi Albert Luthuli who, according to the apartheid government's official report, was struck and killed in 1967 by a freight train, which had only three people on board, the driver, the conductor and stoker, who could corroborate the story? A passenger train in the same circumstances would have had many, many more on board who would have had to have the same story.

- The African continent constantly cried foul that the West was hoarding Covid-19 vaccines in what was generally termed 'vaccine nationalism'. My question to my fellow Africans, all 1.4 billion of us, is, where was our own African vaccine?

- Did the South African Reserve Bank (SARB) sign any BEE deal, giving a smallanyana stake to politically connected black individuals, in the post-1994 era? The question really is: what is the BEE rating of a company that – through the monopoly on the monetary policy not only issues banknotes but also manages the gold and foreign reserves, manages the national payments system as well as regulates and supervises financial institutions – holds more power than any arm of government?

ACKNOWLEDGEMENTS

The Johannesburg Institute for Advanced Study (JIAS) is whole-heartedly appreciated for giving me space, headroom and time to focus on editing this book and researching my next one. I also revered the intellectually stimulating conversations and engagements I had with the other Writing Fellows – in alphabetic order – Molly Andrews, Amos Darkwa Asare, Stefanie Bognitz, Liz Gunner, Stephanie Jenkins, Jill Kelly, Tinashe Mushakavanhu and Janet Remmington as well as the Post-Doctoral and Visiting Research Fellows.

From where I am seated, JIAS provides the air that sustains creative and critical thought.

To my editor, Tracey Hawthorne, and the entire Penguin Random House publishing team, for advice, suggestions and asking those probing questions, and thus helped consolidate my manuscript into something very readable: I cherish your contribution.

And last but not least, to my wife and two kids, Nala and Zawaadi: I hope the publication of this book may finally answer some of your questions, including:

'Why do you spend so much time in front of the computer?'

'Why are you not talking to us?'

'What are you writing about?'

'When is your next book coming out?'

'Is it really worth it being an author in South Africa?'

'Why do you watch mainly aliens-focused TV shows?'

'Why are you not talking to us?'

'Why are you such a loner?'
'Who are your friends?'
'Why are you so self-absorbed?'
'Why are you not talking to us?'
'Why are you so weird?'
'Are you sure you are not an alien?'